Into the Blue and Beneath The Waves

Navigating the deep waters of life

By
Christopher de Beaufort

MAPLE
PUBLISHERS

Into the Blue and Beneath The Waves: Navigating the deep waters of life

Author: Christopher de Beaufort

Copyright © 2025 Christopher de Beaufort

The right of Christopher de Beaufort to be identified as author of this work has been asserted by the author in accordance with section 77 and 78 of the Copyright, Designs and Patents Act 1988.

First Published in 2025

ISBN 978-1-83538-830-3 (Paperback)
    978-1-83538-831-0 (Hardback)
    978-1-83538-832-7 (E-Book)

Book Cover Design and Layout by:
    White Magic Studios
    www.whitemagicstudios.co.uk

Published by:
    Maple Publishers
    Fairbourne Drive, Atterbury,
    Milton Keynes,
    MK10 9RG, UK
    www.maplepublishers.com

A CIP catalogue record for this title is available from the British Library.

All rights reserved. No part of this book may be reproduced or translated by any form or by any means, electronic or mechanical, including photocopying, recording or by any information storage and retrieval system without written permission from the author.

The views expressed in this work are solely those of the author and do not reflect the opinions of Publishers, and the Publisher hereby disclaims any responsibility for them. This book should not be used as a substitute for the advice of a competent authority, admitted or authorized to advise on the subjects covered.

CONTENTS

Chapter One – My Family Roots 4

Chapter Two – My Early School Years. 8

Chapter Three – My Teenage Years... 10

Chapter Four – The Start of My Diving Career............................. 16

Chapter Five – The Underwater Training Centre, Fort William, Scotland.
.... 27

Chapter Six – The Start of My Second Diving Career. 37

Chapter Seven – My Start to Offshore Work with Mini-Subs. ... 57

Chapter Eight – In IRAN. 71

Chapter Nine – The North Sea & Hartlepool. 80

Chapter Ten – Abu Dhabi, U.A.E. 95

Chapter Eleven – The North Sea; Holland. 102

Chapter Twelve – Saudi Arabia... 111

Chapter Thirteen – Lemen Bank, Great Yarmouth. 124

Chapter Fourteen – CCCUE and the Middle East. 126

Chapter Fifteen – My Many Stamps, NPCC WB1 & 1000. 165

Chapter Sixteen – TOTAL ABK.. 176

Chapter Seventeen – Our home life and problems. 182

Chapter Eighteen – Mixed gas diving off Sharjah and to Oman
and PDO SBM maintenance. 186

Chapter Nineteen – Away from Home, French Royalty and being exoceted.
.... 203

Chapter Twenty – Selling my Blood, getting banned from Kuwait to
Thailand, Penang, India and Saudi Arabia. 218

Chapter Twenty-one – Back in Oman for PDO, my last operation at ABK,
onward to Salalah for one of the best diving operation
adventures I've ever had. 257

Chapter Twenty-two – My last operation for CCCUE in Oman was on the
Conoco 111, and then I returned to the UK. 292

Chapter One
My Family Roots

I once read that everyone had a book in them. My wife and friends kept telling me to write about my life adventures, which to me were nothing special; it was just how my life had panned out. When you are dyslexic, you hate writing and spelling, not to mention grammar, so it's not easy to sit down and write about yourself; as for a computer spell checker, well, that is not as good as you may think because how do I know if the computer spell checker is right or wrong? I am writing this life story as I speak, not as English is written or spoken; for me, being dyslexic means that poorly written English or badly spoken English is not wrongly written or spoken in my dyslexic head.

My Dad was from Calcutta, India. He was born on 14/4/1921 and baptised on 24/4/1921. He was a French Anglo-Indian, Roger Clement Pierre de Beaufort. My grandparents on my Dad's side were Clarence Clement and Marie Josephine, but I never recall meeting them. My dad spent his youth living and being educated in India. The de Beaufort name refers to Henry 2nd of England, whose father was Geoffrey V (or Geoffrey), Count of Anjou. The family's history dates back to Jean Nicolas de Beaufort (b. 1723 – 1780) of Moyenvic and Joinville in Champagne, France. His son was Henri Nicolas (1753-1817), the de Beaufort who went to India, thus starting our long association and history with India. Through the family's connections with The Knights of the Order of St Louis, Henri Nicolas met a 21-year-old Mary Eleanor de Palmas, born in Goa (a Portuguese Colony in India), the daughter of Captain John Alexander Simon de Palmas, an army engineer and also a Knight of the Order of St. Louis. On November 22nd 1784, they married in the Union Territory of Pondicherry.

Through this marriage, the French royal 'de' was added to Beaufort's name; it's how we became the de Beauforts. The de Beauforts moved to Chandernagor, and on the 20th of June 1785, Henri was promoted to Grand Voyer Architect for Chandernagor. Chandernagor had been restored to French control in 1763 but was retaken by the British in 1794 during the Napoleonic Wars. The city was returned to France in 1815. The family was originally pure French. However, once they emigrated to India and married Indian nationals or those of mixed European and Indian descent, they became Eurasians, now known as Anglo-Indians, a generic term for those of mixed blood. The last of our family left in Calcutta were the half-brothers of Roger de Beaufort: Joseph Fanshawe de Beaufort and his wife, Thelma, and the other half-brother, Clarence Duncan, and his wife, Margaret. Joseph and Thelma left India in the 1980s and died in the UK. Clarence Duncan de Beaufort b: 1911 in Calcutta, India d: 1975 in Calcutta, and his wife and their three daughters emigrated to Australia. My Dad's family left India in 1947, with my Dad settling in Liverpool, and his parents and siblings around Bristol. Dad died in Liverpool in 2002. His first language was Bengali, and most of his friends in Liverpool were from Bengal. He had four boys and two girls. Dad was one of five boys and one girl, Madge, who died in 2023 at the grand age of 100. The Madges (Stephen Madge) made good, and there is a road in Calcutta called Madge Street named after the family.

My dad's life is sometimes a bit of a mystery, as he would disappear for long periods, travelling around the world, but no one has ever found out where he went. Dad came to England after the Second World War, serving in the navy as a marine engineer.

Mum & *Dad*

Dad had joined a ship called the Empire Raven, and he served on her as a fourth engineer from October 15, 1947, until December 16, that year. Dad's ships sailed in and out of Liverpool, and it was about this time that he met my Mum, Eleanor Daley, in Liverpool. Dad was a very handsome man, with his dark looks and French surname; Mum was a lovely dreamer who fell in love with Dad at first sight. During their courtship, Dad visited the tenements in Dingle, where my Mum lived with her family. Dad found Mum cleaning the outside steps with soap and water. He asked, in all seriousness, where the servants were! (In India, Dad would have been used to the family having servants.)

Dad and Mum married on February 26th, 1949, in Mount Carmel Church in The Dingle.

Mum & Dad on their wedding day

They married in February because at the time, if you were Catholic, you were not allowed to get married during Lent. None of my dad's family attended the wedding, even though they were living in England at the time. Their first child, Eleanor Madge (my older sister), was born on December 11, 1949, at Sefton Hospital. They lived above a fish and chip shop in Cockburn Street, Liverpool. Dad was employed as a marine fitter by A & R Brown Ltd, Engineers and Ship Repairers, Regent Road, Liverpool, between August 24, 1948, and March 31, 1950. Dad joined Grayson, Rollo & Clover Docks Ltd as a fitter in January 1950; in March 1951, he left of his own accord. On 8th March 1951, he joined the SS Argolit as a 3rd Engineer and was discharged in Hamburg on 2nd July 1951, soon after their second child, my brother Roger Pierre, was born on 27th July 1951.

Mum and Dad had four more children: Andre Eugene (21 June 1953), Christopher Denis (me) (1 October 1954), Robin Marc (17 March 1957), and Karen (17 July 1959). Mum and Dad moved from Dingle to Speke and then onto a three-bedroom house at 4 Lulworth Road, Lee Park Estate, Gateacre, Liverpool, in 1957. Dad died there in 2002. Mum stayed at the same address until she entered a care home a few years back, but sadly, Mum has passed away now. Still, even that left everyone laughing as mum had been in a coma for around 10 days and my sisters, brothers plus nieces were there looking after her 24 hours a day. When they heard I was on my way from Cornwall Little Maria, my brother Andre's daughter said jokingly, "Bet nan passes away now that her favourite son is coming," as nan was only hanging on for me to arrive. True enough, that early morning, my mum passed away. We all laughed as I told everyone that Mum was waiting for me to say goodbye, "Sleep tight now, Mum."

Mum was in a care home for a long time. Mum summed up her feelings for my Dad (who had passed away many years ago) in a pub called the Grapes in the Woolton area of Liverpool. I was in the pub with my other brothers, Andre and Robin. We laughed together about anything related to Mum and Dad in the past. Suddenly, Mum tells us all, "Your Dad was handsome. I loved him at first sight, and when we married, I was a pure woman untouched by any other man." "Yoooo, stop there, Mum," we shouted. "Steady on, Mum. We don't want to know this, steady Mother, control yourself," we all said. "There was too much information there, Mum," but at the same time, we could not stop laughing. Mum asks Andre, "Are you married?" "Yes, Mum," Andre says, "to Mary." Mum then says to Andre, "Do you have any kids with Mary?" "No, Mum," he says, "not with Mary." Mum then says, "Why? Is your pecker not working?" Well, we could not stop laughing at Andre, and by now the bar staff and customers were also laughing.

Anyway, back to the council house in Liverpool. By now, it was a happy home full of laughter and fighting with my other three brothers and two sisters. We never had much, but as kids, you never know what you have or don't have at that age. I was a happy kid. I just loved to run, and I still do. I didn't know that I looked any different from other kids until I went to school; even then, I didn't understand what they meant when they would say words like 'nigger', 'Paki bastard', or 'monkey'. It all meant nothing to me; I was five, what did I know?

Chapter Two

My Early School Years.

It was only when I went to Junior school that I began to hear more and more about my colour, as, by then, the Indian side of my father was evident to everyone but not to me, and for whatever reason, I was always much darker than my other brothers and still am. I was called all sorts of names in and out of school, but it just went over my head; I was just a kid at school. But one day, it all came to me from, of all people, a school teacher.

This teacher was talking about monkeys. Anyway, he was talking about the colour of the monkey's hands. He told all the kids that the monkey's hands were white compared to the rest of its body. He looked at me, as did the other kids in the class. The kids started shouting at me, "Show us your hands, show us your hands." I looked down at my hands, and my palms were whiter than the rest of my arms. "Monkey, monkey," the kids would shout at me. I ran out of the classroom and into the playground, where there were loads of kids. I hid amongst the other kids, thinking it would go away. The other kids had come out and started shouting about what had happened, and then all the kids joined in shouting, "Monkey, monkey." I ran home, thinking it would all go away. It never did.

From then on, I was called names every day. I would always fight, which did me no good at all, as the name-calling never stopped. Because of this, it was very hard to make friends at school, but I had to persevere. School was never good for me, as I could not understand English lessons. I discovered the reason when I was in my thirties. I have always wondered why failing the 11+ mark would define kids at such a young age. I excelled in maths, history, PE, and RE, but struggled with English, writing, and pronouncing English words; this led me to distance myself from engaging in conversations and writing. Naturally, I failed my 11+ exam and was sent directly to a secondary modern school. My English never improved, nor did any other subject, as I always felt the teachers were not very interested in our education at the secondary modern school; it was as if they were being punished by teaching jobs in a secondary modern school.

The only teacher I enjoyed lessons with was the PE teacher. I loved any sport, including football, athletics, and boxing. The name-calling never stopped in school or out of school, but I had stopped trying to fight all the time. As my older brother Roger said, "What's the point, as you always get beaten up? They will keep coming back at you." He was right; I learned to walk away and make jokes about the name-calling, which always confused the other guys, as it did not bother me anymore. The name-calling never stopped, but I could deal with it much better.

Chapter Three

My Teenage Years

I left school at the age of 14 without any grades. I just thought I would get a job, which would be easy. I was in the real world, and life was not that easy. I would write away for jobs, any jobs, and apprenticeships mainly, but I was still waiting for replies. I was not surprised I was not getting replies, as my writing, spelling, sentences, and paragraphs were just a mess; I would write as I spoke, with no grammar anywhere, as if I knew what grammar was. Ultimately, I would knock on factory doors to see if they were hiring. I got a break at Wingrove & Rogers, a factory that made electrical components for TVs and radios. They were looking for young personnel to work on the factory floor, and if I joined them, they would send me to a polytechnical school once a week to do electrical engineering. Finally, I had a bit of luck; I was delighted. I was offered a paid job of £ 5-11p a week and had the chance to become an electrician.

The work was different from what I had imagined it to be; I was assembling TV components, the same components every day, four days a week, with one day at Polytech spent learning electrical engineering. The electrical study was difficult to understand; it wasn't sinking in at all, but the practical work was excellent. I could do that, and I could put anything together practically. It was so natural to me, and I enjoyed that side of electrical engineering, but the electrical engineering theory was hopeless; it did not make any sense. To my surprise, one of the instructors noticed something in me. As much as I had failed my first year's electrical exam, the instructor, Mr Gibson, who was mainly into mechanical engineering, convinced Wingrove & Rogers to let me sign up at the Polytech in mechanical engineering craft practice. This was the first time I felt like I was making progress. It was a subject I could understand both practically and theoretically, and it opened up my world, allowing me to finally do something besides running around and playing football, which I loved and was very good at.

I even had two handwritten letters from the great Bill Shankly: one inviting me to have a trial at Liverpool's Melwood training ground, which I loved, and another informing me I had not made the grade. I wish I had kept those handwritten letters from Bill Shankly, but in those days, who thought of memorabilia? Anyway, back to my early years. My Polytech course was going well both practically and theoretically. I hated working in the factory and indoors, but I had four years to complete my City & Guilds in mechanical engineering craft practice. I met a girl called Rose in the factory, and we got on very well, but at that age, what did we know about life? You think you know it all, but you know nothing. Rose and I enjoyed being with each other. Rose's family was very different from mine, and my parents never got on with each other. Rose's family was happy and lived as they saw fit. I always got on very well with Rose's younger brother, Bart, and I still enjoy meeting him when we bump into each other. Rose and I just got on with things, but never knew anything about life. We were just two people who were too young to think about marriage, but in those days, you were left on the shelf if you did not get married by age 21. Not many people know this, but Rose and I got married twice. I don't think even our kids know this, but let me explain.

I had finished my City & Guilds in Mechanical Engineering, and I was thrilled that, at long last, I qualified. I still do not know how I passed the exam. I always thought I was too thick to pass any exams and lacked confidence or belief in myself. Not long after I passed my exams, I was back in the factory, and I always remembered this moment as the turning point of my life. The factory foreman, Tom Hooper, is a name I have never forgotten, as he changed my life in many ways. He had been working on the same lathe machine for nearly 40 years. The wooden pallet had been shaped to his feet because he had been standing on it for so long. He had stood there for almost 40 years in his brown coveralls, staring at the same white walls; he turned around to me and said, "Lad, I will be retiring soon, and all of this will be yours." That's when life shot past me.

I was looking at him and seeing myself in 40 years, and then it hit me with shock and horror: I was staring at him and seeing my life. I was him; he was me. There and then, I decided that was not the life I wanted. I wanted more than standing at the same spot, looking at a white wall for 40 years. I quit my job immediately and realised there had to be more to life than working in the same spot all your working life. Thanks to Mr. Tom Hooper, he saved me in more ways than he would ever have known.

I didn't know what I was going to do. I had my City & Guilds but no longer wanted to work indoors. The only other thing I excelled at was playing football, which I thoroughly enjoyed. I even turned down jobs because that involved working on weekends, which meant I couldn't play football. I worked as a builder's labourer, which was challenging physical work, but I enjoyed the work. It was outside and interesting. I learned many things as a builder's labourer and still use those skills. Little did I know it would get me into diving, but that will come later. I was still with Rose. I had very few girlfriends and very few male friends back then, as I was never the easiest person to get along with. I was never relaxed in company due to my dyslexia, which I never fully understood. I would talk very fast so that people wouldn't know I couldn't pronounce words correctly, which frustrated me; it didn't make me very pleasant company. I did have one very good friend, a guy called Colin Pauline. He always remained friendly with me, likewise his wife, Lyn. I still keep in touch with them through Facebook.

As much as I enjoyed working outdoors as a builder's labourer, it was not a promising long-term career. I watched my brothers' careers in the military flourish and saw how much they enjoyed their lives in the Service. Anyways, let me get back to Rose, and us getting married twice. I found a job advert for a football coach in the Faroe Islands, but the coach must be married. Rose and I decided to get married in a registrar's office without telling anybody, even our families, as we knew they would object. That's how much we knew about life; it was a crazy thing to do. We were married in March 1973 with no family present. We did it without understanding the consequences; we did it just so I could apply for this job as a football coach, which I never got because playing football was not a qualification. That's what Rose and I knew about understanding life: nothing. So, what do we do now? We were married, but no one knew about it apart from my only mate, Colin Pauline.

I decided to join the Army because my two older brothers, who were already in the armed forces, were doing well. Don't ask me why I joined the Army; I just did. I ended up in the Royal Artillery, and off I went to London to the Woolwich Barracks, the home of the Royal Artillery. But this is where real life caught up with me. As I was married, the army needed to send my married man's allowance back to my wife, but no one knew I was married. I managed to stop any payments from being sent back to Rose for the time being, anyway. I enjoyed the army training, being outdoors, and the physical exercise; I was doing well in my training and was glad I had decided to join the army. I had gone past the period when you had to choose between staying in the Army or leave, but now my problems had started. The Army had begun sending Rose a married man's allowance, which was picked up by her mother, who did not understand why the Army was sending Rose a married person's allowance. The Army was unhappy with me. I was told to man up and sort out the mess I had gotten my personal life into, as it was affecting my army training, and I could not concentrate. I was given a weekend pass to return to Liverpool and explain everything to my in-laws, my mum, and my dad. Understandably, the news did not go over well with either family. Real life had caught up with us. After the weekend passed, I returned to London to continue my army training. But by now, I could not concentrate properly on my army training; a discussion between the army careers officer and me that, as much as they did not want me to leave, I could not continue as my mind was elsewhere. It was decided that I would leave the Army but join the Territorial Army to maintain my training, and if I wanted to rejoin the Army full-time, the time spent in the Territorial Army would be considered. I joined Liverpool's 'Royal Electrical & Mechanical Engineers' territory army.

I also got a new job as a builder's labourer after completing a builder's labourers' course; surprisingly, all these different jobs and experiences led me into diving. I enjoyed working as a builder's labourer, and life seemed settled with Rose and her family. We were not living together, but we were still together and carried on as if we were just a courting couple. I was still looking for jobs; then, one day, in the local paper, I saw an advertisement for trainee divers with no experience required, but they must have worked on a building site. I was fascinated by this advert: "Trainee diver needed, no experience needed, but must have worked on a building site." Well, this just excited me. Who wouldn't be! I wrote in my best English, but I never expected a reply. After a few weeks, I received a letter from the Manchester Ship Canal Company inviting me for an interview.

I went to a place called No Man's Land in Runcorn underneath the Runcorn Bridge. I went inside the building where the interview was being held, but then I saw that many people had been invited, much to my horror, as I now realised I didn't think I had a chance. The man leading the interview with everyone at the same time was a man called Les Brown, an old navy-trained hard-hat diver, which at the time meant nothing to me apart from the fact that I had seen those diving suits in the movies, not in real life. His first question was, has anyone been diving before? Many of them put their hands up; well, that's the end of the interview for me, I thought, but no; he then asked the guys who had been diving before to leave the interview. Very odd, I thought, as surely you want people who had dived before. The next question he asked was how many of us had worked on or were working on a building site. About 10 of the 20+ people remaining raised their hands. He said the rest of those who have not worked on a building site can leave. To my amazement, I was still in the interview. "Right," he said to the remaining 10, "Follow me to the dive boat."

Once on board the dive boat, the Jessie Wallwork, he gave me some warm woolly suits and told me to change into them. As I sat on the deck of the dive vessel, he brought out the hard-hat diving suits, called Siebe Gorman's dry suits. They were identical to diving suits I had seen in the movies. The idea was that I would get dressed in the Siebe Gorman dive suits and try to enter the water, then dive to the bottom, which was not very deep, but to me, it felt like a long way down. As the diving suit was cumbersome, few of us could stand in them. The ones who could not stand up were asked to leave. It was now my turn to get dressed into the diving suit and then walk to the dive ladder. (Due to all the heavy work as a builder's labourer, I was used to lifting heavy material up and down ladders for the plasterers and the bricklayers). As they put the diving hat over my head, I wondered what I was doing there; all I could hear was the noise of the air being pumped into the diving hat, and then I listened to a command inside the diving hat to stand up and walk to the dive ladder, I did not know where the sound was coming from, but I did what I was told which was to stand up and walk across the deck to the dive ladder. I stood up with a bit of a struggle, but I did manage to stand up; now I was standing. It was a case of walking across the deck to the dive ladder, which seemed miles away but was only about 8/10 feet away. I managed to walk across the deck to the dive ladder that ran down the dive vessel's side.

Now was the most difficult time for me in the dive suit, you had to turn around and try to put your legs onto the dive ladder, which meant lifting one leg up and over to the first rung of the dive ladder. This was very hard as you now had all the weight of the dive suit, which had lead weights over your chest, the lead diving boots, the weight of the diving hat, and an air hose connected to the diving hat. It was not easy. I managed to lift one leg onto the dive ladder without falling over, then the other leg, so now I had both legs on the diving ladder; all I had to do now was walk down the dive ladder and get into the water.

As I entered the water, which was pitch black, I felt a tremendous pain in both ears. I did not know what was going on, and I shouted out in pain, and all I could hear was, "Come back up the ladder." Once I got to the top of the ladder, they took the diving hat off me and asked what the problem was. I told them I had a lot of pain in my ears. "Good lad," they said. They then put a nose clip over my nose and said, "Go back down, and when you feel pain, blow against the clip." I thought it was all very odd, but I said, "Okay." They put the diving hat back over my head and told me to return to the dive ladder. As I entered the water, I felt the pain again, but this time, I blew against the nose clip as I was told, and the pain went away. I continued going down until I could not go down further, as I had reached the seabed. It was still pitch black in the water. As I had never dived before, I knew nothing different, and I later discovered that Les, the senior diver, did not want people who had dived before, as they would have been accustomed to diving in clear water. Les told me that diving in pitch-black water requires a different approach than working in clear water. Anyway, back to my dive, as I had reached the bottom and could not go any further, a voice said, "Return to the surface." I still did not know where this voice was coming from, but why should I? I never had a diving hat on my head before. After the dive, Les, the senior diver, interviewed me face to face. He asked me what I had done on the building sites. I told him what I had done, from making concrete to laying concrete, jackhammering, hod carrying, helping the bricklayers, laying pipes, working with cranes, etc. He asked me about my short time in the regular army and the TA, which I was still in at the time of the interview, and that I had learned to understand teamwork and to follow instructions. To my surprise, a few weeks later, I received a letter from the Manchester Ship Canal informing me that I had been successful in my interview and asking when I could start my new job as a trainer diver.

Chapter Four
The Start of My Diving Career.

In January 1975, I started my long diving career as a deckhand/linesman and trainee diver on a Siebe Gorman diving equipment vessel called the Jessie Wallwork, using Siebe Gorman/Frogman diving equipment on the Manchester Ship Canal.

The other divers and I.

Frogman's Diving Equipment   ***Siebe Gorman's Hard Hat diving equipment***

It was an exciting but very nervous start on my first day, joining the diving boat in Runcorn harbour underneath the Runcorn Bridge, known as 'No man's land'. Les welcomed me and introduced me to the rest of the diving team. One of the divers was a very experienced hard-hat diver named Dave Wilding. Another trainee diver, Adrian Shannon, was motorbike-mad. I remember he had a Honda motorbike, a Golden Eagle 1000, and he took me out for a ride one day. I had never been so frightened in my life. Boy, could he drive that bike fast!

The first few weeks were spent learning how the dive boat worked and what was required of me on and around the vessel. First, I had to learn how to become a deckhand and care for the dive boat, as well as the vessel's equipment above and below deck. When I joined the dive vessel, it was winter time, so I had to familiarise myself with where everything was stored and how to maintain the vessel's cleanliness, tidiness, and warmth. One of my main jobs was to keep a bucket of water on top of the metal fire stove. This water had to be kept very warm, and we also had to keep the fire stove topped up with coal to keep the boat warm.

The bucket of warm water was for Les and Dave when they emerged from the water after a long dive. I would remove their diving hats and gloves; they would then place their hands into the warm water to warm them up and to remove the numbness they had experienced after being in the cold water for long periods. I had to keep the fire stove clean and polished in the summer. I was told I had to use black shoe polish on ladies' nylons and rub it over the fire stove, as it helped keep a lovely shine on the black fire stove. Les was just what you would think a hard-hat diver would look like. He was a tall, good-looking man, rough around the edges, and he even had blue eyes, if I remember correctly. He was a very calm, patient man. He would take all the time needed for me to do things correctly the way he wanted. He knew what was required and how to do things on his vessel. He would try to teach me everything, from steering the ship to securing it to the harbour walls, throwing the mooring ropes from the boat to the shoreside bollards, and hitting the bollards with the mooring ropes while the boat was moving past them. It took a lot of practice, but I can still do it.

It came in handy one day, many years later. I was on a two-masted schooner in the 150-year 'America's Cup' celebration around the Isle of Wight. After sailing around the Isle of Wight, we sailed into Portsmouth's harbour as part of the Tall Ships Race. As we approached the jetty, the schooner's skipper was having problems getting the schooner alongside. I picked up the stern mooring rope and hit the jetties' shoreside bollard from 20 feet away. Then, I placed the mooring rope around the stern of the ship's bollards, which slowed the schooner down, and the skipper could bring the schooner alongside. The skipper looked at me in amazement and wondered if I meant that or if it was a lucky throw. I won the bet when he asked me if I could do that again.

As time passed, working as a deckhand on the Jessie Wallwork, I began to learn how to be a diver tender and linesman. A diver tender would look after all the divers' needs; the tender would help the diver get into his diving equipment, which meant learning how to dress the hard-hat diver correctly and the diver into the Frogman's diving equipment. The linesman was to look after the diver once he was in the water. Most of the time, we did not have radio communications, so we had to learn how to communicate with the diver using hand signals on the diver's air umbilical. The air umbilical was just the same as the umbilical you are born with; it was your life support. It was an umbilical from the surface that supplied air to the diver, either from hand pumps or a mechanically or electrically driven low-pressure air compressor, directly to the diver from the dive boat.

When the handles are turned, the air diving hand pump supplies air to the Hard Hat Diver. The linesman had a series of hand signals that he and the divers were familiar with; either the linesman would signal the diver by a series of hard pulls on the umbilical line, or the diver would respond by pulling on the umbilical line.

The hard-hat diver with his umbilical attached to his diving hard hat.

The water in the Manchester Ship Canal was pitch black; you couldn't see anything underwater or even your own hands if you put them in front of your eyes. Les would try to teach me how to think and work in black water, which was one of the reasons he did not want anyone who had dived before in clear water; he wanted to teach me his way of thinking and working in black water. I learnt how many pulls on the air umbilical would mean, whether the diver would come up to the surface or start moving left or right on the seabed or if a winch wire was coming down or being lifted from the vessel. I also learnt how to respond in an emergency if something went wrong, which fortunately never did. However, I had to know all of these pulls on the air umbilical to work underwater. I had no prior knowledge of diving theory; I followed his instructions. Les would decide when I dived and what equipment I would use on each dive. Les made it quite clear that 'Diving' was just transport to the job, nothing more, nothing less; I was just an underwater labourer. Les took his time teaching me how to dive and work underwater. He wanted people with building site experience because the Manchester Ship Canal was a man-made canal with five lock gate areas, from Manchester Salford Quays all the way to Eastham Locks on the Wirral. The lock gates at Eastham Docks opened into the River Mersey. The Manchester Canal is 36 miles long and was started in August 1887. It was completed on December 7, 1893, and opened in January 1894. As a man-made canal, it required considerable maintenance. It required extensive underwater building repairs along the canal from Manchester to Eastham Docks.

Everything was going well. I was enjoying my new career, and things were good with Rose, but we knew we had to address our marital situation. We could not ignore the fact that we were married, and no one knew about it except our parents. We decided to have a church wedding in West Derby, Liverpool. We had to ask the vicar if he could conduct a typical church wedding and pretend we were just an average newlywed couple getting married for the first time. Everything went well, and we married for the second time on May 11, 1975; nowadays, I think it is called renewing your wedding vows. We couldn't afford to go anywhere for our honeymoon, but we now have a council house in Runcorn, at 48 Palace Fields Road, Runcorn, and that's where we spent our honeymoon. Rose continued to work in Liverpool while I continued to work on the Manchester Ship Canal. We were settling into life in Runcorn, and I was getting better at my job as a trainee diver. I also played football for the local semi-professional club, Runcorn FC, in what was known as the Northern Conference League. As mentioned, I was never taught any diving theory; I just did what Les asked me to do. I never knew anything about decompression stops or anything else. I just dived when Les told me to dive and returned to the surface when I was told to. If I had been in the water for an extended period, the underwater comms or hand signals would inform me when to return to the surface. I would go down on a downline, a rope with a weight lowered into the water from the dive boat before each dive. I would follow that downline down to the seabed until I got a signal to return to the surface. At this point, I would go back to the same downline to follow it to the surface.

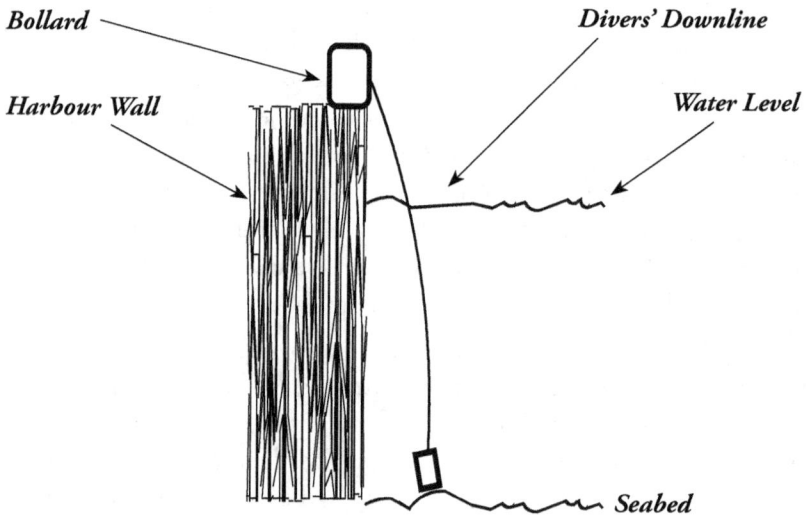

Drawing of a downline running from the bollard on the harbour down to the seabed.

The only time I would stop travelling upwards on the downline was if I came across a chisel fitted inside the downline; if I came across that chisel, I knew I had to stop. If the chisel started to move upwards, I would follow it until it stopped, then I would stop. I was not aware that this was our decompression stop, which at the time still meant nothing to me. I followed the downline with my hands and kept going up until I felt a chisel in the rope; I would then stay there until the chisel started to move. I did this until I reached the surface. I never asked what it was for; I just followed my instructions. I recall the first time I encountered 'Health and Safety'. We were working at the Eastham lock gates, using a water jet to clear away the silt with a fire hose. The fire hose had a brass nozzle at the end, which blew away all the silt from inside the floating lock gates and from the tram lines that ran along the seabed. We usually dived for a couple of hours daily in the docks in the Siebe Gorman hard hat diving equipment, and came up to the surface when we received hand signals on the umbilical. We did have underwater comms in the diving helmet, but it was so noisy that we could not hear the voice communications most of the time, so it was easier to feel the pulls on your air umbilical.

On this particular day, Les was diving; he had only been in the water for about an hour and a half when one of the management team members came along the jetty and asked for Les, as the man next to him wanted to discuss something with him. We said, "No, we can't do that just yet, as Les hasn't completed his couple of hours in the water." The management team said, "Bring Les up now, and he will take all the blame for stopping the dive." "Okay," we said. We gave Les 4 pulls and then two pulls, which meant he had to return to the surface. Once Les had got on the boat, we took off the Siebe Gorman hard hat and put the bucket of warm water next to him so he could put his hands into the warm water; he then asked what was going on. I pointed out to Les that the harbour manager on the jetty and the man beside him insisted that we bring him out of the water, as he wanted to speak to him. The man turned out to be an HSE inspector, which meant nothing to me, but Les knew this day was coming. It marked the beginning of the end of hard-hat diving. I was not involved in any discussions and would not have understood what they were discussing anyway, but as the HSE had not yet stopped us, so we continued diving with the hard hats.

We were still diving in the hard hat equipment, but on one particular day, just before my dive, the brass nozzle on the water jet hose came off at the surface and dropped into the water. I had to go and look for it as I had not fitted it correctly. As mentioned, the water in the Manchester Ship Canal is pitch black, so it was not easy to find anything. I had been in the water for about an hour, still searching through the silt for the brass nozzle, when all of a sudden, I felt sick, experienced headaches, felt clumsy, and became confused. I did not know what was going on. As I was not water jetting, I was able to inform the guys on the dive boat through the in-water communications inside the hat that I was not feeling very well. I was told to return to the surface. I began to feel better once the diving mask was removed, but it was all very odd to me to experience these strange feelings while underwater. This issue concerned me because I was unsure of its nature. It was decided that I should consult the company's doctor for an examination and a discussion to determine my feelings about it. After consulting with the doctor and discussing the matter, it was decided that I should refrain from diving for the time being to see if any symptoms reappear. I was assigned to work with the sandbag crew in Runcorn, filling sandbags that would be used to reinforce the sides of the canal banks whenever they started to collapse. I even had to fill them up for the dive crew and load them onto the dive boat, which was not a great experience, loading up the dive boat and watching it sail away to a diving job somewhere. There was a big diving operation at Eastham floating lock gates, and a big dive company was hired to do the diving work. The dive company was called 'Strongwork'. They were replacing all the tram lines on the seabed, which the floating lock gates used to operate. On-site, they had the first-ever Decompression Chamber I had ever seen. It looked like some space rocket; Strongwork divers only dived for an hour, and when they returned to the surface, they would go away for an hour's rest.

Due to the ongoing large-scale diving operation, the dive team I was part of now needed new divers, so I was replaced, as no one knew when I would be able to dive again. I was now in an odd period; I had lost my job as a trainee diver and was back working as a labourer filling up sandbags. After four weeks, an opening turned up at Eastham Locks. The dive team based in Eastham needed a linesman/tender, as the old guy, called Jack Bird, was retiring, and they needed a replacement. My first dive leader from the Jessie Wallwork vessel, Les Brown, recommended me for that position. Due to the experience, I had gained as a linesman/tender on Siebe Gorman diving equipment with Les, I was selected to replace Jack Bird as a linesman/dive tender. I was delighted to be back working with the dive team at Eastham's

Locks as a linesman/tender. At the end of the winter of 1976, I started working as a full-time linesman/tender with an old diver called Eric Mottershead, who had the biggest hands I had ever seen. I had to conduct a handover with Jack Bird before taking over from him, and Eric also had to approve me before I could take over full-time. Luckily, Eric and Jack were friendly people to work with. They were happy to show me everything they knew and how they liked to operate. It was usually a two-man team, but it was handy for Eric and Jack to have the extra man as we were busy around the harbour area. Our main task was maintaining the lock gates to ensure they were always operational, as cargo ships and oil tankers constantly came in and out of Eastham's lock gates.

Not many ships go all the way to Salford Quays in Manchester anymore. Most of the ships that came through the lock gates mainly went to Ellesmere Port Oil docks, and many more just entered through the Queen Elizabeth 2 floating dock gates at Eastham docks. There were two sets of lock gates at Eastham: the floating lock gates, which were being repaired by Strongwork, and the more conventional lock gates that required opening and shutting using heavy chains, which we worked on. I would occasionally see the dive team on the Jessie Wallwork, but I had my new job to concentrate on and not think about what might have been. I enjoyed working with Eric and Jack. They were both very helpful. I look back at the operation now and laugh at how we used to dive. If we had to dive inside the lock gates, we would load up two or three three-wheel wheelbarrows with all the diving equipment. We would load all the Siebe Gorman hard hat diving equipment in one wheelbarrow and the air hand pump in the other wheelbarrow. We would push them around the docks to the dive areas. We did have a small wooden dive boat, but Eric was usually happy just diving from the harbour wall.

That's me driving the wooden dive boat around the Manchester Ship Canal.

As much as I was enjoying myself, I kept wondering if I could return to being a diver. Still, there did not seem to be any way back, or so it seemed at the time, in the summer of 1976, which was a long, very hot summer. Jack, the old linesman I was taking over from, would always fall asleep without warning when it got too hot, and it was very hot in 1976.

One job we had to do each day during that summer was to check the weather, not to see if it was bad or anything, but to see if our old dive tender, Jack Bird, who was 75 years old and still going, was asleep. That day, we checked the weather; it was very cloudy. Eric, the senior diver, told me to prepare the dive gear for him, and Jack would be the tender for the dive today. Eric would inspect the main running wheels inside the harbour wall, but these running wheels were 60 feet down. Eric would have to climb the harbour ladder 30 feet in heavy diving equipment to reach the water. Jack and I loaded all the diving gear into the wheelbarrows and set off down the harbour to the area where Eric would be diving, so he could check the running chains. We sent up the hand pumps for the Siebe Gorman diving gear, and Jack would stay behind and keep turning the hand pumps to supply air to the diver. Eric had to descend the ladder to the water. This is not easy in heavy, standard diving gear. As it was cloudy, Eric sent me back to our wooden diving canal boat to prepare the fire to keep it nice and warm, and I had to tidy up the dive boat. After a while, I looked outside and noticed the sun was shining. To my horror, I realised it was warm. As I looked along the harbour wall, I could see the diving hand pump wheels turning over independently, with no sign of Jack the tender. I ran as fast as I could to the dive area. Looking down inside the harbour wall, I could see Eric, the senior diver, in all his Siebe Gorman diving gear, which weighed 100/120 lbs, running up the ladder as fast as he could, which was not easy. I then started turning the hand wheels on the pump to give him air.

Once I got Eric to the top of the harbour wall and took his hard hat off, he lay there breathing very heavily and said, "The fucking sun wasn't shining or warm when I started the fucking dive." Then we heard snoring at the back of the harbour fenders where Jack had fallen asleep in the warm sunshine. So, Eric and I loaded Jack and the diving gear into the wheelbarrows, returned to our wooden dive boat, and had a cup of tea while we waited for Jack to wake up. Jack retired soon after this, and I became Eric's full-time linesman and tender. I was very pleased about this, but I was still wondering if I could return to diving. There did not seem to be a way of doing this on the Manchester Ship Canal. I heard about a new professional diving centre opening in Scotland, based in Fort William. The more I read about it, the more I realised it was an opportunity for me to become a fully trained professional diver with all the correct qualifications. The training was free, and accommodations and food were also included, along with the train fare to Fort William, which was a significant added benefit.

I went to the job centre to get all the information about the diving training course. I learned that they would prefer people with diving experience, and I had to pass a diving medical exam. Before I filled in the application form, I asked Les, my first senior diver, for his advice and opinion. I had spent 18 months working for him as a trainee diver/linesman. He advised me to go for it. He would give me a reference to help with my application form. In July 1976, I submitted my application form, accompanied by a reference from Les. I waited and hoped to be selected for the air diving course. After two weeks, I was invited to an interview in Newcastle. I did not know what to expect.

They asked if I had a diving logbook, which I said I didn't, as I didn't know what that was. The only proof I had that I had been diving was a reference letter from Les, plus some photos I had taken with me, which they seemed to be satisfied with. "That's fine," they said, "that will do." That was the first box ticked. I was then sent away for a diving medical, which involved a lot of exercises, breathing tests, heart checks, blood pressure checks, and weighing, all of which seemed to go very well. After a few questions about the type of diving work I had carried out, which was all inshore diving, the interviewer seemed very pleased with my interview. I travelled back to Runcorn and waited to see if I had been selected. I continued working as Eric's dive tender and linesman. I told Eric about the diver training course I had applied for in Scotland; he said he would be very happy for me if it all worked out.

Finally, in August 1976, I received the good news I had hoped for: I was accepted to participate in a three-month Training Services Agency air diving course at Fort William, Scotland, Underwater Training Centre. The course began on September 13, 1976, and concluded on December 3, 1976; it was the 13th air diving course at the Underwater Training Centre. I asked the management of the Manchester Ship Canal if I could take three months of unpaid leave to attend the course. This request was refused as they could not keep my position open while they waited to see if I would complete the course. Plus, the ship canal itself did not currently require any divers to be qualified to a Training Services Agency standard, as it was not yet a requirement for employment. After discussing the situation with Rose, we agreed that I would put my notice at the ship canal to participate in this new adventure. We didn't know where it would take us, but I had to give this new opportunity a try. On September 11, 1976, I completed my notice period at the ship canal and boarded a train from Runcorn to Fort William, Scotland.

Chapter Five

The Underwater Training Centre, Fort William, Scotland.

I travelled to Fort William two days before the air diving course started to get a feel for the Underwater Training Centre's surrounding area. I walked down the jetty to inspect the Deep Diver 1 barge; I looked on in amazement at what I saw. As you can see from the picture below, I had progressed from Siebe Gorman hard hats, Frogman diving equipment, and air hand pumps to seeing this diving barge; I wondered what I had volunteered for, as all this seemed beyond me.

Deep Diver 1

Deep Diver 1 Control Room

I was soon informed that the above systems were not part of my air diver training.

My first week was getting to know the staff at Fort William, **(little did I know then that one of the staff would become my diving manager over 20 years later, a nice guy called Bruce Cobby),** how they operated regarding the setting up of the diving equipment, how each one of us would be a lead diver for a week and which week I would be the lead diver which meant making sure all the diving equipment that was required for that week's training was fully charged and in place on the jetty platform ready for diving.

The first few days also involved getting to know the other people on the diving course. From what I remember, there were around eight to ten guys on each course, and different diving courses were being conducted simultaneously.

I am the one with the moustache, with two Fort William Diving Instructors on the left and eight divers.

The first few days were a bit of a blur for me. I was accustomed to diving, but I was not prepared for the extensive classwork we had to complete, which involved in-depth theory on diving mechanics and laws. This concerned me as I hated writing and had a bad understanding of English. It all came back to how bad my schoolwork was. I would sit away from the front of the class as much as possible. I did not understand what the diving instructors discussed: Boyle's Law, Dalton's Law, Archimedes' principles, decompression tables, carbon monoxide, oxygen poisoning, nitrogen narcosis, and decompression illness. It just went over my head. I was very nervous. I was very concerned about what I had gotten myself into and whether I would be able to complete these three months of diver training. I was not great company, as I felt inadequate compared to the other guys, who seemed to take all the classroom studies in their stride.

As the first week progressed, we learned how to wear the diving suits, charge the air cylinders, and assist in dressing the other divers. This side of the diving operation was good for me, as I was accustomed to it; it helped me settle down a bit more. Towards the end of the first week, I had done a couple of dives in about 10 feet of water. I used surface-supply diving equipment with a communication system to talk to the topside controller. I was also learning the hand signals associated with the diving air umbilical; this was fine, as I was accustomed to these hand signals from my ship canal diving operations.

At the end of the first week, I had to jump off the roof of the jetty toilet building, which was about 40 to 50 feet high. I don't know why we had to do it, but we all had to jump on the roof. It was a case of jumping, but I didn't think about it. At the same time, it was great fun.

Two of us jumped off the roof of the jetty toilet.

I spent most afternoons in the classroom. At the end of each week, I had exams on the diving theory I had been learning. I was hopeless. I couldn't understand any diving theories, and my exam results were poor. I was at the bottom of the class every week, which concerned the diving instructors. I was not grasping any of the diving theories, but I was excelling in the practical side of diving. I think it was because of this that I was not dropped from the course. One instructor, John Foster, told me to keep listening and learning. It would come to me no matter how long it took. If they could see me working on the theory, the instructors would continue to help me.

I enjoyed the practical side of the diving course, but I knew I had to study each night to understand the theory. This was not very good for my roommate, who found the theory very easy and was often out drinking most nights. I could not understand the theory. I must admit that, unlike my roommate, a charming guy from Australia, I was not pleasant to be around; my frustration of not understanding any of the diving theories unsettled me.

Each day, I would dive to different depths to build my resistance to nitrogen narcosis, which was like getting drunk the deeper you dived. At times, we all took turns dressing as standby divers to rescue divers who may have encountered difficulties in the water during their dives.

I am the standby diver.

At times, the diving instructors would arrange with one of the divers to pretend they were having difficulties, so they could observe the reaction of the entire diving team when they were called into action to rescue a diver in trouble. I was slowly improving my understanding of diving physics. I recall a particular day when the instructor discussed carbon monoxide poisoning. The diving instructor explained that if carbon monoxide enters a diver's air supply from the air compressor intake valves, it may be because the intake valve was placed too close to the engine's exhaust or if the oil in the compressor becomes too hot. If this happens, the oil partially combusts, producing carbon monoxide, which the diver breathes in. The bit that interested me was when the diving instructor explained the symptoms: nausea, headaches, weakness, clumsiness and confusion. These were all the symptoms I experienced when I had my diving incident on the Manchester Ship Canal. I then realised the importance of the diving theory I was being taught; it was my watershed moment.

After six weeks, we were all due a long weekend break from our training; I decided to head home while a few of the other lads chose to stay in Fort William. I used to call home from a phone box about once a week. We never had mobile phones or the internet in those days. I got home after being away for six weeks. Rose had done very well looking after the house while I was away. She spent most of her time back in Liverpool, which was fine as that's where her family and friends were. As much as I had been away for six weeks, I hadn't earned any money. I only had £10 every two weeks to cover any outgoings while I was in Fort William, which meant I rarely went out in the evenings apart from walking around the town. This is why I spent most of my time studying in the hotel room.

Dangerous Dave is in the middle, with me in the background.

My first week back was interesting. We were going to learn a bit about explosives from 'Dangerous Dave'. It's an apt name for the man teaching us how to blow up things. It was fascinating and dangerous. Dave would show us how to blow holes downward using the base of wine bottles. If you ever look at wine bottles, the bottoms of some of them are concave. Because of its shape, if you pushed an explosive material into that indent at the bottom of the bottle, it would blow up in a confined area, but the explosion would blow downwards to give you a clean hole. It was a great couple of days of blowing up things. I enjoyed those few days, which relaxed me after returning to Fort William. I also took a few exams to see if I had forgotten any of our diving physics while I was away. It was the start of multiple-choice questions, but this format worked for me because I didn't have to do much writing. I understood them and knew the answers because I had a choice. At last, I was beginning to understand what the instructors were teaching me, and my exam results were heading in the right direction. I started to feel like a part of everything concerning the diver training, and as a result, I became more relaxed.

As I went deeper and deeper with my dives, I learnt more about decompression stops. As I began to understand more, I could not stop laughing, to the amusement of the diving instructors and the other divers. One of the diving instructors asked me what was so funny about them. I began retelling the story about the chisel. Our decompression stops were not calculated using fancy diving tables, but rather by a chisel fitted inside the downline. I mean, who would not laugh at this? During this period, I started to learn how to use the decompression chamber, how to control the flow of air into the chamber, how to supply oxygen to the divers, how and when to flush the chamber due to high oxygen levels building up, and how to use the diving tables for the chamber's operations. If I remember correctly, we used the United States of America Decompression Tables because they were the diving decompression dive tables primarily used by offshore diving companies worldwide. Many diving companies also had their own diving tables that they would use. I had to learn how to use the in-water and oxygen decompression tables, correct the timing between each water stop, and calculate the travelling time to get the diver from his last water stop to the DDC (Deck Decompression Chamber). There was a lot to learn. The diving instructors were very patient and thorough in teaching me the correct methods until I fully understood what I was doing and how to use the diving tables correctly for any in-water and oxygen stops during the DDC. If you got any of this wrong, a diver could end up with the bends or, as it was known, 'decompression sickness'.

Decompression sickness results from the formation of bubbles in the blood or body tissues and is caused by inadequate elimination of dissolved gas after a dive. It may occur from seemingly trivial no-decompression dives or on decompression dives, even when the correct procedures have been followed. Every diver had to be aware of decompression dives, decompression sickness, and the importance of understanding diving tables thoroughly. The diving instructors reviewed every dive I had to carry out as a diver. I continued to dive deeper and deeper in my build-up to 50 metres or 165 feet. I was now starting my week as the lead diver. The other divers knew I had spent my early days as a diver using Siebe Gorman hard hat diving equipment, so I was selected as the lead diver for that week. At the time, Fort William had an old-standard diving instructor named Whally Salsby. (I'm sorry if I misspelt his name.) Whally provided us with instructions on how to dress the diver in the dry suits, how to fit the shoulder collar onto the diving suit, and how to fit the diving hat, among other details. All this was great for me as I had done it many times before. The dive team and I were sent down to the jetty to prepare for our dives, but Whally got delayed, so I took it upon myself to start getting the first divers ready for the hard hat diving to save time, as I was used to doing this. However, this did not go down well with Whally; this was his baby and no one else's. After I apologised to him, he allowed the divers to go ahead.

Divers are ready and waiting.

Final checks before diving.

That's me getting dressed & the final checks from Whally in the red hat.

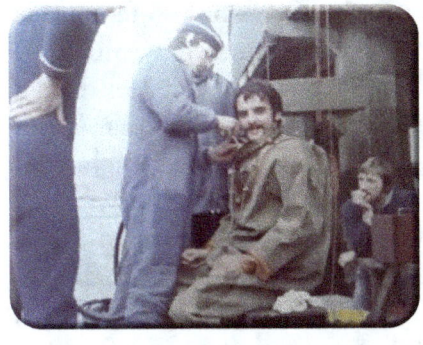

The week spent diving in hard hat diving equipment was very good. Everyone enjoyed the opportunity to explore the Siebe Gorman equipment, but now we had to prepare for the deep dives that followed. We started diving in Aquadyne helmets; they were very light and secured to your head with a neck dam and jockstrap, which was very uncomfortable, especially around your nether regions.

Aquadyne diving helmet with a neck dam and a Jockstrap.

We started going out in a Dory craft to conduct our deeper dives, as diving from the jetty was no longer suitable due to its shallow waters. I started diving to 60 feet and doing tasks like rope splicing to have something to do while at that depth. We also began doing in-water stops, but now I understand why I was doing them. I still laughed at these water stops, as all I could think of was the chisel in the downline. The build-up to the deep dives was becoming increasingly serious. We now had to be blown down to 50 metres or 165 feet inside the decompression chamber. This was to build up our resistance to nitrogen narcosis. I think the diving instructors enjoy this part of our training. We all had to be blown down to 50 metres or 165 feet inside the decompression chamber with exam papers to see how much we could concentrate at that depth. At that depth, you did feel drunk. We all filled in the exam sheets and thought we handled that depth without problems. Once we had returned to the surface, we climbed out of the DDC and handed our exam sheets to the diving instructors. I saw them laughing, but did not know why until we returned to the classroom. On the exam sheets, we were then shown what we had filled in at 50 metres/165 feet. We all had to laugh; the exam sheets looked like we were all drunk. Our classwork became more intense, focusing on diving deep, understanding diving tables, and, of course, all the diving theories. By now, I was beginning to understand it all. My weekly exam results were in line with those of the rest of the divers. I have now started diving at 30 metres and then to 40 metres. Everything was building up to my last couple of weeks. I had grown accustomed to diving deep. My exam sheets were still multiple-choice, which was great for me as I could understand the questions and did not have to write out the answers. I had passed all my exams, and now I just needed to complete my final dive. I entered the last week of my training, and everything depended on my deep dive to 50 metres/165 feet.

I started my descent to 50 metres. Upon reaching 50 metres, I was tasked with splicing a back splice at the end of the rope that I had been given to take down with me; it was a simple task to assess my ability to work on the seabed with nitrogen narcosis. This was fine with me, as I had spent many hours doing rope work while on the Manchester Ship Canal as a deckhand. This ended my practical underwater deep dive and diver training. All that was left was my final exam, but this time, I was not worried or concerned, as the diving instructors had taken the time to help me with the diving theory. I had no problems. I passed my final theory exam, and at long last, I was a diver again, qualified as a 'Training Services Agency Air Diver No. 227'. In those early days of diver training, it was not an HSE Part 1 certificate; that came ten years later.

Chapter Six

The Start of My Second Diving Career.

After we said our goodbyes to the Fort William staff and the other divers, we headed to the underwater training centre, our diving certificates in hand. Most single guys headed straight to Aberdeen. We had been informed that the best way to break into offshore diving was to knock on the doors of diving companies, let them know you were available, and hang around close to Aberdeen, hoping to get a call if a company needed divers at short notice. I could not do that. I had to head home with a list of diving companies and their telephone numbers, which were given to me by Fort William. I arrived home on December 4, 1976, with great expectations. Now that I was a fully qualified professional air diver, I would get a diving job in no time. Well, I soon realised that the real world of professional diving does not operate that way; most of the time, the phone numbers I had been given were never answered, and if you did manage to get through, you never got further than talking to the receptionist. They would tell you that you would not be considered anyway because you don't have any offshore diving experience. Plus, it was the winter season, and not much was happening offshore for air divers. Frustrating! In the end, I had to sign in at the job centre as I had no money coming in. Rose was still working in a factory in Liverpool, which was a great help, but for me, nothing was happening. We decided I would have to wait until after Christmas, as nothing would change until the New year.

A few days after the New year in 1977, I received a letter from Fort William inviting me to participate in trials for a saturation course. A diving company had a large saturation diving operation but needed trained and qualified saturation divers. They wanted to train divers on the 'Deep Diver One' barge in the Fort William saturation system. They also ran trials on underwater welding and 02 cutting, as the offshore contract required extensive welding and underwater cutting. I had to make a couple of dives from the diving bell to see how I would get on with diving from this position. They would conduct a 10- to 12-day trial to determine which divers would best suit them for the saturation training. I set off to Fort William again, but this time, I was beginning a new adventure as an offshore diver in the North Sea, or so I thought. I arrived at Fort William at the end of January 1977. I checked into the same hotel but was given my own room this time. All meals were covered, and I was given a small allowance for other out-of-pocket expenses. I could not wait to get started.

The first day was spent understanding what was expected of us concerning diving from the diving bell, including how to get dressed inside the diving bell, how to leave it, and how to re-enter it. The diving supervisor inside the bell with us would control each dive from the bell. I wouldn't dive too deep, as a quick turnaround was needed to ensure all divers completed the required number of dives. The training centre had a whole crew of instructors on the saturation diving barge for each day's diving. The main thing was to listen carefully to all the bell-diving instructions. My second day involved diving off the jetty with the underwater cutting equipment. I had to cut three 12-inch-high H-beam sections in half within a specified time frame. Each diver had to complete their underwater task and the bell diving. Depending on the time we had each day, we had to do two or three diving bell runs. I was getting ready for my first introduction to bell diving. In a few short months, I went from Siebe Gorman hard hat diving to diving from a diving bell, which was a fantastic step forward.

The diving bell on the barge Deep Diver One.

After my bell diving safety instructions, I was instructed to get ready and follow the supervisors into the bell. Once inside, I followed the instructions I was given. The diving bell was not going deep, just deep enough for me to practice leaving and returning to it. My first dive inside the diving bell went well; I was very pleased with myself. I removed my diving suit and returned to the jetty to continue with the other divers in the ongoing underwater cutting and welding operation during the bell runs. I was looking forward to my second dive of the day. Unfortunately, I never did get my second bell dive. An issue occurred during one of the diving bell runs, and one of the divers inside the bell had to be treated for decompression sickness. We were not informed what went wrong, except that all the diving bell runs would be stopped until further notice. The diving health and safety executive had to get involved in conducting a safety check. The rest of us were informed we would continue our underwater welding and cutting tasks while the HSE investigation into the bell diving incident was ongoing. The following day, we were all asked to go to one of the classrooms to produce our diving log books for the HSE inspector to inspect. We also had to stop all diving operations until the HSE inspection of our diving log books had been completed.

After a few hours, we were informed to proceed to one of the classrooms, where we were told that only divers with logbooks that had a minimum of six months of offshore diving experience would be allowed to continue the assessment for the saturation diving course. There and then, my hopes of getting into offshore diving, saturation diving or air diving had disappeared. I had no offshore diving experience. How could you gain any experience diving offshore if you couldn't get offshore without any diving experience? It's a catch-22, as they say. I remember returning home feeling deflated; I had gone away thinking I was about to secure my first offshore diving job, only to return with nothing – no job and no diving log book to document any offshore diving experience. I realised I needed to secure a diving job locally and stop looking offshore for the time being, as that was unlikely to happen.

I consulted the local Yellow Pages to find out which diving companies operated in the North West of England or Liverpool. I discovered two diving companies in Liverpool: Manor Divers and Housden Diving. I phoned the first one, Manor Diving, based in the Sefton Area of Liverpool. Amazingly, the call was answered, and I spoke with Ken Marlow, who occasionally worked for them. I told him who I was and that I was looking for diving work. He replied that he did not know if they were looking for divers, but if I left my phone number, he would pass it on to Mark, who owned Manor Divers. I left my phone number, but I did not expect anything to come of it.

The following day, I received a phone call from Mark, the owner of Manor Diving, who said he needed a diver that day and asked if I could arrive at the Liverpool docks within one hour to meet a diver named Sam Musket at the dock gates. "Yes," I said and headed off with my dive certificate and logbook. I saw the Manor Divers' van when I arrived at the gates. I went over, knocked on the driver's door, and introduced myself to the man behind the wheel. He introduced himself as Sam Musket. He asked me to get in the van so he could drive through the lock gates to get to the diving job. Once we arrived at the docks, he introduced himself a bit more. I handed him my dive certificate and logbook. Sam just looked at them and told me he would decide when I would be called a diver. He said no certificate or logbook would make me a diver, as no certificate had become a diver, and walking around with a piece of paper in my hand and a logbook saying I was a diver meant nothing to him. In the meantime, he would contact the dockers to find out where the ship's cargo had fallen into the water and to prepare a crane.

He told me to prepare the diving ladder and tie it to the harbour wall so he could start his dive when he got back with the dockers. I thought it was no problem, as I was used to securing a dive ladder to the harbour wall from my days at the ship canal. On his return, he said nothing. He just checked the dive ladder with a few pulls and noticed I had connected the air umbilical to the air cylinder and the dive mask. He also noticed that I had his dive suit ready, the downline in place. He said nothing; he got ready for his dive to locate the cargo once he was at the bottom of the dock. He walked down the dive ladder with his admiralty fins, checked his dive mask, and swam over to where the dock foreman pointed to where the cargo had fallen overboard. To save Sam from swimming, I pulled the downline and Sam over to the area the dock foreman was pointing at. I secured the downline and gave Sam a thumbs-up. He followed the downline to the bottom of the dock. The crane wire was already in place at the bottom, next to the downline. As the dockers and Sam had done this operation many times, they knew how much crane wire had to be lowered into the water. Sam started to pull on the diving umbilical, and he told me what signals he would pull to move the crane wire left, right, or up and down. After a few minutes, he signalled that he was returning to the surface. Once he reached the surface, he climbed back up the diver ladder and told the dock foreman to come up on the crane wire. Sam had secured the lifting straps around both sides of the cargo so it would not slip out during the lift from the bottom of the dock. While Sam was talking to the dock foreman, I started disconnecting all the diving gear and putting everything back into the van. Sam never said anything apart from, "Thanks for helping." He took me back to my car, dropped me off, and said hopefully, "See you again sometime." Hopefully, I had done well and would get another call, fingers crossed.

The following day, I received another phone call asking if I was available again, as Sam had another job, and if I could meet him at Seaforth docks, as he had to work on a vessel's propeller. "Yes, of course," I said. I arranged to meet Sam at around 1300 hrs at the dock gates. I arrived at the dock and spotted his van by the gates. I parked my car and walked over, but this time, Sam got out and said, "Hello, lad, nice job yesterday, get in, and let's go and remove the rope from the ship's propeller." When we arrived at the boat, Sam said, "OK, lad, get the dive gear ready." He then went on board the vessel to speak with the captain and chief engineer to ensure that no one turned on the ship's engines while he was working on the propeller. Everything went very well. Sam asked me if I would like to come for a pint at the local pub with him. Of course, I would, as it was a chance to get to know him. He was a very experienced hard-hat diver from the Navy. He was one of the original Navy divers who discovered that breathing oxygen underwater was not a good idea. He had many stories to tell me, but he was only interested in me and my diving experiences in and around the docks. He was pleased to learn that I had gained most of my knowledge from working on the Manchester Ship Canal. He knew Les and Eric and realised that I knew how to set up the diving equipment on the docks when he was getting ready to dive. He had put in a good word for me to Mark Berry, the owner of Manor Divers, and I received more phone calls to join up with Sam again.

The next bit made me laugh. He said, "Look, lad, I know you have just finished a diving course, and you may think you're a diver, but you're not; in my day, it took years to be recognised as a diver, so in the meantime, you are just my dive assistant. I will decide when and if you will be marked down as a diver. I must let you know that, and are you happy with that before we do any more dives together?" I was delighted with that, I said. I was working with a man who had so much diving experience to learn from; what's not to like? Plus, I was back working as an assistant diver, which was fine. I was back working and diving, which is all I wanted. I may have missed the saturation diving course, but the future was looking bright. The money was not great—£10 a day and £5 for each dive—but I wasn't too bothered as I had to start somewhere again. I still hadn't met Mark, the owner of Manor Divers, but I knew that would happen in its own time. For the next few weeks, I continued to receive callouts to work with Sam, who would occasionally give me a dive assignment, although Sam did most of the dives. If he didn't dive, he wouldn't get his dive money. I never had to collect any diving equipment, as Sam had it all in the back of the van. After every job, Sam would fill in the time sheets concerning which job we had completed and post them to Mark. I did wonder how Sam charged up all the air cylinders, and I found out that he would go to the local dive shop and use their high-pressure (HP) compressor, for which they would send a bill to Mark. This seemed to suit everyone.

After four weeks, Mark called me into the office to discuss something. Finally, I would meet Mark and see the setup and whether all the stories I had heard about Mark were true. Anyone who met Mark would tell you that he was the original Del Boy, before anyone had even heard of Del Boy. I drove to Sefton in Liverpool and found the base. Well, what can I say? The garage was full of diving equipment scattered everywhere, but Mark seemed to know where everything was. There was a phone and paperwork everywhere in the garage. Mark welcomed me in and asked how everything was going and how I was getting on with Sam. "Fine," I said, "no problems at all. I enjoyed working with Sam and learned a great deal from him." I was still wondering why Mark had asked me to come and meet when he started talking about moving the company to Birkenhead on the Wirral, which would have a proper office and a small workshop area to store all the diving equipment. He then asked me if I would like to work for him full-time in his new setup. "Well, yes, that would be great," I said. "That's good," he said. I asked him what he would expect from me. I could continue working with Sam, but he expected me to report to the new office or workshop every day, except when I received a call to go diving. No problems. I was pleased to be offered a full-time position. "Great," said Mark. "Leave your car here and go over to the new setup so we can start planning the move of the diving equipment. Jump into my car." Mark said it was the Ford Pontiac Firebird. I got inside and noticed it had an old dial-up phone in the centre console, the same type you had in your house, where you put your finger in a hole and turned the dial. I never said anything. I just looked at this phone and wondered how you could ring anybody by turning the dial and driving simultaneously.

I kept quiet as I was starting my new full-time diving job. Once we arrived, he told me how he had started Manor Divers. He was a deckhand from the Merchant Navy. He received an offer to work as a dive tender for a company based in Liverpool called the Liverpool and Glasgow Salvage Company, a prominent diving company in its time. When the company stopped operating, Mark got a payoff of around £3000. He then bought a small diving company that someone was getting rid of in Liverpool; it came with all its dive equipment plus some phone numbers of a couple of local divers that he could call up when he needed as these divers did not want to work away from home anymore. It also turned out that Mark was not his real name; his real name was Stan. However, he did not think Stan Berry was a good business name for the owner of a diving company, so he adopted Mark Berry as it looked much better on his business cards and contracts. So now Mark and Manor Divers were moving on to bigger and better things in the inshore diving world. I was happy to be fully employed again and looked forward to better things in my diving career.

I spent the next few days moving all the diving equipment from Mark's old base in Liverpool to Hamilton Square in Birkenhead. The new place did not have a yard, so all the equipment had to be fitted inside a large room at the front of the building.

Sam came round to look at the new place, as he didn't live far away, and to give me a hand. I also learned more about Sam, whose real name was not Sam. His correct name was William Musket, but in his Navy days, an old expression was used: "Sam, Sam, pick up my Musket." Hence, the nickname 'Sam' stuck with him. He was a great character. I enjoyed talking to him about his past. He was an old Navy hard-hat-trained diver; he had even dived with a Siebe Gorman hard hat in the North Sea. He lived close to the new setup and had to return home to pick up some diving equipment. He asked me to go with him and have a cup of tea. While he was making tea, I was sitting in his living room, looking at all the diving memorabilia around him. An odd thing that stood out in a glass cabinet was his wedding picture and a letter. Once he sat down and had a cup of tea, I had to ask Sam why his wedding photo and a letter were among his diving memorabilia. He smiled and asked me if I had ever heard of a diver called Buster Crab. "Yes," I said, "it was rumoured that he was a Russian spy and his headless body was found in his diving suit after he had gone missing." Sam smiled and laughed. "Well," he said, "if you look at the wedding photo on my left, that was Buster Crab." Buster was Sam's best mate at his wedding. The letter next to the picture was from him, congratulating Sam on his wedding. He never believed all the stories about Buster Crab being a Russian spy, as he had known him throughout his navy days and training as a navy diver. Sam decided that, given all the stories about him, it was only fitting that the wedding photo and the letter from him accompany his diving memorabilia.

Sam started giving me more and more dives, not because he had to or because I was asking him, but he decided I could handle more. At first, it was just a couple of hull inspections on cargo ships, as the vessels might have hit something while steaming across the seas from harbour to harbour. The shipping companies did not want to risk damage to their ships, as they could have the hull inspected while the vessel was in the harbour. On one particular dive, I learnt a valuable lesson. As I was getting ready for my dive, I put on my diving fins, which Sam never does. He always walks down the dive ladder and puts on his old Navy dolphin dive fins before entering the water at the water level. He said to me, "Hang on, lad; you have got your dive fins on; you can't walk down the dive ladder with them on." "Don't worry," I said. I would jump into the water from the harbour wall and off I jumped. Once in the water, I swam to the side of the vessel and began my hull inspection, starting from the stern and progressing to the bow of the ship. Once I had completed my dive inspection, I returned to the dive ladder. But as I was treading water I could not see the dive ladder. When I looked up to the top of the harbour wall I could see Sam, but not the dive ladder, when all of a sudden I heard a voice shout down at me saying, "Well smart arse, you jumped into the water, you can bloody well jump out." I guessed Sam was not amused by me jumping in. Eventually, he put the dive ladder back into the water, and I climbed out. Once I was on top of the harbour wall, and I took off my diving mask, Sam said to me, "Look, Mr Trained Diver, look at what is bobbing around in the water." As I looked down, I could see this giant tree trunk floating about. I looked at it a bit surprised. "Yes," he said, "you could have landed on that or any other piece of rubbish that is floating around the docks; hence smart arse, walk down the bloody dive ladder, or you are going to hurt yourself one day jumping into the water in the docks." Sam was right; I had not looked around before jumping into the water. I never jumped in again while I was working with Sam. As Sam got used to me, he began assigning me more complex underwater tasks, not just inspection work. On some of the diving jobs we did on the ships, we had to clean out the sea-chest grills on the sides of the vessels, which would get clogged up with marine growth. Sometimes, they would become clogged inside the sea chest, and we could not reach inside to remove the marine growth from the intakes, which would cause problems for the ship's engines as they could not draw enough water through the intakes to cool them down. What we needed to do for this operation was fit, a limpet box over the intake grill.

Sam always had, in the back of the van, different size limpet boxes with rubber seals around the edge of the limpet box and a long screw pole in the middle of the limpet box, which would fit through the sea chest grill. We would then tighten up the screw fitting as the screw fitting had a curved end which would fit against the grill so we could tighten the limpet box against it. Once I had fitted the limpet box onto the grill, I would bang on the side of the ship so the Chief Engineer would know the limpet box was in position. He would then remove the intake valve inside the engine room and safely remove all the marine growth inside the cooling pipes. As the intake valve was removed inside the engine room, water pushed the limpet box against the ship's side, and the rubber seals came into contact with the ship's hull to form a solid seal. Sometimes, water would leak through the limpet box into the engine room. If that happened, I would return to the sea chest with a bag of sawdust and hold it around the limpet box. The suction would draw up the sawdust and block the leaks. The sawdust would swell up as it got wet and expanded, which stopped any leaks.

Ships Sea-Chest.

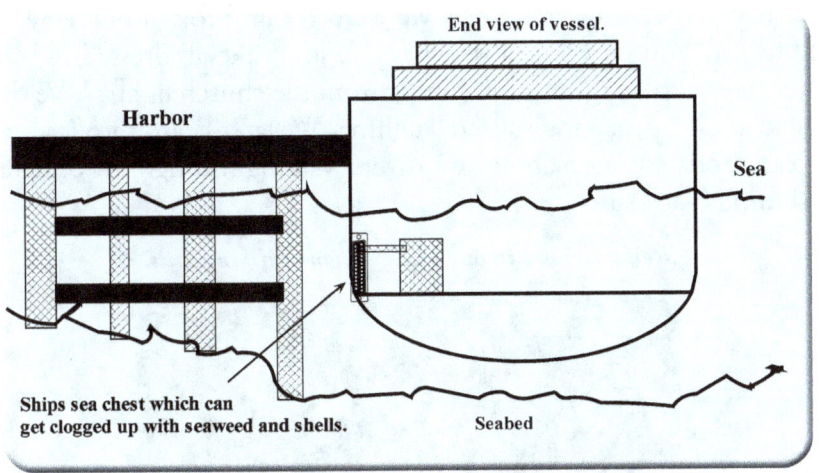

Sam was increasingly trusting me with diving work, but on the time sheets, he still listed me as his assistant diver. When Manor Divers had operations that required working away from home, Mark would bring in other divers, as Sam would no longer work away from home, having had enough of it. The first diving operation I had to travel away with Manor Divers was in Warwickshire. The other diver, Ken Marlowe, conducted underwater inspections on road bridges crossing rivers. In the winter, the rivers flood, sending a fantastic amount of water rushing downstream, carrying all sorts of debris, mainly fallen trees. The fallen trees would smash into the supporting pillars on the road bridges and cause damage. Our job was to inspect all the supporting sections for damage and any undercutting on the water bed under and around the bridge supports. We typically conducted our operations early in the morning as we had many structures to inspect. We would generally change into our diving suits wherever we could. On one particular day, Ken and I were getting changed into our diving suits by a cemetery at around 6 a.m. It was raining heavily, but we thought nothing of it as we would get wet anyway. However, to reach the edge of the riverbank, where we were going to start our inspections, we had to pass through the church cemetery to access the Zodiac we had placed earlier by the riverbank, so that we could proceed downstream to the following road bridge support pillars. As we walked through the cemetery, we heard an almighty scream from one of the graves when we saw a couple of people running away in an almighty rush, screaming and shouting for their lives. The vicar, who knew we were going through his cemetery, said to us, "You two do realise what you look like all dressed in black rubber that's soaking wet and shining from the church lights?" We then looked at each other and started laughing. We later heard the vicar gave a great Sunday sermon about two divers walking through the cemetery in shining black suits.

Ken and I are in our black Frogman diving suits.

The diving operation in Warwickshire lasted around six weeks. We would come home every weekend with our reports and time sheets. On these timesheets, I was listed as a diver, but as soon as I started working with Sam again, I was listed as an assistant diver, which always made me smile.

I never managed to get many pictures of Sam. When he saw the camera, he said, "We have come to work; if you want to take pictures, go on a bloody holiday." If there was no diving work, I would hang around the diving equipment room, organising all the diving equipment in some order. I would also repair any diving suits with holes in the arm cuffs and the neck dams. On this particular day, a yellow Lotus car pulls up outside the office, and a guy gets out of the vehicle and asks where it is. "Mark," I say, "go up the stairs, his office is on the left." He throws me his car keys and says, "Keep an eye on my car, mate, while I have a coffee with Mark." Who does he think he is? I said to myself. I will look after your car, mate. As I was working in the equipment room, I picked up a load of grease and accidentally covered the top of his lovely yellow Lotus. It was raining when he came down, he ran out of the office door with his head down and never noticed any of the grease on the top of his yellow Lotus as he drove away. Mark came down as well. I asked him who the visitor was, and he told me he was an old pal who had gone on to dive and supervise in saturation operations, his name was Keith Davis or 'Scouse Davis' as he was known offshore. Mark asked what was that on the top of Keith's car. "Don't know," said I as I walked away smiling. Years later, I would work offshore with Keith in Saudi Arabia, and in many ways, he saved my life, but that story will come later.

Another job came up to inspect all the bridges that trains crossed. This time, the other diver, Mike Rutherford, and I would be carrying out this work. I had done a few small jobs with Mike before. He was a small but powerful individual who had engaged in extensive weightlifting, weight training, and running. He was fit. We were based in Barrow, as we worked all over Cumbria. The first thing Mike did when we got our accommodation in Barrow was to look for the local gym. Once he obtained a temporary membership, he was all set. Our first inspection went very well, with no problems to report. We went back to Barrow for the night, and the first thing Mike did was head to the gym. Once he had done his weight training, he would then run for about an hour. Mike asked me why I didn't join him in the gym as well, which I was happy to do. However, I had never really done any weight training or known the difference between weight lifting and weight training. Mike knew his stuff about lifting weights. He taught me many helpful things about it, which I still apply to this day, and boy, could Mike run!

The job went very well. We dived all over Cumbria, but the most surprising diving inspection we had to do was at Lake Windermere, as all the jetties belonged to British Rail. Our biggest job was to remove fishing lines from the support posts, as swimmers would get their legs tangled up on the fishing lines wrapped around the support posts.

Mike at Lake Windermere

The inspection lasted about six weeks, and we encountered no issues with the bridges. I came home very fit and with new knowledge, not about diving but about weight training, all thanks to Mike. Winter was starting to arrive, and Mark would often hire local divers from the North Sea to take on small diving jobs as they wanted to pass the time in the winter months, as the North Sea saw a significant decline in diving work due to the harsh weather conditions.

An emergency job came up at Camel Lairds' shipyard in Birkenhead, and Mark could not get anyone at short notice apart from a guy called Dave Kean. At the time, he was running saturation diving operations, but he also enjoyed keeping his hand in at the docks during the winter months. The main lock gates would not close, as there was something at the bottom of the ledge. I will give Dave his due; he asked me if he could do this dive. It was not a nice dive. It was on the River Mersey, which is very dark, with no visibility, and the water was very choppy. Dave entered the water and went down the downline; after about 15 minutes, he gave me a pull on his umbilical to let me know he was coming up. Once he was on the surface, he asked if we could pull up the downline, as he had attached a big tyre that was stopping the lock gates from closing. After we finished the dive, I asked Dave why he was diving in the docks when he was a big wheel in saturation diving. He told me that doing diving jobs like this occasionally kept him grounded. I never heard of him again until one day, like everyone else,

I was watching all the news about the recovery of the gold on HMS Edinburgh; Dave was one of the supervisors on that diving operation.

Although I was working and enjoying my job, there wasn't much money. I was still on £10 a day and £5 a dive even when I worked away from home. I heard all these stories about how much divers were earning in the North Sea, and everyone thought I must be earning the same money. Rose was now pregnant with our first child, due in February 1978, the same month as Rose's birthday. I stopped thinking about the money divers were earning in the North Sea. How could I get a diving job offshore, as I had never worked offshore before? I carried on working with Sam, who still did not mark me down as a diver. Sometimes, after we had finished a diving job in Liverpool docks, Sam would take me over to meet his old dive buddy, Tug Wilson, who worked for the Liverpool port authority. He was an old hard-hat diver who would not wear any other dive gear in the docks; he would only use Siebe Gorman hard hats.

Every time the HSE came to Liverpool docks for an inspection, Tug would hide all his Siebe Gorman diving gear until the HSE left. On a couple of occasions, Sam and I would help him and his divers use the hard-hat diving gear, as Sam missed using it. Sam and Tug also liked catching up and discussing the good old days. On that particular day, Sam and Tug discussed how the Liverpool docks were changing due to the new container berth at Seaforth Docks and the decline in cargo ships visiting the docks. At first, this did not bother me, as I did not understand the difference it would make. I was to dive on the next cargo recovery job we had to do in the Liverpool docks.

I got dressed for the next dive. Once dressed, I went down the dive ladder and put my head underwater. As soon as I did this, I could see the cargo at the bottom of the dock. I took off my diving mask while on the dive ladder and asked Sam to lower the crane wire to the area I was pointing at and lower away. Sam stopped everything and asked me what I was doing. I told Sam I could see the cargo from the dive ladder and to lower the crane wire where I was pointing. Sam got annoyed and asked me to get out of the water, saying if I was going to play around, then I should get out of the water, as he would dive. As Sam entered the water, he lifted his head, took off his mask, and said,

"Lower the crane there," which confused me, as that's what I had asked for. He apologised to me after the cargo was lifted clear and all the dive equipment was put away. He explained that he had been working in these docks for many years and had never had any visibility in these waters.

He was surprised when I told him I could see the cargo from the surface. He then explained to me that this was a bad sign, as it meant that not enough cargo ships were operating in the docks anymore, which was why I could see the cargo. It meant that the bottom of the docks was not being disturbed, the sediment had settled, and the water had cleared. Because of this, Sam began to think that his time as a diver in the docks was coming to an end. It was the same story with his old buddy Tug Wilson. That's what they were talking about on that day when I helped him out with his mate Tug Wilson's diving equipment. I could do nothing about this situation. Sam started giving me more diving work as it came in.

One job I had seen Sam do many times was stemming a stern gland on the ship's propeller shafts. The idea was that if we could seal the propeller shaft underwater, the chief Engineer could remove the protection cover in the engine room and then replace the internal seals around it that were leaking oil. This meant the ship did not have to go into dry dock to get this work done. I had to make a rope sausage using Denso tape and a rope. Denso tape is a great adhesive tape for sealing various items; plumbers and pipeline workers use it mainly.

The first thing we did was measure the gap between the propeller shaft and the rope guard to determine the diameter and length of the rope required, ensuring it wrapped all the way around the propeller shaft. Once I had that information, I would roll up the rope inside the Denso tape like a big sausage filling. This was the first time Sam had allowed me to carry out this diving operation; usually, it was Sam's responsibility, but this time, he had allowed me to do it. If I got it all wrong, I would flood the engine room—not good.

The drawing below shows the area where I had to fit the rolled-up Denso rope sausage to create a seal on the ship's propeller. Once I fitted it into the gap, I would cover it and the propeller shaft with more Denso tape as an added protection. I also had a bag of sawdust with me. Once I had finished fitting the Denso sausage and Denso tape, I would bang on the side of the ship four times so the Chief Engineer would know he could remove the propeller guard inside the engine room, and hopefully, the engine room would not flood.

Once the Chief Engineer removed the cover, he would give me four bangs back. I would then open the bag of sawdust, which would get sucked into any small gaps. The sawdust would swell up and seal any small leaks. The Denso tape sausage was fitted around this part of the propeller shaft.

Propeller Shaft set up.

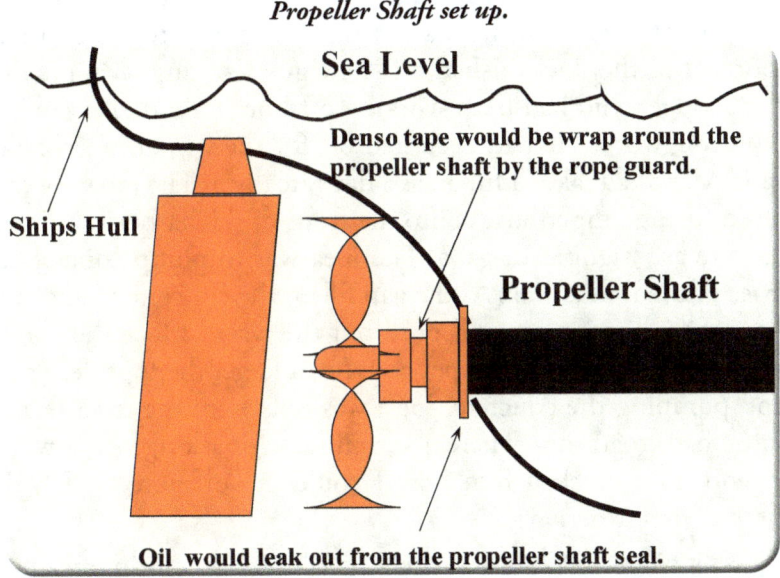

The Chief Engineer would fit new seals around the shaft to prevent oil leaks. Depending on the depth of the water, the seal would experience a significant amount of water pressure pushing against it. Occasionally, I would re-enter the water to check the seal by walking around it with a bag of sawdust, which would be sucked into any leaks. Once the Chief Engineer had fitted his new seals, I would remove the Denso tape and the Denso rope sausage from the propeller shaft. If everything had been fitted correctly, the engine room would not have flooded with seawater. Everything went well, and Sam was very pleased with me. Sam asked me to get the Chief Engineer to sign off on the timesheet; I noticed that Sam had put me down as a diver, not the assistant diver. I was very pleased that, at long last, Sam finally recognised me as a diver. Hearing this from someone with his knowledge and experience in the diving world meant a great deal to me.

That night, I had a few drinks and got drunk. After that weekend, I went back to work feeling very pleased with myself. Mark noticed that Sam had listed me as a diver on the timesheet and said, "Well done," but there was no increase in my wages. That just stayed the same. Winter had started; it was getting cold in the water or while standing on the harbour. I was working at Garston Docks in Liverpool, repairing the harbour wall as a ship had lost control and smashed into the wall very heavily, causing many sandstone blocks to crack or fall to the bottom of the docks. I had one new guy working with me called John Burridge, who had been working offshore for a diving company called Strongwork. He had been laid off for the winter, or so he told me, and Mark had taken him on as a day rate diver. The job we were on involved fitting limpet boxes onto the front of the harbour wall where there were any significant gaps. The idea was to pump concrete into the base of the limpet box. As the gap filled, the concrete would rise to the top of the limpet box and push out the water. Once the concrete came out at the top of the limpet box, I would get the topside foreman to stop pumping the concrete. John was only with me for a few days when he had to go somewhere else, but he kept asking why I was not diving offshore. I asked him how I could get offshore, as I had no offshore diving experience.

This job lasted approximately five weeks, continuing up to Christmas and into the New Year. After the new year, I returned to work, and I was doing a few jobs around the equipment room when John Burridge walked in, wished me a happy New Year, and asked if I wanted to work offshore as a diver. "Yes," I said, "but how?" "Don't worry," he replied, "I've had a word with my friends. They'll be able to help you get started." "Great," I said. "How?" "Give me your CV and a copy of your dive certificate, and I'll pass them on to the right people." "Great," I thought, and went home to talk to Rose. However, our first child was due in February, so we decided it was not a good time to go offshore.

The following day, I had some diving work with Sam, or so I thought. Instead, I was told to meet Mark in the office. Okay, no problems; there must have been a change of plan. I got into the office early, but no one was there, so I just waited in the equipment room. After about an hour, Mark said, "You in my office now," Very odd, I thought. I headed up to his office, and Mark told me I was sacked for trying to get his mate John Burridge to help me get a job offshore. Hang on. I said he asked me if I would like to go offshore, as he has contacts, and requested my CV and dive certificate to pass on to his contacts. Mark then informed me that he was not waiting around while I decided whether I wanted to work offshore. He gave me my P45 and wages and sacked me on the spot. He then told me he was giving my job to John Burridge, who didn't want to work offshore anymore and told me to get out. I drove home in a state of shock. I had been set up hook, line, and sinker by John Burridge, who I later discovered had a bad reputation and could no longer get a diving job offshore.

It was January 1978. I was out of work, and our baby was due in about six weeks. It was not a great start to the new year. Sam called me to find out what had happened. After I told him what had happened, he was not very happy with Mark or John, who had not been getting any offshore work due to his poor reputation, which was unknown to me at the time. John had just seen an opening regarding my job. I had to sign on at the job centre, explaining why I had been sacked from my diving job. The job centre then informed me that I could take Manor Divers to an industrial tribunal court for unfair dismissal and get compensation for my unfair dismissal.

In the meantime, our first baby was born in February 1978, but Rose suffered severely from post-natal depression, which, at the time, I did not understand what it was or how to adjust to life with a baby and being out of work. After listening to all the advice from the job centre, the case for unfair dismissal was heard by the tribunal court in March 1978, and I won my claim for unfair dismissal. I received £950 in compensation, but that money went to the Jobcentre, which took back all the unemployment benefits I had received and taxed them. I ended up with about £400. As Rose was still suffering from post-natal depression, we ended up staying at Rose's mum's, as Rose was not getting any better when, out of the blue, the local Barrow Gazette came in the post. I had forgotten that I had left my address at the local gym in Barrow when I was there on the railway inspection operation. They sent me an article about their gym in the Barrow Gazette, as they had won an award and just wanted to show people how well they were doing. I started reading the Barrow Gazette when I noticed an advertisement in the job section for divers with an engineering background, either mechanical or electrical, to work as diver maintainers for Vickers Oceanics Limited on their mini-submarines. As I had my CV ready, I decided to send it off, having nothing to lose. However, I did not expect anything back as I had not worked offshore.

Chapter Seven
My Start to Offshore Work with Mini-Subs.

After two weeks, during which I had forgotten all about that job, I received a phone call from Vickers Oceanics Limited, based in Barrow. They asked me if I was available to work for them as a diver and maintainer on their mini-subs and if I could travel to Norway within two weeks. I could not believe it; at long last, I was getting offshore as a diver maintainer on mini-subs. They were not interested in the fact that I had not worked offshore before, as the work for a diver maintainer mainly involved releasing the mini-sub from the A-frame lifting wire on the stern of the vessel and reconnecting the lifting wire to the mini-sub once the sub returned from its operation. My main job was to assist the sub's Chief Engineer in maintaining the mini-sub's hydraulics. Amazingly, my City and Guilds in mechanical engineering was my most important qualification for this operation. Being a qualified diver was just a bonus, as they needed qualified divers with an engineering background. I made my way to Leith Docks in Edinburgh, Scotland, in March 1978, where I had to sign my contract, get measured for all my working clothes and safety equipment, and obtain travel information as I was travelling to Stavanger, Norway. Once the documentation was completed, I met with six other individuals travelling to the same operation. Two were mini-sub pilots, one worked in electronics, one was a deckhand, and another was a diver maintainer who also served as an electrician.

On March 30, 1978, I boarded the company's private plane with the other guys for Norway. It was not a jet plane; it was a twin-propeller plane, and the flight was not comfortable due to the strong winds. As we approached Norway, the weather remained windy, and snow was falling heavily. Once we landed and disembarked, I couldn't believe how cold it was. It was freezing, and I was eager to get indoors. After we had gone through customs, we were met by the company's operations manager, who welcomed us and introduced himself to everyone. He then took us to the coach that would transport us to Stavanger harbour, where the vessel was berthed. Once on board the ship, I was shown my cabin. I unpacked and had something to eat, and as it was getting late, I decided to get some sleep. The following morning, I was informed that there would be a group meeting after lunch for all the new crew members to familiarise themselves with the vessel and get their bearings. After breakfast, I went out onto the deck and was surprised at the weather; it was warm and pleasant.

My first morning and afternoon in Norway.

The mini-sub on which I worked as a diver maintainer.

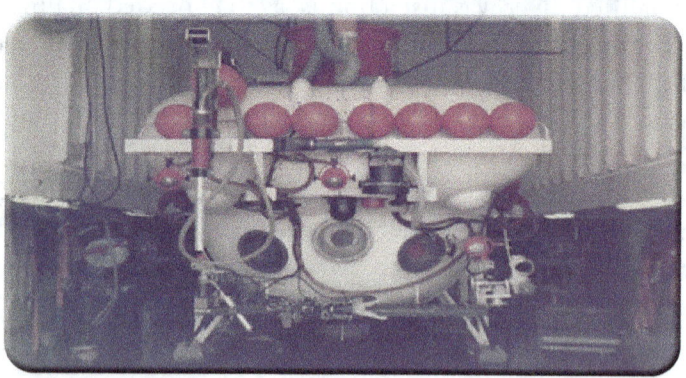

During the group meeting, we were informed that we would be conducting sea trials for the mini-sub and the various crews on the vessel for the first month, so we all understood our duties concerning the mini-sub operation. The main objective of this operation was for the mini-sub to record all the backfilling from a drill ship that had been converted to drop gravel over a pipeline. The pipeline was already in a trench running from offshore to an inshore supply line to Denmark, and the gravel had to be backfilled to protect it. Trenching of subsea pipelines is widely used as a means of stability enhancement in that the pipeline within a trench is partially shielded against hydrodynamic loads. Additionally, the method is also suitable for providing protection against damage caused by fishing gear, scour, and ship anchors. The mini-sub would be working in water around 250 feet deep. Our shifts would be 12 hours each day. The mini-sub could not operate on 24-hour shifts, as we had only one mini-sub, which required maintenance and recharging after each dive, and the pilots needed to rest after each operation. We were also informed that we might occasionally need to act as observers in the mini-sub for small operations, allowing the mini-sub pilots a break, but this would be decided as required. We sailed into the fjords around Stavanger, where the sea trials would start. While sailing, I was shown around the mini-sub's hydraulic systems, which controlled the hydraulic arms at the front of the mini-sub (as shown in the photograph) and all other hydraulic components. Each pilot preferred the hydraulic arm controls to be set to their personal preference for the hydraulic controls inside the mini-sub. Once I was notified which pilot was in charge of that day's dive, I would meet with them to set up the flow of hydraulic oil, ensuring the pilot was comfortable with the operation of the manipulator arms, as well as any other hydraulic units that might be fitted to the mini-sub, if required.

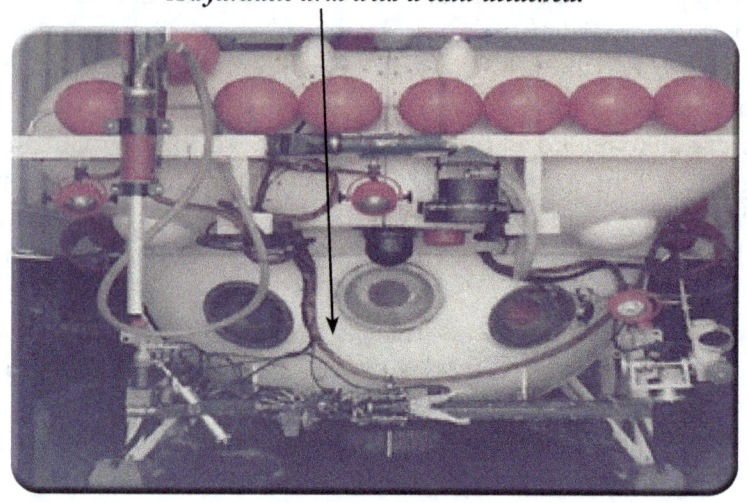

A hydraulic arm with a claw attached.

Safety was one of the most significant issues concerning manned mini-sub operations due to a severe incident in August 1973, which few people realised had occurred. However, during our manned mini-sub operation, they ensured we were aware of the risks associated with its maintenance and recovery, so no risks were taken lightly. The information regarding the serious incident in August 1978 was shared with all of us on our manned mini-sub operation, so we could fully understand the risks to our pilots and observers if we did not take safety seriously when recovering the manned mini-sub. One incident made me realise what I could be involved in if I did not take my responsibilities seriously. The story of Pisces III shows the risks personnel took in the early days of underwater exploration. Here's some information I received at one of our safety meetings on how the incident and rescue effort unfolded in August 1973.

The below information was referanced from Wikipedia.

The mini-sub pilots were waiting for the towline to be attached so they could lift the mini-sub and take it back to the mother ship. As is normal, during this phase of the operation, there was a lot of banging of ropes and shackles. Suddenly, the mini-sub hurtled backwards and sank rapidly. The mini-sub was dangling upside down as it was hanging onto the towing line, and then, due to the sea swell, it heaved up like a big dipper. The aft sphere, a smaller watertight sphere where the machinery was located, had flooded when the hatch was pulled off. Suddenly, the sub was over a tonne heavier. As it sank, the biggest concern was whether the mini-sub was anywhere near the continental shelf, because if it had struck it, it would have been crushed due to the water's depth. The mini-sub had sunk to a depth of around 1600 feet. Nobody realised that the mini-sub had hit a gully on the sea bed, so half of it was below the sea bed, which made it difficult to detect. The mini-sub carried 72 hours of oxygen but had already used 8 hours on their dive.

When the mini-sub was located, the operation to rescue the mini-sub was underway. The other mini-subs encountered problems trying to attach lifting ropes. Eventually, a line was attached to the mini-sub, and the slow process of recovering it to the surface began.

The rescue of the mini-sub pilots occurred between late August and early September. Pisces III was trapped on the seabed at a depth of around 1600 feet, 150 miles off Ireland in the Celtic Sea. The 76-hour rescue effort resulted in the deepest successful submarine rescue in history.

The Canadian commercial submersible Pisces III was launched in 1969. Pisces III originally had tail fins, which were removed to improve access and handling when Vickers Oceanics purchased the submersible. Apparently, if the fins had been retained, they might have prevented the entanglement of the towline on the craft's machinery sphere, which caused the 1973 accident.

The lead pilot crewed the Pisces III submersible, Roger Chapman, a former Royal Navy submariner, and 35-year-old engineer and senior pilot, Roger Mallinson. In late August 1973, Chapman and Mallinson began a routine dive. They were working on laying transatlantic telephone cable on the seabed, around 150 miles off Cork in southern Ireland.

The submersible would typically take approximately 40 minutes to reach a depth of 1,600 feet. For Mallinson, this dive was additionally fatiguing, as he had spent over a day previously repairing a broken manipulator on the submarine. Luckily, during the repair, he changed the oxygen tank to a full one. During each dive, the pilots had to ensure that after every 40 minutes, they turned on a hydroxide fan to remove carbon dioxide from the atmosphere and add oxygen.

They also maintained a video commentary record during every dive. With the submersible about to be lifted out of the water by a towline back onto the ship, a water alarm sounded in the aft sphere, a self-contained part of the submersible that contained machinery and oil storage. The towline had fouled on the aft sphere hatch and wrenched it open. The crew heard the sound of water entering the aft compartment as Pisces III became inverted and began to sink back to the seabed. The aft sphere was entirely flooded with over a tonne of water. At around 165 to 175 feet, the submersible jolted to a stop, held at the maximum length of the nylon towline. The mini-sub swung about in the sea currents until the rope snapped. The pilots immediately closed down all the electrical systems, which left the sub in total blackness. They also released a 400-pound lead ballast weight as they descended, until they hit the seabed very hard.

The pilots reviewed their surroundings using a flashlight and called their mothership to report their status. The entire tank of oxygen Mallinson had added could last approximately 72 hours, but eight hours had already been used, leaving around 64 hours. Mallinson and Chapman spent the first few hours sorting out the submersible, which was almost upside down. They checked all the watertight doors for leaks and prepared for rescue to come. They knew they had to make as little physical exertion as possible to preserve oxygen, not even speaking. They made themselves as comfortable and high up as possible to avoid the foul air that sank. The pilots had just a single sandwich and one can of liquid on board. They also decided to allow the carbon dioxide in the air to build up beyond the standard 40 minutes to conserve oxygen, which resulted in lethargy and drowsiness for both men. The support ship *Vickers Venturer*, then in the North Sea, was ordered to return to the nearest port with the submersible Pisces II aboard. At midday, the Royal Navy survey vessel HMS Hecate steamed to the accident location to offer assistance with special ropes.

The United States Navy also offered a submersible belonging to the U.S. Salvage Department, called a Controlled Underwater Recovery Vehicle, sent from California, and a Canadian Coast Guard ship left from Swansea. Eventually, the Vickers Voyager arrived in Cork and loaded the submersibles Pisces II and Pisces V.

At the end of August, the Vickers Voyager reached the scene and launched Pisces II with a polypropylene rope attached. However, the lifting rope broke free of the manipulator's arm, and the submersible had to be returned to the surface for repairs. An attempt made by Pisces V failed to find the crashed Pisces III and returned to the surface after it ran out of power. The relaunched Pisces V had more success. However, an attempt to attach a rope failed. Pisces V now remained with the stricken Pisces III. An attempt to send Pisces II down again had to be called off when it suffered a leak. Even the newly arrived ROV was unable to launch due to an electrical fault. The Pisces V was ordered to the surface. They were running out of oxygen and lithium hydroxide to scrub the carbon dioxide from the deteriorating atmosphere in the submersible. The rescue operation of Pisces III commenced at the beginning of September, with the rescue submersible Pisces II. Within a little over an hour, it had successfully attached a purpose-built toggle and polypropylene tow rope to the rear sphere of the distressed Pisces III. The remotely operated underwater vehicle also joined the operation. It managed to fasten another tow rope to the stranded submersible. The lifting of Pisces III began. This procedure caused the submersible to jolt significantly. The lift was temporarily halted, and the lifting process was paused again to allow divers to attach heavier lifting cables to the submersible. Pisces III finally broke through the surface. Divers immediately attempted to open the hatch to allow fresh air into the submersible. However, it took nearly 30 additional minutes to achieve this. When the hatch finally opened, both crew members struggled to exit the craft, having been confined inside for around 84 hours. It was an incredible rescue that nobody ever wanted repeated, which was emphasised at our safety meeting on the vessel. Roger Chapman has written a book about the incident titled 'No Time on Our Side'.

I continued to learn more about the operation and maintenance of the mini-sub. My job was to understand every aspect of the operation, not just mechanical engineering and diving. I had to learn how to act as the radio operator for the mini-sub from the radio control room and relay the correct information to the bridge/navigator, the mini-sub pilot, the winch operator, and the divers. All communication from the radio operator was recorded. The lead pilot of the mini-sub had to complete a comprehensive checklist to ensure that all the sub's operating systems were functioning correctly. Once the pilot, operational supervisor, Chief Engineer, vessel captain, and client had signed off on all the check sheets, everyone was aware of the mini-sub's operational status at all times before permission was given for its operation to commence. I also had to learn how to move the mini-sub from the hangar to its launching position under the A-frame, which lifted and lowered it into and out of the sea. The picture below shows the A-frame lifting the mini-sub with me as the diver on top of it. I would then be lowered into the sea with the mini-sub and remove the lifting rope once it was submerged.

A-Frame.

Once the mini-sub was in the water, the lifting rope was removed. However, the mini-sub was still connected to the vessel via a towing rope, and it would then drift away from the ship. Once the mini-sub was far enough away from the boat, a command would be given to remove the mini-sub from the ship's towing line. The diver would then remove the towing rope from the back of the mini-sub, remove the camera covers from the underwater cameras, and give a thumbs-up to the pilot through the mini-sub's portholes to indicate that everything was clear and the mini-sub was ready to proceed. The pilot would then receive clearance to start his dive. The diver would then climb into the Zodiac (rubber boat) and be taken back to the mothership. He would stay in his wetsuit for the duration of the operation in case he was needed in an emergency. I continued to learn more about the entire operation of the mini-sub and how Vickers Oceanics worked. The goal was to have as many people as possible fully trained in case of any emergency. In the event of an emergency, personnel may transition to any operational status, depending on the operational pattern. After a few weeks of training in the fjords around Stavanger, we sailed to Kristiansund in Norway to collect all the required stores, spare parts, and final instructions concerning the operation before setting off to Esbjerg in Denmark. In early April 1978, our vessel sailed from Esbjerg to commence the seabed survey of the pipeline that had been previously buried by the converted drill ship. My first day offshore was rough. It took me a few days to stop feeling seasick, which was a nightmare. I don't think I left the toilet for the first few days. Gradually, I got my sea legs, and I started going outside for some fresh air and to get used to working on the mini-sub vessel while we waited for the weather to calm down. I was getting used to working on a rolling ship and my duties on and around the boat.

After a couple of days, we started our first mini-sub operation. The mini-sub had to follow a plotted line along the trench, as an underwater navigation system had been laid alongside the pipeline trench. The mother ship recorded the mini-sub's position via the navigation system on the vessel, which enabled plotting of the mini-sub's location. The first run went very well, so we fully commenced the operation. That night, I worked late, setting up the hydraulic flow on the hydraulic arm. By now, I knew which pilot would be starting the first dive, so I had everything marked down for his settings and the required oil pressure from the hydraulic pack he prefers to work with. The following morning, I was assigned winch operator duties. It involved simply lifting the mini-sub and lowering it into the water, after which I could sit back and relax for around 6 to 8 hours, depending on the dive's duration. Once it returned to the surface, I resumed my duties as a winch operator to lift the mini-sub out of the water. Upon reaching the deck, I checked that the hydraulic oil pack had no leaks. I then checked all the hydraulic pipes and topped up the hydraulic oil tank. At the end of each day, I would review the work roster and schedule for the following morning, so I knew what to do after breakfast and when I was required to work. My usual daily routine was to check the work roster. I was always pleased when assigned as a diver, which I enjoyed, as it fulfilled my ambition to be an offshore diver.

That's me releasing the towing rope from the back of the mini-sub once it was far enough away from the vessel after it was lowered into the water.

The operation was going very smoothly. It was a fascinating job; not everyone gets a chance to work with mini-subs. I was fortunate to be working on this operation, as news was emerging from Vickers Oceanics that this mini-sub operation could be one of the last ones they would ever conduct. One day, the whole operation came to a halt. The converted drill ship had a significant problem with the pipes used to drop all the backfill. One of the main lifting wires had broken approximately 100 feet down, and they could not lift the pipe on the other lifting wire, as it would come up at an incorrect angle. The operation's supervisors discussed various ways to resolve the problem. None of the discussions involved me, as I was just a diver maintainer. I was having lunch when I heard about the situation. It was suggested that if they could get a new lifting wire connected to the pipe pad eye at 100 feet, they could lift the pipe and fix it properly. I just happened to say, "Why not send a diver down to attach the lifting wire?" They just looked at me as if I were daft or stupid, or both; I thought no more of it until a couple of hours later, when I got a call to go to the client's office on the ship. I was asked how I would go about this operation. I informed them I would take a downline to the pad eye and attach it to the pipe. Once connected, they could lower the lifting wire down the downline. After numerous discussions with senior management, it was decided that if I were sure I could do this, they would proceed. The following day, the weather was good, the water was calm, and permission was given for the job to proceed.

That's me before heading down to attach the lifting wire.

I started my dive to 100 feet. Once I had attached the downline to the pad eye, I gave the signal on the downline for the crew on the surface to take up the slack and lower the lifting wire. It came straight to the pad eye, allowing me to connect the shackle/wire without problems. I removed the downline and signalled that I was returning to the surface, but due to the depth, I had to do a 3-minute water stop at 10 feet. Once I was back on the surface and returned to our vessel, I could see that everyone was delighted, amazed, and happy because I had resolved a significant problem in the operation.

The converted drill ship with our Zodiac is heading back to our vessel.

This was my first deep dive in the North Sea and my first decompression dive without a chisel in the downline! The drillship sent me a good bottle of whisky as a thank you, but I think that was a big mistake. I woke up the following day with a thumping hangover, and I had thrown up all over my cabin, much to the dismay of my roommate.

The following day, the drill ship's operation continued as they had fixed the pipe casing. They could continue the backfilling operation, and the mini-sub could continue monitoring the backfill over the pipeline. The operation was coming to an end, and the mini-sub was spending less time surveying the backfill in the water. As one of the video surveys was very foggy, a minor operation was required to inspect a part of the backfill using the mini-sub. The inspection would be brief, lasting approximately an hour.

As I checked the work roster, I noticed that I was listed as the observer in the mini-sub, so I double-checked to ensure this was correct. I was informed that, as it was a short inspection and the regular observer was feeling ill, they had decided that if I was willing, I could serve as the observer. I was more than happy; a chance to go down in the mini-sub was just too good an opportunity to miss. While in the mini-sub, I went through all the debriefs with the pilot, and my primary operational duty was to ensure the pilot stayed awake by supplying him with coffee. I also underwent another operation: pressing a button while we were on the seabed, following instructions from the pilot. Once the mini-sub left the surface and headed to the sea bed, it was a fantastic experience for me, from Siebe Gorman diving with a hard hat to an observer in a mini-sub. Once we reached the seabed, the pilot had to review his checklist to ensure everything was working correctly in the mini-sub. When the mini-sub had been cleared to start its survey, the pilot told me to get ready, so I was waiting for his instruction with my finger on this one button. He then hit the flood lights outside the mini-sub and said, "Now, I hit the button." It was a tape recording of ABBA singing 'Dancing Queen'. He told me to look out of the sub's porthole. The water was so clear that a fluorescent light effect was visible all across the portholes. It was unbelievable. It was just like a big disco. The pilot then informed Surface that we were good to go.

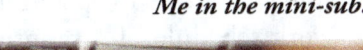

Me in the mini-sub.

The dive only lasted about an hour, but it was something that not many people would get a chance to do. I loved the experience. The operation was now coming to a close, and I was informed that no further operations were ongoing due to the introduction of a new underwater vehicle called a Remote Operating Vehicle (ROV), which was proving to be more cost-effective and efficient. On July 10th, the vessel sailed back to Stavanger, completing the operation. I enjoyed the operation; I went offshore, did my first deep dive in the North Sea, worked on a mini-sub, dived in a mini-sub, and listened to ABBA singing 'Dancing Queen' under a couple of hundred feet of water. What's not to like? I was flown back to Scotland on July 11th, but I was out of work again and wondering where I could find a job.

There was no internet or mobile phones back then. While waiting to catch a train back to Liverpool, I was reading a newspaper and noticed an ad with a phone number for qualified air divers who "must have offshore experience" for a diving job overseas. Well, I thought to myself, I have now been offshore, dived offshore, so what have I got to lose? I called the phone number in London, and it was a diving company called Solus Schall; I spoke to a man called Nobby Foreman. I told him I had just finished an operation in Norway and Denmark and was available and ready to go. "Great," he said, "can you get to London for an interview in three days?" "Yes," I said. "Great," he said. "See you then." I went home to Liverpool; well, I say 'home'. Rose and Chris were still living with my in-laws, but that was fine as Rose continued suffering from post-natal depression. I arrived in London for the interview and was accepted for a diving operation in IRAN on a 12-month contract with a work schedule of 4 months on and two weeks off. I was happy to sign, as it was a long-term job that I was delighted to accept. I returned to my in-laws' house to have a break with Rose and Chris while waiting for the flight details.

Chapter Eight
In IRAN.

I flew to IRAN on July 16, 1978. I landed in Tehran on July 17, where I was picked up by a Solus Schall's driver and taken to their office to finalise my work visa. I spent a couple of days in Tehran. It was a lovely city, and the people were welcoming and friendly. I enjoyed my few days there, even if it was sweltering. I found it impressive that you could see the mountains surrounding the Caspian Sea, with their tops covered in snow, which I wasn't expecting to see, given the extreme heat in Tehran.

On my fourth day, I was flown to a city called Ahvaz, located a couple of hundred miles inland, essentially in the desert. I was taken to my accommodation, where I met the other divers and the diving supervisor, Mr Ivan Whatly. One of the other divers I had worked with a few times in the North Sea and the Middle East over the years was a charming individual named John Kent, who had a fantastic life. I discovered more about it many years later when I met his brother. John himself was very quiet and experienced in many different things. The accommodation was a big villa surrounded by a tall wall. We were based inland, which seemed strange as we were nowhere near the sea. It turned out that the area where I would be working was a city called Bushehr, and I would be working offshore in the Pars gas field. At that time, the city of Bushehr was too uncivilised to live in, so we were based over 430 km away in Ahvaz.

What shocked me in Ahvaz was the poor treatment of the locals. They did not have nice accommodations and were made to eat outside in the gutters. I was shocked, but as this was my first time in the Middle

East, I just got on. I was told to ignore everything, as I would get used to it in time. The Iranian people were friendly and pleasant, considering their living conditions. Most of the time, I spent my days sunbathing at the villa, as there was nothing to do. I was getting tanned; in the end, I was mistaken for a local, but that was fine, as the locals who spoke English would speak to me about anything and how they hoped one day they, too, could live in a lovely villa and not in the shanty houses they lived in.

My tan and I are on top of our villa.

I would have gone out with my camera, but I was informed that I could not take any pictures outside the villa, as the local authorities did not permit it. No problems; I thought I did not want to cause any issues with anyone. One thing I did notice was how poorly the American oil workers treated the local workers. I was glad we weren't getting the same treatment, as I don't think I would have been pleased; little did I know that we would be treated the same as the locals once we arrived in Bushehr.

At long last, we received a call to prepare for our departure from Ahvaz. We would be flying to Bushehr and going offshore to recover drill pipes from around a gas rig. The rig had suffered a big gas blowout, and a recovery programme as needed to recover all the drill pipes from the seabed around it. We flew to Bushehr in an 8-seater plane. It was something that I had never experienced before. We had been up in the air for about an hour when the pilot got out his coffee flasks and some sandwiches; he then turned around and said, "Right guys, pass the coffee and sandwiches around as that's the only thing you're going to get to eat and drink until we land." I got my coffee and sandwich, and then looked out of the window. All I could see for miles was desert and mountains. I was on a real adventure. If only Tom Hooper could see me now, what would he think!? From looking at those white walls in the factory to looking across a desert and mountains, drinking coffee and having a sandwich handed down to me from a pilot just a couple of feet away.

We arrived at a very primitive airfield in Bushehr, where we were met by a big yellow bus from the gas company we would be working for. The company was called O.S.C.O. We were instructed to retrieve our belongings from the plane and find a seat. The bus was mostly full of locals. When we arrived at our accommodation, we could not believe it. It was a portacabin with two double beds on the floor, a couple of dirty sheets, and a disgusting shower and toilet with two towels for five guys. The surrounding area was horrendous. Two large open sewers, about 4 feet across; I did not want to know how deep these open sewers were running down the sides of the roads. We were then informed we would be there for one night before joining the supply boat the following morning, which would take us offshore. I could see that John Kent was not amused, but as I didn't know better, I assumed this was part of life in the Middle East. I did not eat anything that night as the food looked disgusting. We had to eat with the local workers as we were not allowed in the main canteen.

The following day, I could not wait to get on the supply boat, the Malaya Tide, but that was not much better. On board the supply boat were six sets of twin scuba bottles, wet suits, dive masks, fins, weight belts, a zodiac, and an HP compressor. No decompression chamber was supplied, as we were only diving in 40 feet of water.

It didn't take long for us to arrive at the gas rig. We had heard that the famous Red Adair, the American firefighter, was on the rig, having put out the big gas blowout. Once we got alongside the rig, we were all lifted off the supply vessel with our diving equipment and met on the drill floor by the rig supervisor, who told us, "Get ready to dive in one minute." We had just arrived and needed to get ourselves rested and plan our dives. The next thing we heard was Red Adair shouting, "When I say I need divers, all I want to hear is splash, nothing more." That was our welcome on the gas rig. Our supervisor insisted that we be shown our accommodation before we do anything. Now, more shock and horror.

We were taken to the gas rig accommodation area, where we were shown a dark cabin with 16 beds, one light, and a toilet in the corner of the room. Two shifts worked from the same room. It was disgusting, and I wondered what I had gotten myself into. Now, this is where John Kent decided enough was enough. He would no longer be treated like this by the American gas workers. At least John could do something about us, but not the locals. Their treatment and conditions were disgusting. "Right," John said, "all of you get your gear and come with me." John decided to take over, thank God. He took us all to the main canteen and informed us that this would be our sleeping quarters until we received proper treatment. The rig supervisor did not want anything to do with us, so we spent two nights sleeping in the mess room. We were not going to start any diving until our facilities improved. On the third day, we were instructed to pack our belongings and disembark from the rig, as a supply boat had just arrived with another dive team. This was great for me. I could not wait to get off. I saw the supply boat with a decompression chamber on the deck and some diving gear as I looked down.

The Supply Boat from a personal basket with a decompression chamber and a zodiac.

As we were lowered onto the vessel from a personnel basket, we were met by another dive team. They were all well-educated Iranian divers who lived in America. They noticed our diving equipment lowered onto the deck and asked us what was happening. John told them about the accommodation they expected us to put up with while working from the rig. Most of their diving equipment was lifted onto the rig, except for the decompression chamber and LP compressor. However, that did not bother us, as we were leaving, or so we thought. The supply boat was told to stand by and wait for instructions before sailing back to Bushehr. Next thing we knew, we could see all the Iranian divers and their diving equipment being lowered back onto the vessel. Once we spoke to them, they informed us that they, too, had been given the same accommodations and facilities. They were also told they could not bring their decompression chamber onto the rig, so they said, "Right, we are not doing any diving or living in that accommodation." The gas company had two dive teams on the supply boat, and no diving occurred.

Both diving supervisors were called back onto the rig to discuss the next steps. The outcome was that both dive teams would live and work from the supply boat. On July 30th, I made my first dive in 40 feet of water in the Persian Gulf, not the Arabian Gulf, as we were diving in the Iranian sector of the Gulf.

I searched the seabed around the gas rig with a twin-set scuba bottle, looking for the drill pipes that had been blown across the seabed. The water in the Pars Gas field was dark brown, and the tide was swift and strong. Due to the strength of the tide, we could not stay down for long periods, around 40 to 60 minutes. Once I had located the drill pipes, I had to mark them off with a rope that went to the surface, with a marker buoy on the surface to show the position of the drill pipes for the crane on the rig or the winch on the supply boat to lift them out of the water. During the evening, I got to know the Iranian divers very well. They were all former Iranian Navy divers who had been trained as divers in an exchange programme between the American and Iranian Navies. The supervisor was the owner of the Iranian dive company. He was a nice guy and a good diver.

My last dive, searching for the drill pipes, was on August 4th; the operation was completed on August 5th, 1978. As we sailed back to Bushehr, the Iranian boss asked us if we would like to work for him on a two-week-on, two-week-off contract, with paid leave and flights to wherever we lived in the world. I could not believe my luck that what started as a terrible experience would hopefully end well with a fantastic new contract.

Once we returned to port in Bushehr, the Iranian divers and we went our separate ways, but we exchanged all our contact details. We were picked up from the supply boat and taken back to the first portacabin we had arrived at, but by now, John Kent was no longer taking any more nonsense. He told us to wait in the portacabin while he went to sort something out. About an hour later, he returned with transport, and we were then taken to a much better portacabin, where we could eat in the main canteen. I don't know what John did or said, but I was very grateful. I was not sorry to leave Bushehr. I did not understand why we were getting treated so poorly by the American gas field workers. Everyone seemed to think they were John Wayne and could do what they wanted. I felt sorry for the locals. At least we could do something about our conditions, or John certainly did for us. We got the same plane back to Ahvaz with the same pilot. The pilot informed us that there had been some trouble while we were away. A few locals had started shooting in the evening, so it was unsafe to go out at night, but he reckoned it would all blow over very soon.

We arrived back at our accommodation on August 7th, which I was very pleased about, as at long last, we would get a proper bed and some good food to eat. However, we were again informed not to go out at night. That evening, I could hear gunshots in the distance, but I did not know if someone was out celebrating or shooting at something or someone. The following morning, our supervisor, Ivan, went to the main office to discuss our successful operation, the poor conditions, and the shooting we had heard overnight. While he was gone, I finished all my laundry and relaxed, listening to the BBC World Service, as there was nothing else to listen to: no TV, no internet, no phones, no newspapers, and no mail. I decided to walk around the town; I still could not believe the locals' living conditions and how they were being treated. At least we had John, who improved our conditions, but the locals did not seem to have anyone, including their authorities, to improve their conditions. I kept hearing on the radio about the trouble brewing in Iran and protests against the Peacock King, the Shah of Iran. Still, at the same time, I heard news that the Queen of England was planning a state visit, so I stopped paying attention to the BBC World Service.

Our supervisor, Ivan, had returned from a meeting with the operations manager, who told him not to be concerned about the shooting. It would all blow over in a couple of days. Our supervisor heard that I had gone out for a walk around the town; he looked at me and said, "Well, that's okay because you look like one of them." I just shrugged my shoulders and walked away. More shooting was going on that night, but this time it was getting closer to our accommodation. This was when I learned that John was ex-military and highly trained, more so than I had ever known. However, I didn't discover his military experience until many years later. The following morning, John noticed gunshots had hit our accommodation, and the riots were getting worse. We were told not to worry, to keep our heads down, and no matter what, not to go outside, day or night. It would all blow over, we kept being told. The next few nights got worse; more gun shootings were going on, and our villa was getting hit more and more; during the day, riots were happening all the time. I kept listening to the BBC World Service, as did the rest of the guys; we then heard that the Queen's visit to Iran had been cancelled due to the continuing troubles. I was unaware of what was happening back home, as I had no means of contacting them or even knowing if they were aware of the situation in Iran. Yet our operations manager kept saying, "Don't worry; it will all blow over."

I don't remember the exact date we were told to prepare to pack up, but we were instructed to be ready to move out of Ahvaz on a Friday at 5:00 a.m. We were told to take what we could carry, no more. There will not be enough space to bring everyone and their belongings. We all met up at a convoy of buses that were to take everybody out of Ahvaz and onto a town called Bander, which was 110 km away through the desert. There would be one plane left to fly us all out to safety. As we approached Bander, it was clear that the town was in chaos, with people running around and riots erupting; it was not a pleasant sight. I did not know what would happen.

The local army met our convoy of buses, and we were taken straight to the aeroplane and told to get on and sit anywhere, including the aisles. The plane was full, with no space available anywhere, and people were seated all down the aisles, but no one seemed bothered; they just wanted to take off and get out. We took off, but we were not allowed to leave Iranian airspace. The plane was instructed to fly to Tehran, but we were flying farther into the country than where we had travelled from.

I did not know what was going to happen. I did not have my passport because back then, the company you worked for took it from you and kept it. Once we landed in Tehran, we were instructed to disembark and proceed to our company's office. Great, where's that? I thought. But luckily, Ivan knew how to get there. Plus, he had somehow managed to get a taxi. As we were travelling through Tehran, there was rioting all over the city. My impression was they were not interested in us; they had just had enough of being kicked around and being treated poorly by their rulers and, in my opinion, the American oil/gas workers. When we got to the office, there was no one there. It was empty and had been completely emptied. Suddenly, an Indian got out of a car and asked us if we were the divers from Ahvaz. "Yes," we said, great, and he said, "You are the last ones I need to help." He held up our passports, plane tickets, and money, told us to get out as soon as possible, and then left. We looked at each other and headed straight back to the airport with the same taxi driver. We managed to find a flight and left Iran, heading to the UK. I arrived home around the middle of August. Rose was delighted that I was home safe and sound, plus she was a lot better with her post-natal depression. Additionally, it was great to see Chris's progress.

While I was home, more and more news was coming in about Iran and the riots; in many ways, I did not blame the Iranians for the uprising. To me, they just had enough and wanted a better life. Have they achieved that? I am not sure. I found them to be friendly and well-educated. Did I think the uprising was all about religion? No, to me, it was about them just having had enough of being mistreated. If they had been treated better by the Shah, I am sure the country would not be in its current state.

I never did get that two-week on-and-two-week off contract. I never heard from those Iranian divers, and I don't know if they ever went back to Iran once the troubles started. My contract was also cancelled, but I received payment for those few weeks I spent in Iran. However, once again, I was out of work and once more wondering where the next job would come from. Rose was getting better, and I was considering moving back to our home in Runcorn. Living with your in-laws is not ideal, even if they are helpful. We needed to move back home to have our own lives.

So much about **it will all blow over in a couple of days**. Problems persist in Iran.

Chapter Nine

The North Sea & Hartlepool.

On August 20, 1978, Solus Schall called to ask if I was available for a diving job for Mobil in the Beryl A Field in the North Sea. "Yes, no problems," I said. On August 25, I arrived in Aberdeen to catch a helicopter flight to the Beryl A platform on August 26. I had never been on a helicopter before, so I was nervous. The helicopter was a twin-rotor Chinook, which I had only seen on TV. It was a fantastic experience to fly on.

Once I arrived at the platform, I was taken to the main deck to be lowered to a supply ship with all my diving equipment in a personnel basket. Once onboard, I was introduced to the supervisor, who introduced himself as RT. He explained that the operation involved fitting mid-steel limpet boxes to the concrete structure legs, as the platform had to accommodate new water intakes. To achieve this, the rig engineers had to drill four 12-inch diameter holes inside the legs to install the new intakes. The concrete legs were enormous; it was unclear how anyone would determine which areas to dive on. The diving supervisor called a meeting with the rig operations manager to explain what we had to look out for.

Scaffolding frames had been erected around the concrete leg above the water level where we would be working. The mild-steel limpet boxes were 4 feet square. They would be lowered down on the inside of the scaffolding frame to about 10 feet to the water. Our job was to ensure the centre of the limpet boxes was in line with the small 4-inch boreholes that were to be drilled from the inside of the concrete leg. Once the safety plug had been removed from the inside of the concrete leg, sufficient water suction from the 4-inch borehole would draw the limpet box against the concrete leg, creating a seal.

On August 31st, the first limpet box was lowered into position at the 10-foot location. I was scuba diving from the zodiac, using hand signals with a rope back to the zodiac. Once I signalled on my downline that the limpet box was in place, removing the borehole safety plug could commence. As soon as they removed the borehole safety plug, the water would rush in, and the limpet box would be sucked in immediately. The fitting of the first limpet box went perfectly. Everyone was very pleased; the engineers were happy to start fitting the new water intakes inside the concrete leg.

On September 1st, we had to prepare to start fitting another limpet box in 10 feet of water, this time on the opposite side of the concrete leg. The scaffolding frame was in position, and the limpet box was lowered. The borehole was already drilled, and the safety plug inside the leg was in position. The same procedure was followed for the next limpet box, which was sucked onto the concrete leg. We then returned to the supply vessel to eat and drink, as the limpet box was being fitted. About an hour later, our supervisor, RT, was asked to check the limpet box. Too much water was leaking through the seals, and they could not continue working unless the leaks were stopped. I went back into the water and checked all around the seals, noticing that some of them had been sucked inward. Our supervisor reported my findings to the operations manager, who asked our diving supervisor if we could come up with any ideas to stop the leaks. "Do you have any ideas?" he asked us. I said I could make Denso sausages with rope to fit around the limpet box. He gave me a strange look and said, "What the fxxk are you on about?" I told him about my time on the docks and how I used to stop leaks when replacing stern glands on cargo ships using rope and Denso tape. I had noticed that the supply ship had plenty of Denso onboard, as they used Denso tape to seal the ship's pipes in the winter. He said, "OK, get on with it and go and make some Denso rope sausages." I did not find out until later that he had not informed the rig engineers of what we were doing, as he told me he did not want to look foolish if it did not work.

I finished making my rope sausages and started my next dive, fitting the Denso sausages around the limpet boxes. It was sucked in immediately, and due to the soft Denso material on the rope being squeezed in, it stopped the leaks. When I got out of the water, RT, our supervisor, could not stop laughing. He couldn't believe that such a daft idea worked. I guess my time on the docks was not wasted. He ensured we had some Denso rope sausages ready for the subsequent dives, just in case more limpet boxes leaked. On September 6th, we fitted our last limpet box, and the engineers had completed all the internal drilling. We commenced our operation to remove all the limpet boxes, which was very simple. We just removed the Denso rope sausages, which allowed water to enter the boxes, equalising the internal pressure, and the limpet boxes came away from the side of the concrete legs. The fitting of the limpet boxes went very well, and I began to feel comfortable with what I was doing offshore. I was still wet behind the ears, but feeling better within myself.

I arrived home around the 9th of September. I say 'home', but in reality, we were still living with the in-laws, which had been going on for eight months. Although it was helping Rose, I was beginning to find it overwhelming. I started returning to our house in Runcorn so we could plan to go home for Christmas. Still, at the same time, I knew Rose was not happy to be heading back to Runcorn, so I asked if we could be put on the Liverpool Council housing list to see if we could get accommodation back in Liverpool. We secured an interview for accommodation very quickly, as Rose's mum had connections with the council due to her involvement in local politics. I remembered from the interview that I was still very tanned from my trip to IRAN. I tan very quickly, and the weather in the North Sea was good, so as far as I was concerned, I looked very healthy. However, the person interviewing us commented on how dark I looked and asked how long I had lived in the UK. I wondered if this would stop us from getting a council house in Liverpool. I came away from the interview very annoyed; Rose never really said anything about it, as she never thought about how I looked or mentioned how other people always looked at me.

After a week or so at home, Solus Schall called again to ask if I was available for a 6-8-week offshore diving job off Hartlepool. Yes, I said, I was. I set off for Hartlepool on September 18th for one of the best diving operations I have ever been on. I worked with some of the friendliest and funniest people I have ever worked with. One person stood out from any other divers I had worked with. That person was a tall, gentle giant named Graham Potts, who always called me Frenchy and still does. I also worked under one of the best diving supervisors I had ever encountered, Antony Hart. He was a great guy in my eyes. I arrived at Hartlepool on the evening of September 18th and joined the M/V Gallustrum. We were going to work for Phillips Petroleum on one of their permanent rigs off Hartlepool, which required the removal of all marine growth from the supporting members on the platform.

This is the Phillips Petroleum platform on which I will spend the next six weeks working.

I felt this was my first real offshore diving job compared to the other diving jobs I had done before. All the other diving jobs had always been in scuba, but this operation would use Kirby 10 diving hats, which I had never used before. It was also the largest dive team I had been involved with—an 8-man diving team. Apart from one or two guys, the rest of the divers were the same as me, starting in the offshore diving world. Our first day involved sailing offshore and preparing our diving equipment; the diving operation had two decompression chambers. They were not fitted into any air-conditioned containers or similar equipment; they were simply placed on the deck of the ship and secured in place. We had two LP and two HP compressors, two air quads and two oxygen quads, two water jet machines, and a Zodiac. The containers we did have were an equipment container and a dive control room.

On September 23rd, I carried out my first dive on the 36/22 Phillips Petroleum Ekofisk platform. I was to set up the downline and wait for the water jet gun to be lowered to me. I was working at the 70-foot level, and the other diver was working on the platform members at the 20-foot level, but that diver was using hand scrapers. Graham Potts was the diver above me, working on the members at a depth of 20 feet. The water was crystal clear, allowing us to see each other working. I started the water jetting to remove the marine growth, which was approximately 18 inches to 24 inches thick in places. It was especially thick around the platform members. The first dive with the water jet went very well. It only lasted around 41 minutes before I was informed to stop my dive, secure the water jet, and make my way to my water stop, which was at 10 feet for 10 minutes. I could see Graham working away at 20 feet with the hand scraper. To pass the time, I broke bits of marine growth on my 10-foot stop and started dropping lumps of marine growth to see if I could hit Graham's head with any of them. I could see them dropping nearby, but I don't know if any hit him. My in-water decompression time was up, and I returned to the surface. Graham was only working at 20 feet, so he worked for around another 30 minutes before returning to the surface. Graham and I got changed into our working gear. It was our working gear, as no one gave us overalls back then, not even foul-weather gear. However, I had kept the foul-weather gear I received while working on the mini-subs. We went for a coffee and had a good natter about anything and everything, but all the way through, he just kept smiling and nodding at me; I soon found out why when we dived together again. The following day, our supervisor, Tony, wanted everyone to become accustomed to the decompression chamber, as he planned to extend dive times to 70/80 feet for the members.

Into the Blue and Beneath The Waves

I am in my lovely working gear, doing a 02 decompression in the deck decompression chamber (DDC).

After a couple of days, Graham and I were diving together again, me on the 70-foot member and Graham on the 20-foot member. "Don't worry," I said to him, "one day they'll let you dive deep with the big boys." We both just laughed.

I am getting ready to dive using a Kirby 10 diving mask.

In those days, we used neoprene wetsuits and a fenzy jacket as safety garments to quickly get us to the surface if we got into trouble. The big problem arose from wearing the fenzy jacket. A hilarious incident happened to Graham with the fenzy jacket, but that's for later. We both jumped into the water. I went down the downline to the 70-foot member and Graham to the 20-foot member. I was water jetting, and Graham was using the hand scraper. After about 20 minutes, big lumps of marine growth started falling on me. At first, I thought nothing of it, but suddenly, two big lumps of marine growth landed on me. What the fxxk was going on? As I looked up, I could see Graham waving at me, and then I realised what was happening: He was getting his own back on me from the other day. We both could not stop laughing. Tony, our supervisor, put us on joint communications and asked what was going on, as all he could hear over the communications was us laughing. He told us both to stop pissing about and get on with our jobs. After the dive, we both had a good laugh about dropping the lumps of marine growth on each other over a cup of coffee. Graham and I got along well throughout this job. We got along well with all the guys; it was a great job with plenty of laughs, and everyone pulled their weight to remove the marine growth from the platform members. However, one incident did show us how crazy it was to have a fenzy on with a full diving mask, and at the same time, it had its humorous side, as you will see from the incident narrated below.

Graham and I are getting ready to dive on one of the funniest dives I have ever been on.

On this particular dive, I was diving again with Graham Potts. We were wearing wetsuits and Kirby 10 diving hats. We also wore fenzy air jackets around our necks as an extra safety measure in case we got into trouble or had to surface quickly. I was working on the 40-foot platform member, cleaning off all the marine growth, and Graham was below me on the 70-foot member, also cleaning off the marine growth. What was good was that the water was always clear; you could see down to about 90 feet. All of a sudden, I heard a lot of shouting over the diver's radio concerning Graham; as I looked down, I could see Graham was trying to stab himself with the diver's knife in his chest, and his other hand gripping onto his diving hat. The next minute, the standby diver went past me, heading down to Graham, who was still trying to stab himself in the chest. As the standby diver got to Graham, I saw him kicking the standby diver away. I was then told to go down and help out, but I did not understand what was going on, apart from Graham trying to stab himself, holding on to his hat and kicking out at the standby diver. As I made my way down, I noticed both divers were heading up towards me at a rapid rate; I had to move out of the way very quickly. As they went past me, Graham was still trying to stab himself in the chest while still holding on to his hat; the only thing I noticed was that the standby diver was holding on to Graham's leg as they went past me, heading to the surface. As they hit the surface, the water was so clear that all I could see was splashing around. All I could hear was shouting over the diver's radio. After a few minutes, I was instructed to return to the surface, as the dive had been cancelled.

Once I was out of the water and onto the deck, the diving supervisor, Tony, stood between Graham and the standby diver, as Graham wanted to hit him. Once everything had calmed down, I was informed about what had happened. Graham was working away on the platform member when his air bottle on the fenzy air jacket opened and inflated his fenzy jacket. It started inflating and pushing against his diving hat, trying to force it off his head. The only way Graham could stop himself from shooting to the surface and stop his diving hat from being pushed off his head was to wrap his leg around the downline next to him. He then took his diving knife out to try and puncture the fenzy air jacket that was forcing his diving hat off his head. Due to the noise from Graham shouting, the supervisor was unable to determine what was happening and sent the standby diver down. He just saw Graham stabbing himself and thought Graham was trying to kill himself; he also noticed Graham's leg was fouled up on the downline. The standby diver went to cut Graham to free him from the downline, but Graham knew what would happen if the downline got cut, so he tried to kick the standby diver away. Once the standby diver cut the downline, which had also gone around the standby diver, they both shot to the surface, and they both hit the surface at a rate of knots. Once on deck, Graham wanted to hit the standby diver while everyone else was trying to get the diver's knife off Graham. Luckily, no decompression was needed, and once everything settled down, we all laughed about what had just gone on. It makes me laugh to this day.

Cold, wet suits drying out; it was horrible getting into wet, wet suits.

That's me in the middle with a couple of the other divers. The diver on my left was the standby diver who rescued Graham on that hilarious dive.

To me, life was great. I enjoyed working offshore as a diver, gaining valuable experience and spending more time at sea. The operation was going well; we had no more incidents with fenzy jackets. Nowadays, there would be considerable investigation, and the diving HSE would be called in. Diving was much more relaxed then. Still, safety must continue to improve to benefit all diving operations. Diving in those days was great fun.

The operation was nearing its close, and it was approaching the end of October. We had just a few more cleaning operations to complete before the diving season ended. The winter was starting, and not much work was required for air diving in the North Sea during the winter, but I was hoping to get some overseas work again with Solus Schall. We were now approaching the end of our diving operation. All we were doing was cleaning up the last bits of marine growth the client wanted us to remove. We didn't have underwater cameras to record anything. All that was supplied was a drawing of the platform, and the areas we cleaned had to be ticked off. We had one diver with a Lloyd's inspection certificate, which we all wondered about, including the client who had the inspection diver sign off on the underwater reports. I was wondering what this inspection certificate is. I later found out when I was sent on an inspection course by Solus.

I was the standby diver.

I am the standby diver for the diver below.

That's me on my last dive of that operation.

We were now down to the last few dives, and knowing I would be going home soon was a nice feeling. For how long, I did not know, but by now, I was sure something would turn up.

Me as the diver tender

I finished my last dive on November 1, 1978, as the diving season had come to a close for the winter. Solus Schall assured me they would call me if anything came up. I had no reason not to believe them, as they had kept me busy for a few months. Additionally, I felt I had performed reasonably well on the diving operations I was involved with during the second half of 1978.

The diving team sailing away from the Philip Petroleum 36/22 Ekofisk Platform

I arrived in Liverpool on November 3rd. Rose was still living with her parents, but after being away for so long, the last thing she wanted was to spend time with them. Being with Rose and Chris was great, but spending your days with the in-laws was not enjoyable. When we moved back to Runcorn, we had to start living our own lives. Rose was fine now, and young Chris was great, so I thanked the in-laws for ensuring Rose was back to normal and Chris was happy and healthy. We were looking forward to Christmas at home. I must admit we had a great time.

We visited my parents and Rose's parents all over Christmas and the New Year, and honestly, we had a great time. After the new year, I got a phone call from Solus Schall, now known as Solus Ocean Systems. Would I be interested in doing a Lloyd's NDT inspection section course in Falmouth starting on February 25, 1979? Plus, they would pay for everything they asked. By now, I had grown accustomed to saying yes. I was available for everything and anything, even if I had no idea what NDT was.

For some reason, I had to have a diving medical with Doctor King, who, over the years, had a reputation with divers. Plus, the medical report had to be in my diving logbook. Back then, no pages were made available for the medical report, so he filled out his medical report on a dive sheet in my diving log book on February 23, 1979.

On the 24th of February, I arrived in Falmouth, ready to start my course at the Pro Dive diving centre. My trouble was that I had no idea what NDT stood for. On the first day, I learnt it stood for underwater non-destructive testing. Holy fxxk! was all I could say to myself. What the hell is this? All my worst fears from my school days came flooding back; if I couldn't pass my 11+, what chance did I have with this?

It was a nightmare once they started discussing magnetic fields, ultrasonic field readings, Krautkramer D-meter thickness gauges, permanent magnets with adequate field strengths for magnetic particle inspections, cathodic potential measurements, magnetic particle crack detection, and CCTV inspections. All this had to be done in one week. Knowing how to make a Denso sausage roll with a rope to seal a leak would not help me now. I just fell into my shell. All my fears of being thick came back; what was I doing here? All the other nine guys seemed to take it in their stride. I was utterly lost. I didn't know any other guys or learn how to speak to them without feeling stupid.

My only saving grace was Fawlty Towers. It had just started showing and was on TV every night at the hotel. None of the rooms had TV sets, so we all had to sit in the TV room with a drink to watch it. None of us could stop laughing. What made it even funnier was that we had a waiter named Manuel, who was unhappy when everybody kept saying "Qué." So, Fawlty Towers, Manuel, and our waiter, who hated everyone, saying "Qué," relaxed me, as no one was talking about 'non-destructive testing', which I still had no idea what it was all about.

On February 26th, I began my first dive, taking D-Meter readings with the Krautkramer D-Meter thickness gauge. If you have never seen one of these Krautkramer metres, they are enormous. It was like taking an old TV with handles into the water. It had a nozzle protruding from it, allowing me to take thickness readings from the metal beams I was testing. It was so big that you had to tie it off to take any reading. I spent half an hour practising with that unit before moving on to a cathodic protection meter, which was about a quarter of the size. After an hour, I had finished my first NDT dive. I just thought, give me a jackhammer; it's much easier to understand.

Each afternoon, we spent in the classroom learning about NDT on welds, anodes, steel plates, underwater photography, CCTV inspections, magnetic particle inspection, quartz crystals, the piezo effect, and ultrasonic sound waves. We had to learn all about this in one week, and then we would have an exam at the end of the week. My second dive involved magnetic particle inspection on weld butts, followed by more classroom work. In the evening, after dinner and Fawlty Towers, I would try to spend my time studying, but I did not understand anything apart from photography and CCTV inspections. My third dive involved more M.P.I. testing, additional bathycorrometer readings (Cathodic protection), and then returning for further studies. We now had the weekend off to prepare for the written and practical exams. I spent the whole weekend studying without realising just how much was sinking in. I would see the other guys at meals, and they never seemed bothered by it all. Boy, did I feel out of place?

On Monday morning, March 2nd, 1979, my NDT tests started. The first tests were all the underwater tests, M.P.I., followed by the bathycorrometer test, CCTV, and photography, finishing with the big old TV set called a Krautkramer D-meter. I completed my written and multiple-choice exams in the afternoon, and my head spun. We did not wait a week or so for the results; we were given them after about two hours. The funny thing is that I passed my written and multiple-choice exams but failed my CCTV, M.P.I., and that monster of a unit, the Krautkramer D-meter. Only two of us failed out of the nine; I was very disappointed, but unbeknownst to me, Solus had expected some of us to fail and had arranged a backup test at Fort Bovisand in Plymouth for September 8th, provided I could get there. I thought, why not? What have I got to lose? I arrived at Fort Bovisand on March 8th, ready for my underwater tests on March 9th. I started my dive in their test tank. Around 120 minutes later, I had completed my CCTV test, my M.P.I., and my test on my old mate, the Krautkramer D-meter. Again, I did not have to wait long to get my results. I passed all my tests. I then received my Lloyd's Register Industrial Services Underwater Non-Destructive certificate. I was now a fully qualified Lloyds inspection diver.

I went back home to Runcorn to wait for my next diving job. About ten days later, I received a call from Solus asking if I would be available for a diving job starting on the 22nd of March, 79, in the Middle East, in Abu Dhabi, in the U.A.E. "Come on," I said. "Did you see what happened the last time I visited the Middle East? They had a great, significant uprising, and we had to get out quickly." They said, "Don't worry. Abu Dhabi is a lovely, friendly place; it's nothing like Iran." "I am not sure," I said. "Look," they said, "we will give you an open return air ticket; if you don't like Abu Dhabi, you can come home anytime." "Give me a couple of days to think about it," I said, which they did. In the end, I agreed to fly out on the understanding that I could return home if I didn't like Abu Dhabi. On March 22, 1979, I flew to Abu Dhabi, very apprehensive about what I was letting myself in for.

Chapter Ten
Abu Dhabi, U.A.E.

On 23rd March 1979, I landed in Abu Dhabi, one of the best places I could have hoped to work from. It marked the beginning of a long and successful diving career that spanned until my retirement. I landed at Abu Dhabi's international airport, Al Bateen, which was then in the heart of the city. I was picked up and taken to the guest house, a lovely villa in Abu Dhabi. It had its bar, cleaners, a cook, a houseboy, and everything you could wish for.

After a night's sleep to get over the jet lag, I got up the following morning to get ready for work, but to my surprise, no one was interested. I was taken to a hotel called the Ali Pally, where we would have a few beers by the swimming pool to relax and meet the other guys. It was just not what I expected; there I was with my new Lloyds inspection NDT certificate and my diving qualification, and the reaction was, "Nar, we're not interested in that shit. We want to know if you can dive and swim around in circles, checking the oil rig legs to see if any deep holes or obstacles may cause damage to the oil rig legs when they drop them into the seabed to anchor the oil rigs."

After the weekend, I was taken to the Solus office to hand over my passport and have a work visa stamped. Once that was completed, I was instructed to return to the villa, relax until needed, and get to know the other staff members. The diving supervisor was Dave Holding, a great, easy-going guy. As far as I could tell, he had been in Abu Dhabi for a long time.

Eventually, I joined the Pacific Builder vessel to carry out oil rig leg and seabed inspections. We would locate anchor blocks by swimming down the anchor chains at the stern of the ship, where we would then prepare them for lifting back onto the stern of the supply vessel, which had an A-frame for lifting and lowering the anchor blocks in and out of the water.

Pacific Builder with A-Frame and anchor block.

Once we lifted the anchor blocks out of the water, we inspected them and the floating buoy to determine if any maintenance was needed before re-submerging them at a new location. Our main operation was offshore field maintenance for ZADCO. The client informed our supervisor each evening of the details for the following day's diving operation. On some days, we lifted and repositioned anchor blocks; on other days, we conducted pipeline surveys and removed debris around the fixed platforms. We also conducted extensive seabed surveys for any jack-up oil rig platforms relocating to new locations. Before lowering the jack-up rig legs to the seabed, we had to survey the seabed to ensure the platform's legs could be safely positioned.

There are different types of offshore jack-up oil rigs, which are equipped with three legs that are lowered to the seabed after we conduct our seabed surveys.

Once the oil rigs were in place, we would place the anchor blocks in and around them, allowing the supply vessels to connect the vessel's bow to the anchor block floating buoy. The vessel's stern would then go astern and moor up to the oil rigs.

The picture shows one of the anchor blocks being lowered into the water from the A-frame, which would lift the anchor block and drop it to the seabed; once the anchor block was on the seabed, the vessel would go ahead and play out more anchor chain, until it was far enough away, so we could dive on the anchor block and release the A-frame wire from the anchor block, The vessel also dropped its anchor at the bow to secure the ship before we started our dive.

That's me and the diver getting ready to dive to release the anchor block from the A-frame.

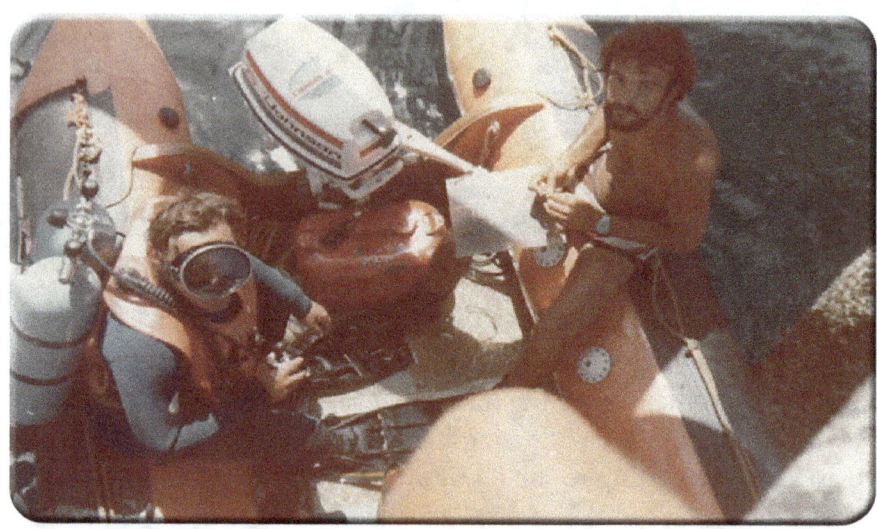

The operation of the offshore maintenance vessel varied from day to day. I enjoyed it; all the divers were friendly and helpful. I had never been in an operation like this before, but the supervisor ensured I was involved in everything. Each oil rig leg on the jack-ups was different, but the inspections on the seabed were the same. The key was to ensure that nothing was in the area on the seabed where the jack-up rigs dropped their legs. Once we had completed our seabed surveys and no more jack-up rigs needed to be moved around for a while, I changed vessels and proceeded to survey 'Free Standing Wellhead Jackets'. However, before I changed vessels, one of the jack-up rigs had lost a drill head while jacking up. We had to go alongside the rig, as they had stopped their jacking-up operation until we located the lost drill head.

Alongside a jack-up rig, looking for the lost drill head.

Once we had located the lost drill, I completed my dive on the M/V Pacific Builder. On April 9th, I was transferred at sea to the M/V Brootor to initiate an inspection operation on free-standing wellhead platforms for ZADCO. Our diving operation involved conducting seabed surveys around free-standing wellheads, verifying the depth of each wellhead, and removing any debris encountered.

I did two to three dives daily using scuba diving equipment and USN repetitive dive tables, which I had never done before. It was my first time using these tables. Most of the dives ranged from 40 to 70 feet in depth. We had approximately 11 free-standing wellhead platforms to inspect, measure the depth of each wellhead, and remove any debris. I enjoyed the work, diving in scuba and learning more about USN repetitive dives. Once we had finished all these surveys, I was transferred back to the M/V Pacific on April 19th, where I worked on placing anchor blocks and conducting surveys around the seabed to facilitate the arrival of more jack-up rigs on location. On April 24th, I was transferred to another vessel, the Penrod 56, where we inspected the condition of the cement around conductor pipes on the free-standing wellheads. We had one last operation: surveying the seabed around the main offshore complex, checking it for debris, and removing any marine growth from the water intakes.

The main complex.

On April 26th, I completed my last dive. I had been away for around four weeks and enjoyed working with the divers in Abu Dhabi. I wish I could have stayed longer. It was a great job and a lovely city. I enjoyed my time in Abu Dhabi. Besides, I had never considered using the open-return air ticket Solus had given me before I set off. I flew home to Runcorn around April 28th, but now I am no longer wondering about the next job. So far, Solus Ocean Systems has been in touch with me regarding more diving jobs.

Once home, I could see that Rose was not settling in Runcorn and wanted to get closer to her family. As I continued working away from home, it was fair enough. We had not been contacted about an interview for a council house in Liverpool. Although I was earning a living, we had not yet saved enough money for a deposit to buy our own home. Additionally, being a day-rate diver was not what a mortgage company wanted; they only sought full-time employees.

I had around four weeks off, which was a nice break. Rose, young Chris, and I would go out and about on different days, and every few days, we would head into Liverpool to see both families.

Into the Blue and Beneath The Waves

My Dad, Rose's Mum, me, Rose, young Chris, and my mum.

Chapter Eleven
The North Sea; Holland.

Around the 20th of May, Solus called to see if I was available to travel to Holland for an inspection diving job off Den Helder in the North Sea. Solus required divers with inspection certificates, which I had, as I held a Lloyd's NDT certificate. I flew to Amsterdam and caught a train to Den Helder to join the M/V Scot Oil Four vessel.

When I joined the vessel, the diving superintendent met me, Jack Frost, the dive supervisor, Jim Sheppard and the lead diver, Pete Dickenson; he was a real East Enders boy, the real Danny Dyer of the diving world, he took no prisoners, always said what he wanted to say and didn't cut any corners if he had something to tell you he said it. I went down to the mess room where I saw Graham Potts, which was great as we got on so well with each other. I was pleased to see him. Plus, John Kent from Iran was there, so it was great to meet the guys I had worked with on previous diving jobs. Another person I met was TC (Keith Mobbs), who went on to do well for himself and helped me return to the North Sea many years later.

We sailed on the evening of the 23rd of May, and the vessel was set up for diving by midday on the 24th of May. At 13:51, I began my first dive, descending to approximately 70 feet to inspect the anodes and the impressed current anode system circuit. So, finally, I could put the skills I learned from my Lloyd's NDT course to use. I was unprepared for how dark the water was and how fast the tide was around the platform. You had to hold on tight to the support members on the platform. It was May, and the water was freezing, so diving in neoprene wetsuits was not great. You could only get warm by having a wee inside the wetsuit. I was glad when the first dive was over. After my dive, I spent the next few hours being a tender for the other divers. After a few days, the more experienced divers requested dry bags to dive in, as the water was freezing. But in those days, you were just told to "put up and shut up". If you did not like it, then go home. I never understood why some supervisors had that macho attitude; getting cold was not much fun.

I was conducting more and more inspection dives, and the dive times were becoming increasingly longer. As a result, we had to start carrying out 02 decompression in the deck decompression chamber, which was not in a container; it was located on the deck and was freezing inside. This meant you were cold during your dive and your decompression inside the chamber. Again, the more experienced divers asked if Solus could supply dry diving suits or dry bags for diving, as we knew it was necessary, given the low sea temperature. However, the reply came back: "If you're not happy, go home."

What eventually changed everything was when one of the divers got hypothermia while diving and went into shock. His body shut down, and he drifted away from the platform at around 70 feet due to the strong tide. When the dive supervisor could not communicate with him over the diver radio, the command was given to take up the diver's slack on the diving umbilical and pull him to the vessel. The only trouble was that the diver had drifted through the platform, so the standby diver had to be deployed to rescue him. However, more problems came as, in those days, we did not use dive baskets or any pulley system on the stern of the vessel to bring the diver out of the water. Once we got the diver to the dive ladder, it was simply a matter of getting a rope around him and dragging him up the stern of the vessel. From there, we got him and the standby diver into the DDC for their decompression treatment and to warm up the divers. Not long after that, a decision was made to head to Den Helder to pick up a supply of dry suits.

That's me and Graham Potts in our dry diving suits.

After that photo, Graham and I got told to stop pissing around being fxxking models and get ready for our dive. Our dive this time was to the seabed, which was approximately 120 feet deep. We then began conducting circular searches around the platform for any debris and brought any we found to an area where a winch wire would be lowered from the stern of the vessel. At that depth, we did not have much diving time, so we had to be quick and not pissing around. "Get down, get looking and get busy," we were told. Graham and I just laughed at this. As we were getting ready, we kept saying to each other, "Get down, get looking, and get busy." We both reached the bottom and started to gather a pile of debris in the area where the winch wire would be. We only had around 24 minutes on the seabed when we were told to stop our dive and prepare to leave the bottom. Upon your arrival on the surface, you will proceed to the DDC for decompression stops. We completed our dive in our nice, warm, dry suits and our decompression in the DDC.

The following day, we were both informed that, as we knew where all the debris was, it would be better to recover it as it would save on bottom time. We began our dive and descended directly to the seabed, where we located the debris. We requested that the winch wire be lowered so we could attach it to the debris and make it ready for lifting. Amazingly, the water was clear for a change, and we could see each other on the seabed. There was trouble with the winch wire; it could not be lowered just yet. No problem, we said over our dual comms, as it was taking a long time. Graham started going rat-a-tat-tat at me with a pretend gun. I looked across, and he had a piece of debris as his gun; I started laughing and also picked up a piece of debris and started going attung, attung at him with my pretend gun, when all of a sudden, we heard the dive supervisors shout, what the fxxk are you two doing, Graham replied, were playing soldiers while waiting for the winch wire. Well, all we could hear coming back at us from the dive supervisor was a lot of fxxk fxxk fxxking, idiots, get real and stop fxxking about.

Graham and I looked at each other and waved, dropped our pretend guns on the seabed, placed our hands over the tops of our diving hats, and surrendered to each other. We were informed not long after to return to the surface as the winch was broken. We continued diving for a few more days, clearing the debris once the winch wire was fixed. As the water became increasingly clear, the client initiated underwater photography and CCTV inspection work. The only trouble was that no dive technician was available to print out the photos in the vessel's dark room. The diver who should have been doing that work had gone home and was not expected to return. Our diving superintendent asked if anyone could set up the cameras and work as the diving photo technicians in the darkroom. All of a sudden, Graham stood up and said 'yes'. "Frenchy (my nickname from Graham) and I can do that," he said, "no problems." I just looked at him and wondered what the hell he was on about. I didn't know anything about working in a dark room, nor did he. Before I could say anything, the dive superintendent said, "Right, you two. You're the dive technicians from now on. Get the cameras ready and prepare the dark room."

"Fxxk me," I said to Graham. "What are you doing? We know nothing about photography work in a dark room, don't worry." He said, "I have a plan." I think this was Graham's Baldrick moment; the only trouble was that Baldrick was not around back then. Once we entered the dark room, I asked Graham what he was thinking. Look, he said, it's simple. It's where all the beer is kept. I just looked at him, very puzzled; he said that all the ships' beer is kept in the same room as the darkroom. I was still puzzled. "It's simple," he said. "We take a break from diving for a bit, and we get to sit in the dark room, where we can also enjoy a beer. If anyone knocks on the door, we tell them we can't open up yet because we have the negatives still in the camera." "Hang on," I said. "The client and the superintendent will be expecting us to produce some photos. How do we get away with that?" "He says we follow all the written instructions the photo tech has left behind and see if any images come out." "Great," I said, "what if we can't produce any photos?" "Simple," Graham said, "if we screw up developing the images, we tell the supervisors the divers have not taken any good pictures, and they will have to go and retake the photos."

It sounded like a great idea; setting up the Nikon Mk 3 underwater camera was straightforward; all you had to know was the DIN rating on the film. Say a DIN on a roll of film was 27; all you would do is divide your DIN 27 into the distance, say 27 into 6 feet, which would come to 4.5, and your F stop would be F5; if you divided 27 into 3 feet, your F stop would be F9. Graham and I found some old negatives that had not yet been developed, so we practised on them. Mixing the chemicals was fine, so that was taken care of. Learning to accept the negative roll out of the film casing, fit it onto the film reel, and transfer it into the developing tank was difficult, as it was all done by feel. You did not want to expose any light onto the negative while transferring it. You had to load the film onto a reel and transfer it into a developing tank without exposing it to any light. Then, you would fill the tank with the required chemicals to develop the film.

Amazingly, we began to see some good results in the darkroom. Plus, we could have a beer or two; no one could enter unless we allowed them. We would say we couldn't open the door, so that the negatives would get exposed to light, and then hide the beers we were drinking. I apologise for not keeping any photos from that period. We just threw away the bad ones, and the client took away all the good ones. The diving operation was going very well, but the photography inspections ended, much to my and Graham's disappointment. We had had a good run of getting away with things, plus a few beers, which were from the ship's crew supply.

By now, we no longer needed a superintendent as the operation was nearing its end. We had around two weeks to go before the end of the diving work operation, so the work was being pushed to meet the end date; however, it became hazardous due to the impending deadline.

I was diving with John Kent, and we were both at the same depth, around 60 feet. I could feel the surge of water through the platform as I inspected an impressed current anode system. I was clinging to anything I could wrap my legs around to stop myself from being pushed about, so I could complete my inspection.

I was then informed to gather my tools and return to the surface. I gathered my tools and made my way to the surface; once I arrived, I could see the vessel's stern above my head. I then realised why I felt the surge of water through the platform: the sea was rough. I could see John trying to make his way to the dive ladder, but because the ship was bouncing above John's head, he had to try to time his approach to grab the dive ladder. Each time the boat came down, the surge would push John away from the ladder. Eventually, John caught the dive ladder and held on, then hauled himself up the ladder and onto the vessel's deck. It was my turn to try to time everything so I could grab the dive ladder as it came crashing into the sea. I grabbed the dive ladder as it came down into the water. As I hung on to the dive ladder, the ship surged upwards. The upward surge pushed me to the top of the dive ladder, and the deck crew just pulled me onboard the vessel.

Luckily we didn't need any decompression, but John was mad as hell that we had been kept diving while all the time the weather was getting terrible because this macho image of being supposed to "suck it up and take it" was fxxking madness in my eyes. This surge convinced the Captain, Client and supervisors that we may cancel the day's diving. After a couple of days of downtime due to adverse weather conditions, the operation resumed. The next underwater operation involved underwater cutting using oxy/arc cutting equipment. I was the next diver, and my diving operation involved cutting off old grout pipes that had to be removed from the platform legs. Everyone enjoyed underwater cutting, and I was fortunate enough to have had the opportunity to do it while diving on the docks, so I was very comfortable using the cutting equipment.

The vessel remains moored to the platform in adverse weather conditions.

The diving operation was now coming to an end. I had been on this operation for around two months, so I was looking forward to going home for a break. My last dive was on July 16th, during which I conducted a visual inspection of an impressive current anode system, and I took the last few pictures of the operation. Before I left, I was informed that Solus had no more diving work scheduled. If you manage to secure another diving job from another diving company, please take it, as Solus was not expecting any more air diving operations until 1980.

When I arrived home in Runcorn on July 17th, it was evident that Rose was not enjoying living there and was spending most of her time back in Liverpool with her family. While I was away, Rose received a letter from Liverpool Council requesting that we attend another interview. I noticed the interviewer was the same lady who had asked me how long I had lived in the UK.

As I had been away throughout the summer offshore in Holland, I was looking very well-tanned. The guys used to ask how I was getting such a good tan, and I would tell them it was from the French side of my family, which was fine, as they were used to Graham calling me Frenchy. I was determined not to face any awkward questions from the interviewer, so I made sure I was well-prepared. Even though it was hot, I wore a whole shirt with long sleeves, a high collar, and trousers. I didn't want anything to harm our chances of getting a council house, as Rose needed to move back to Liverpool. Luckily, the interview went well. The interviewer asked if I had been away, as I was looking well. I just smiled and said I had been to Europe. We waited for a letter from Liverpool council to see if we were approved for a council house. Although I was now earning a good income, I still couldn't get a mortgage. I was unemployed again and looking for another diving job.

I was reading a national newspaper when I noticed a company called CCCUE advertising for divers for an operation in Saudi Arabia. I called the number and asked the guy who answered the phone if he was still looking for divers. "Yes," he said, "do you have diving experience?" I said I had just finished working offshore as an NDT inspector diver. I had also done other offshore diving work, and I was available. "I'm sorry," he said, "you are not the type of diver we seek, so we can't use you." He thanked me for calling and said goodbye. I was very disappointed. I wondered what type of divers they were looking for, so I decided to call him back and ask him. I spoke to him again, apologised for calling him back and asked him what type of divers they were looking for. He said CCCUE were looking for civil engineering divers. I almost started to laugh. I then asked him if he had ever heard of the Manchester Ship Canal and Liverpool Docks. "Well, yes," he said, "why?" "I began my diving career on the Manchester Ship Canal and Liverpool Docks, where I worked as a civil engineering diver for approximately three years." He then asked if I could send him my CV and if I would be available to travel to Saudi Arabia on August 10, 1979. I arrived in Saudi Arabia on August 11th and travelled to an area called Jubail to work on a new harbour for a joint venture company called V/H/CCC. The contract was three months on, one month off, with paid leave. Little did I know that I would spend over ten years working for CCCUE in and around the Middle East and India.

Chapter Twelve
Saudi Arabia

My first day was spent settling in and meeting the superintendent, who explained the operation. It involved mainly building a two-mile breakwater, repair work on the new harbour walls, concreting, and extensive jackhammering. The operation ran 24 hours a day, from 06:00 hours in the morning until 18:00 hours in the evening, with the night shift from 18:00 hours until 06:00 hours. I was expected to work two weeks on the night shift and two weeks on the day shift, but each Friday was a day off, and Friday was the shift's changeover day. I met a couple of the other divers at the canteen, where we were having a meal before my first shift started. They were mainly from Scotland and had been working for a Scottish diving company called Fox Diving. The campsite was excellent, featuring numerous sports facilities, social amenities, and a school, which made it a popular choice for families.

I was on a floating dive team for the first few days, until I could move to a proper shift pattern. During this time, I spent my days inspecting the harbour walls and fixing loose fittings on the fenders. Sometimes, we would dive from a small dive barge towed around by small line boats.

That's me on the left of the dive container.

I met one of the guys I would be working with at the canteen. He was a Scottish diver named Alastair Bruce. He was a motorbike enthusiast, but one of the nicest guys you could have hoped to meet and work with. I was fortunate to work with him many times for CCCUE.

On my first Friday, I was asked if I would be coming for a drink in one of the divers' cabins. I looked surprised and said, "What, but you can't drink in Saudi Arabia?" Alastair told me to make my way to room 24 after lunch. "Okay," I said, "I will see you there," thinking it was just a big wind-up, but no problems; I would be there. Well, once I was there, all I could see in the cabin was this big drum of homemade beer still bubbling. That never seemed to bother the lads. They just put their glass in the big drum and pulled it out full of bubbling beer, which I can tell you was very strong. I continued working from the same small dive barge and sometimes from the small line boats for another week, inspecting the harbour walls, checking for damage to the concrete blocks, and fixing any loose bolts on the fenders. All of this work was carried out underwater using scuba gear.

We occasionally use two of the small line boats for diving.

On August 21st, I began work on one of the main work barges, the Damman 2. I would be with a three-man dive team. We would split the 12-hour shift among the three of us, and all of us would do around four hours of diving. As I walked onto the barge, one of the Indian crew members started greeting me with his head bowed and hands clasped together, which I found very odd. I asked him what he was doing. "Sir," he said, "you are the image of our Prince of India." When I looked around, the other Indians greeted me; I looked at them, I could only see images of my dad.

The other divers started saying to me, "You do look like them," "you are undoubtedly tanned more than the rest of us," and "you have only been here a week or so," but by now, I had learnt to laugh it off. "Ahh, I would say to the guys, it's the French side of the family, plus there's no point being hung like a donkey if you don't have the colour to go with it," which always brought a laugh; their reply was, there must be some miniature donkeys in France. After that, everyone just got on with their work. I don't know if anyone would have been prejudiced, but I had heard many things said over the years, so it was easier to laugh about it and blame everything on the French side of the family.

There were no dive supervisors as such; one of us would do the first 4 hours of diving in about 30 feet of water, another diver would be on the dive radio/dive panel, and the diver radio went directly to the crane driver so the diver could talk direct to the crane driver while diving. The other diver would tend the diver's umbilical. After 4 hours, we would all swap our duties: the diver coming out of the water would then get something to eat while tending to the next diver, the diver on the radio would become the next diver, and the dive tender would sit by the diver's radio and dive panel. It all sounds like a very odd way of working, but it worked; mainly, the diver would talk directly to the crane driver, and the diver on the radio would listen to the conversation, as all the diver was doing was placing large 2/5-ton rocks along the breakwater. We also had to put large Tetrapods along the breakwater, but unlike the rocks, which filled significant gaps, they had to be positioned in a specific way.

One of the other operations we had to carry out on the work barge Dammam 2 was lifting out all the hefty lifting frames used to lift and lower the harbour wall blocks that built the harbour walls. The operation of placing harbour wall blocks had come to an end. All the required remedial work on the harbour walls had to be completed. The main work was the completion of the two-mile breakwater.

Dammam 2 lifting the lifting placement frame for the harbour wall blocks.

Into the Blue and Beneath The Waves

The placement frame is now out of the water.

After the frame was lifted clear, we began inspecting the basement sections of the harbour wall on the seabed to identify any gaps between the seabed and the base of the harbour walls. If gaps were found, we marked the areas and measured them to determine the amount of concrete needed to fill them in. The Dammam 2 was moved back to the breakwater operation while a decision was made about when the concrete operation would start. Due to the required amount of concrete, VHC wanted to conduct the concrete repairs in one stage.

Some nights, I would spend my entire night shift placing the large rocks in any gaps I could locate inside the breakwater; if I could find a gap in the breakwater, I would move a marker buoy to that spot, and the crane driver would then see the marker buoy, he would swing the crane around to that location and drop the rock, I never had to do much talking to the crane driver, nor did the diver manning the dive radio, it was a case of mark the spot, drop the rock, mark the spot, drop the rock.

The grab dropped the 2/5-ton rock.

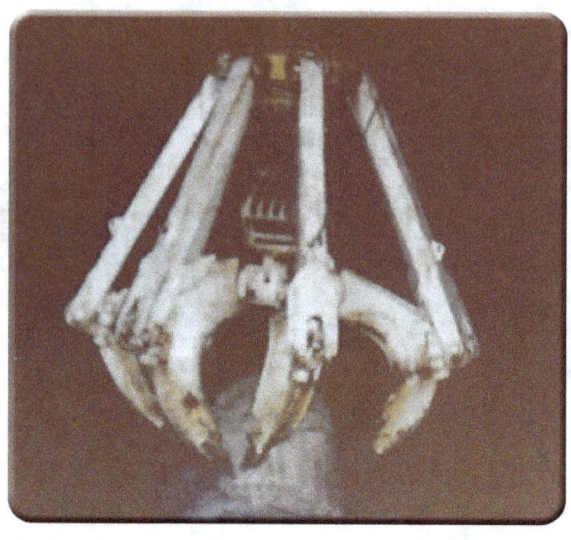

On most Fridays, if I did not go for a drink, I would go into the town of Jubail to shop in the local shops. Apart from a few gold shops, local restaurants, and the local supermarket, there wasn't much, but walking around somewhere different was lovely. The campsite's amenities were excellent, but working 12-hour shifts meant you didn't get a chance to use them much. However, the families enjoyed a lot of socialising each evening as they mainly worked during the day. On Fridays, the families often had BBQs and a few drinks, as everyone was brewing their beer and a powerful spirit. I often wondered what would happen if any local police found out about the homemade beverages being made. However, the local police were excellent; the campsite always received advance notice when any checks were conducted. I was nearing the end of my three-month trip when I was asked if I would mind returning and working over the Christmas period. No, I said that was fine, as I did not like being out of work. Getting work over the winter period was significant, as Solus had not yet been back in touch to see if I was available.

I flew home around the beginning of November. I was looking forward to a good break. I had earned a good amount of money and was on a 30-day paid leave, which included a bonus. Rose was still in Runcorn but had spent most of the time in Liverpool with

Chris, which was fine. When I got home, Rose had some good news: we had been approved for a council flat in the West Derby area of Liverpool, which was very close to her family. Additionally, we could move in immediately, so everything seemed to be falling into place. We managed to move into the flat during the month I was home, which was good as it meant Rose and Chris were in their new home before Christmas. While I was home, I received a phone call from Solus to inquire about my availability for an inspection operation in Great Yarmouth, scheduled to begin around the beginning of April. That was great news, as the Saudi job was set to finish in March 1980. By now, we had saved enough money for a deposit on a house, plus the TSB had told us that if we could put 30% of the house's value as a down payment, they would approve us for a mortgage.

As the return to Saudi Arabia drew closer, it was not a pleasant feeling; it was the worst feeling ever, especially as Christmas approached. I had never been away from home over Christmas before, and knowing I would not be there was horrendous. It was the last day of my leave, and leaving home was a challenge, as all the Christmas festivities had begun. Chris was getting very excited as kids do, but he never knew I was going away. Once I got into the taxi to take me to the airport, the feeling was overwhelming. It was the same for Rose, but as we lived very close to her family, her mother came around after I had left. I landed in Saudi Arabia around the first week of December 1979, but my heart was back home.

When I landed in Saudi Arabia, I noticed a lot of attention everywhere; I didn't know why. Extra security was everywhere. My luggage was double-checked, and my passport was checked three times before I was allowed to go through customs. Once I was outside and picked up by the driver, he told me we would go straight to the campsite, not stopping anywhere on the way to Jubail. There were roadblocks at the campsite; police and the army were stationed at every checkpoint, and my passport was checked at each one. When I returned to the campsite, most of the night and day shifts had ended, which was a welcome relief. If needed, I was assigned to an 8-hour day shift with occasional call-outs for late shifts. The campsite was getting prepared for Christmas, as so many families were staying there. It was nice to see the camp preparing for Christmas, but it was sad at the same time, as I knew I wouldn't be having a family Christmas. Security was tight at the campsite, with the police and armed forces everywhere.

My first shift was on December 2nd. I was working with a guy named Wesley Clash, who was nice but also very odd, still, a lovely character. We had to jackhammer some nasty soft concrete that had to be removed from the roll-on, roll-off jetty. It was only 15 metres deep. Wesley was the first diver that morning, and off he went with a little C9 jackhammer. As he was working away, all you could hear over the dive radio was him humming through his dive. I thought nothing of this; the other diver I was with, Brian Keen, said, "Don't worry, Wesley is always like this." After an hour, Wesley came out of the water, and I was next in. I asked him how the jackhammering went. "It was lovely," he said, "I built a beautiful house and managed to make a family." I just looked confused and wondered what he was talking about. I jumped into the water and made my way down to the job. I couldn't stop laughing when I arrived at the area where Wesley had been jackhammering; as the concrete was so soft, Wesley had dug a big hole about 3 feet deep and 3 feet long, and built a house with a family inside the harbour wall. Brain asked me over the divers' communications, "Has Wesley built another house in the soft concrete? Don't worry," he said; "keep jackhammering away. Wesley will create another one the next time he is in the water."

We were now hearing news that Mecca, the holy site for all Muslims, had been attacked and had been taken over by a religious group in the third week of November '79. I did not know much about the different religious groups back then, but the attack on Mecca was not a very good thing to happen; Saudi Arabia went on a big lockdown, the atmosphere was tense, and no one knew what was happening. Towards the end of the first week of December, my colleagues and I noticed helicopter gunships flying overhead around Jubail. No one knew why, but suddenly, there seemed to be a lot of police and armed forces everywhere; we were instructed not to go anywhere without proper authorisation. The campsite was told that a security inspection might be conducted, but no reason was given. We were not getting any news about anything. Any homemade drinks that had been made would have to be poured away. We were informed that the attack on the holy site of Mecca had ended on the 4th Dec, but tight security would remain in place for the time being; we were also advised not to travel into the town of Jubail until further notice. We were also told not to travel to Dammam for any shopping, as some of the rebels that were caught would be facing a public beheading; if we were there at that time, we would have to watch it.

The below information was referanced from Wikipedia.

In the early morning of late November 1979, the Imam was preparing to lead prayers for the worshippers who had gathered for their morning prayers. The Iman was interrupted by insurgents who produced weapons, chained the gates shut and killed two policemen who were armed with only wooden clubs for disciplining unruly pilgrims. The number of insurgents had been estimated to be around a few hundred. At the time, the Grand Mosque was being renovated by the Saudi Bin Laden Group. The insurgents released most of the hostages and locked the remainder in the mosque. They took defensive positions in the upper levels of the mosque and sniper positions in the minarets, from which they commanded the grounds. No one outside the mosque knew how many hostages remained, how many militants were in the mosque and what sort of preparations they had made.

A team of French commandos from the Groupe d'Intervention de la Gendarmerie Nationale arrived in Mecca. The commandos pumped gas into the underground chambers, but perhaps because the rooms were so bafflingly interconnected, the gas failed, and the resistance continued. With casualties climbing, Saudi forces drilled holes into the courtyard. They dropped grenades into the rooms below, indiscriminately killing many hostages. The remaining rebels moved into more open areas where sharpshooters could pick them off. Nearly two weeks after the assault began, the rebels finally surrendered.

I was beginning to think I was jinxed, as, apart from Abu Dhabi, there seemed to be an uprising in the countries I worked in each time. As the issues started to settle in the holy city of Mecca, our work at Jubail Harbour continued. We were still jackhammering, and Wesley was still building homes inside the soft concrete.

If it had not been for Wesley, I wouldn't have ever changed my way of speaking to people. I used to talk as fast as anybody from Liverpool. It was my way of hiding that I couldn't pronounce words correctly due to my dyslexia, until one day Wesley asked me if I could slow down while talking, as he couldn't understand a word I was saying. So, I started trying to speak more slowly, and I ended up speaking in a kind of pidgin English to avoid saying certain words. Still, the funny thing was that the Indians and the Arabs mainly spoke pidgin English, and I found that I could communicate with them very well. Whenever I talked to the other divers, I would speak slowly in pidgin English and say, "Oops, sorry guys, I'm just used to speaking to Indians and Arabs this way." But in many ways, speaking like this helped me slow down and gave me confidence in pronouncing English words I usually wouldn't try to say. I began to feel more comfortable talking to others. So, in many ways, Wesley helped me face my dyslexia, even if I didn't know it at the time. The campsite was building up for Christmas, and the families organised a panto for the kids. Many adults had volunteered to be in the panto, including our Wesley Clash.

On the Friday before Christmas, I was walking down the corridor of our accommodation block when I heard singing coming from Wesley's room. When I looked in, Wesley was standing by the mirror, looking at himself with a microphone in one hand and bits of cardboard on the top of his head. At the same time, he was singing into the microphone the Spike Milligan song, Ying Tong, Ying Tone, Ying Tone, idle I Po. "Wesley," I asked, "what are you doing?" He said, "As you know, I am in the Christmas panto, so I am practising singing my 'Ying Tong' song while at the same time, I am designing my diving helmet, which will only fit my head. The bits of cardboard around my head are because I am trying to make a profile of the size and shape of my head so my diving helmet will only fit me and no one else." Wesley returned to singing Ying Tong, Ying Tong, idle I Po while still looking in the mirror at the bits of cardboard on his head. I walked away laughing, and the sound of Ying Tong, Ying Tong, went around in my head.

Christmas itself was horrible for me. We were all given a few days off to celebrate, but what was there to celebrate? I was not with my family, and seeing all the other families together did not help. I was happy for them, but I wouldn't say I liked the whole period. The only thing that made me laugh was Wesley singing 'Ying Tong, Ying Tong, Ying Tong, idle I Po' at the panto for the kids. Once the Christmas and New Year period was over, as everyone returned to work, I was happy, and I didn't have to think about what I had missed at home anymore. Our diving operation continued with the jackhammering on the roll-on, roll-off jetty, but the sad thing was that Wesley had gone home on leave, and no one else was building homes inside the soft concrete.

We began fitting the shuttering around the jetty to commence pouring the new concrete, replacing all the soft concrete. The operation took about seven days and nights of continuous pouring, as it was impossible to stop once started, and work had to be completed in one continuous effort. It was January 6, 1980, and we had finished all the diving work on the jetty. We then moved on to diving to the bottom of the main harbour wall, as one of the diving engineers for VHC had discovered a big problem with soft concrete at the base of the harbour wall on one of the main berths.

The main problem was the presence of many undercuts underneath some of the harbour wall's main base supports, which necessitated the initiation of an airlifting operation to remove the seabed and the soft concrete that had collapsed under the harbour wall. I was working at the bottom of the harbour, around 60 feet deep, from a work barge called the Dammam 2, where I was airlifting and water jetting the seabed to remove all the soft concrete from the damaged areas. Once I had cleared all soft concrete and seabed, I had to prepare the damaged area with hessian bags. These bags were filled with dry concrete, which would harden with time and form a concrete wall. This would prevent the concrete from spreading all over the seabed once we began filling the damaged area with fresh concrete. On 1 February 1980, we began pouring concrete into the base of the harbour wall using the longest pipe I had ever used, called a Tremie Pipe, to transport the concrete to the seabed. It must have been around 80 feet long.

80-foot Tremie Pipe, which was used to get the concrete to the seabed

I would lower the Tremie Pipe to the seabed, ensuring the pipe's end was flat against the seabed. Once the pipe was in position, the engineers on the surface would fill it with concrete. As I slowly lifted the Tremie Pipe, the concrete would come out of the pipe and rise above the end, so none of it would get washed away. The weight of the concrete inside the 80-foot pipe would rush out of the end of the Tremie Pipe, and the concrete would flow over the damaged areas. It was another night-and-day operation. Once we started pouring the concrete, we could not stop. After four days of continually pouring concrete, we had completed the operation to secure the base of the harbour wall. We were slowly approaching the end of the operation, and my last few dives would involve installing the remaining Tetrapods around the breakwater.

A barge full of the last Tetrapods will be installed around the Breakwater.

I spent the next two weeks carrying out remedial work on the breakwater and the final installation of the Tetrapods.

The end of the breakwater operation with all the Tetrapods Installed.

I flew home on March 10, 1980, having spent nearly six months working in Saudi Arabia. During that time, we had saved enough money to put down a deposit on a house. Also, for the first time, I was not going home wondering where the next diving job was coming from. Solus Ocean Systems, formerly Solus Schall, had been in touch to see if I could start work offshore from Great Yarmouth on an inspection operation in five weeks.

Chapter Thirteen
Lemen Bank, Great Yarmouth.

On April 24, 1980, I arrived at a platform called the Kilo 49/24 to carry out an anode inspection at 105 feet in the Indefatigable Field before being transferred to a vessel called the Suffolk Shore. Little did I know then that this vessel would be the last one I would work on in the North Sea for the next ten years.

The diving operation itself could not have been more interesting. I inspected and cleaned the anodes on the 49/26 platform, from 105 feet to 25 feet, and used a Krautkramer D-Meter for thickness measurements. However, this inspection instrument was so large that it always required two divers to move around the platform legs and support members to take any thickness readings. Graham Potts was also involved in this operation, and it was the last time we would meet for over twenty years.

We both caught up on what we had been doing over the six-month winter period; as written, I had been working in Saudi Arabia, and Graham had completed his saturation diving course in Scotland. After this operation, we would both be moving in different directions.

I heard from home that CCCUE offered me more offshore diving work in Abu Dhabi. However, CCCUE had many years of diving work available for me if I was interested, and this diving operation for Solus Ocean Systems only lasted for five weeks. I was still determining when more work would become available, but after completing this diving operation for Solus Ocean Systems, I would accept the offer from CCCUE and head back to the Middle East.

All I wanted was to know I always had work coming in. I had a young family, and finally, I bought a house with a mortgage, so a steady income was my most important issue. I completed my last dive on May 18, 1980, on the diving operation in the Indefatigable Field. I headed home to Liverpool from Great Yarmouth on May 21, 1980, to prepare for my long career in diving in the Middle East. I never realised then that I wouldn't see Graham again for a very long time, but those few diving operations we had together were the best I had ever been on throughout my diving career.

Chapter Fourteen
CCCUE and the Middle East.

On September 2, 1980, I flew to Abu Dhabi to start my long diving career with CCCUE, working in the Middle East and India. I would spend the next 90 days working offshore on the NPCC 250 barge, maintaining a 12-hour day shift for the entire duration, which I had never done before. I worked away from home for over 90 days in Saudi Arabia, but had never spent 90 consecutive days at sea. My first offshore operation with CCCUE was on the NPCC 250 barge, where I worked for ZADCO, an oil and gas company. The operation involved the long-term installation of offshore drill head platforms.

Before the NPCC 250 could be positioned, divers conducted a comprehensive seabed survey to ensure that no debris on the seabed could cause damage to the rig legs as they were lowered to the seabed. The heavy-lifting barge was used to lift the drill head platforms onto the seabed. Once the jack-up barge was in position, a supply barge was secured alongside the 250, and the lifting operation commenced.

NPPC 250 Lifting Barge.

The NPCC 250 was a jack-up barge that could move up or down on its legs. To lift the drill head platform, the barge lowered the jack-up to a couple of metres above the sea, making the lift easier.

Once the lift had started, we had to be ready to dive. The crane would swing to the right until the platform was in the correct position to start lowering it to the seabed. Once the platform was on the seabed, divers would dive in scuba gear to verify that the platform legs were not resting on any debris, as the platform's weight on the seabed could sometimes dislodge objects from the seabed.

The Platform is being swung around to the right.

Once the divers had checked the platform legs and had given the all-clear, the operation to level the platform on the seabed would commence. The divers would then fit big, heavy-lifting jacks under the support members at each leg. Once all the jacks had been fitted under the platform legs, the surveyor would start checking the platform level at all four corners. Our diving operation would then involve pumping up or lowering the hydraulic jacks on each corner as an extra backup in case any lifting jacks failed. We would fit sandbags under each member. I was only in 36 feet of water, so I had plenty of time to swim around the four corners of the platform to pack sandbags under the support members and use the hydraulic jacks to raise the platform to the required level specified by the surveyors. Once the platform was level, the lifting barge would lift and increase the height of the jack-up, allowing the drilling engineering team to start their drilling operation on each leg.

The Platform is now level and in position, and the jack-up has been lifted to the correct height for drilling to commence.

The drilling operation would start inside each of the platform legs. Once the drillers had reached the desired drilling depth, which ranged from 20 metres to over 30 metres, depending on the ground conditions, drilling would cease, and the platform level would be rechecked to assess any movement that had occurred during the drilling. Once the surveyors were satisfied with the level, large caisson tubes would be welded together and lowered into each leg.

After the caisson tubes reached the required depth, a grouting operation started to concrete the caisson tubes from the drilled depth to the seabed. Our diving operation then involved positioning the platform on the seabed and waiting for the concrete to arrive at the platform's base. Once the concrete arrived, I would inform the diving supervisor that the concrete had reached the seabed and was below the bottom platform members.

That's me waiting at the bottom of the platform, waiting for the concrete to reach the top of the seabed, which is also my cover photo.

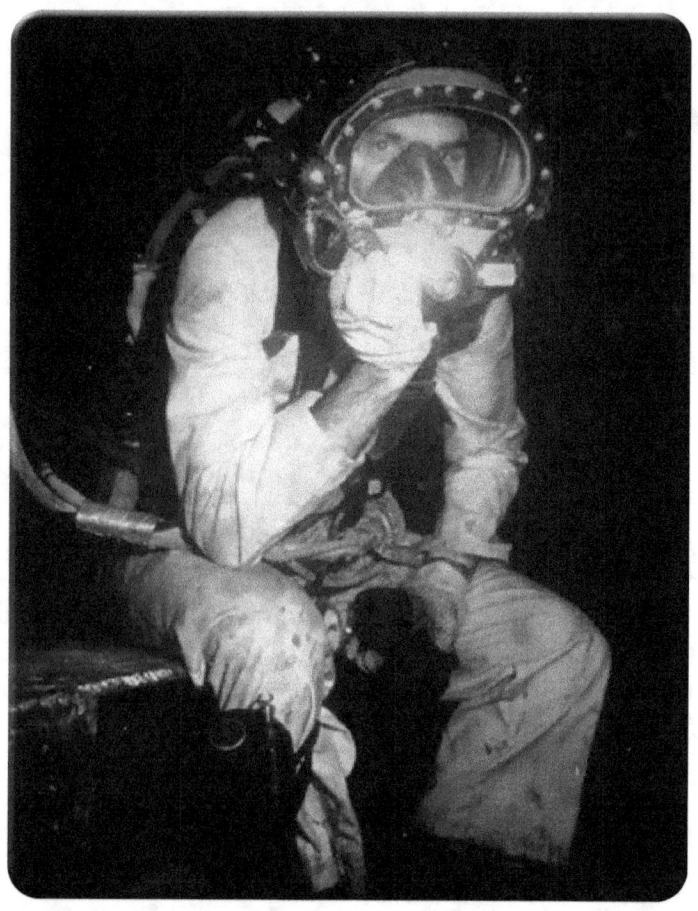

Once the concrete pumping had stopped, our diving operation monitored the concrete until it had hardened all around the base of the platform leg. Then we began removing the mud mats, which were fitted to the bottom support members on the platform and used to support the platform as it was lowered onto the seabed at the beginning of the operation. This operation involved using an air-impact wrench to remove all the bolts holding the mud mats together. Eight mud mats, two on each corner, were heavy and had to be removed from the platform. They had to be lifted back to the deck of the SEP 250 with a crane. The operation went well, and I enjoyed my first experience installing oil rig platforms on the seabed. However, I had only spent four weeks offshore by now, and I still had another two months to go before I headed home.

Pictures of me releasing the bolts from the mud mats & making my way to the next mud mat.

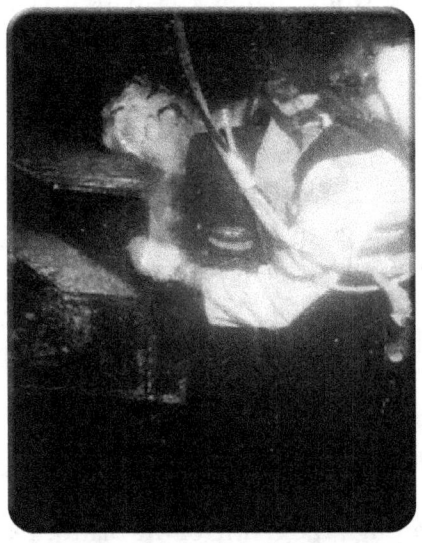
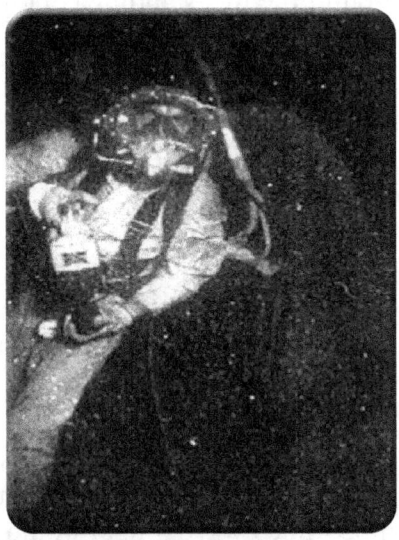

I had just finished removing all the bolts from all the mud mats and was happy to be heading back to the surface after I had finished my dive.

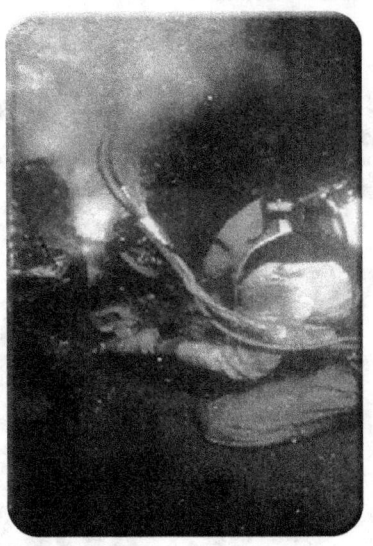

The next four weeks were just the same routine. We would be taken to a new location, a few miles from the barge, on a small tugboat called the Gulf Master to conduct seabed surveys and inspect free-standing conductors. If we encountered any debris on the seabed or around the free-standing conductor, we would remove or mark it if it was too heavy to move by hand. All the diving was carried out in scuba in around 50 feet of water, and the nearest decompression chamber was miles away, but in those days, you never gave it a thought or questioned anything. You just got on with it.

Once we had inspected and cleaned up the areas for the next platform, we would head back to the barge. Many times, we would have to start diving immediately, but we only got a little rest. If you were on a 12-hour shift, then you would work a total of 12 hours. I didn't mind what else you would do, and the more you worked, the quicker the time went. I had completed 45 days offshore and still had another 45 days to go before going home on leave. By now, we had installed about four platforms, but sometimes, we had to fit cover plates inside the platforms, which meant diving through the guide holes. To pass the time while I was diving, I would fly through the centre of the platforms just for a bit of fun.

I flew through the middle of the platform.

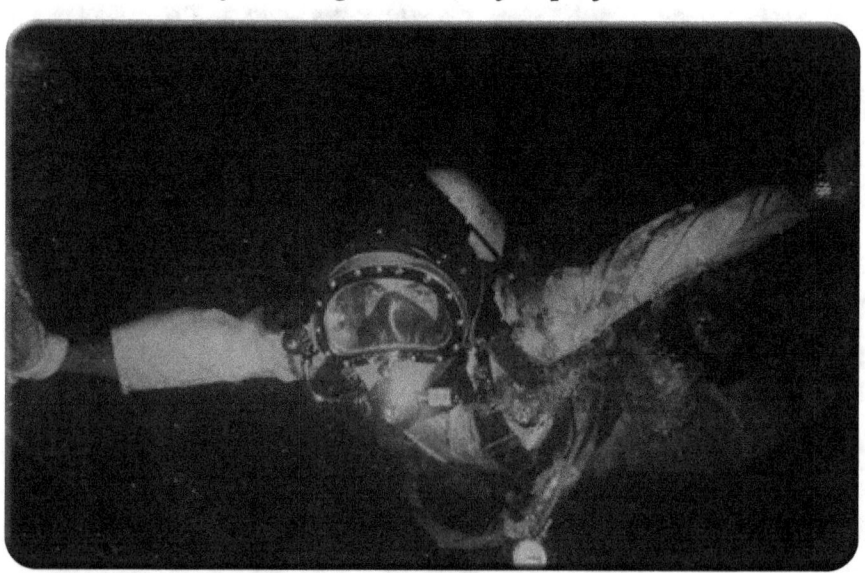

I was now approaching the end of my 90-day trip offshore, the longest period I had spent at sea, and I was looking forward to going home on leave. However, I still had to wait a few more days, as I couldn't leave the barge until my relief arrived. Even when he did come, I had to spend another few days on the supply boat, which also served as the crew boat, as it had to visit all the other rigs and barges to drop off stores and pick up personnel who, like me, were all heading home for some leave.

I landed in Abu Dhabi's free port on September 1, 1980. After spending just over 95 days offshore, I was thrilled to see land, buildings, and other people who were not oil rig workers. I also did some shopping and had a beer, and boy, did that first beer taste good! I was pleased, and I had some good money. I was going home for a few weeks but knew I had a new job to return to in Saudi Arabia, in Jeddah. On September 2nd, 1980, I flew home for a few weeks' rest and couldn't wait.

When I arrived home, Rose had done a great job of making the house feel homely, and Chris looked very well and was a thrilled young kid. I had a great few weeks at home and spent money making the house feel good. Around September 24th, I flew to Jeddah, Saudi Arabia, to start work on an underwater civil engineering operation called Jeddah Four. It was a massive new power station; our operation involved installing five massive 250-ton concrete intake blocks.

However, before these concrete blocks could be fitted, we had to jackhammer and airlift the seabed over an area of 300 to 400 square feet. This was a significant operation, and six three-man dive teams worked 12-hour shifts. We would work two weeks on days, then rest on Friday and change over on Saturday night. My first shift was on the day shift. My first dive was on September 27th. I was diving in 30 feet of water in a 300- to 400-square-foot basin.

The basin is protected from the Red Sea by a wall of sheet piles across the front. The idea was that once we had fitted the massive concrete blocks, all the sheet piles would be removed to allow the Red Sea to flow into the seawater intakes, and the seawater would be used for the power station, which was located around a quarter of a mile away. My first morning work lasted around 180 minutes in 30 feet of water, a long-time of continually jackhammering; by the end of the dive, my hands felt numb from all the vibration. After my dive, the next diver would continue from where I had left off. I would then become the next diver's tender while at the same time getting something to eat and drink on the job. The diving supervisor would then stay on the divers' communications radio for another 180 minutes before we had a lunch break after nearly 6 hours of diving. Our lunch was always curry, the only food available, but that was fine as I just wanted anything to eat after a long dive. After an hour's break, the supervisor would dive for the next 180 minutes and survey our work to see where we would continue working on the following dives.

I continued the same diving operation for the next six days, diving in 30 feet of water and always for 180 minutes, just jackhammering; by the end of those six days, my hands were numb. I then spent a couple of days diving and working on a small drilling rig. We had to prepare for a drilling operation in front of the sheet piles, as we were about to start an explosives operation. For three days, I was diving in 50 feet of water in the Red Sea, moving the drilling machine into various locations. The drill machine would drill down to 30 feet, and then we would have to move 2 metres to the side of each drilled hole. After over 20 holes were drilled into the coral face at the front of the sheet piles, I would start placing the explosives into the designated locations. Once the explosives had been placed, I would guide all the electrical cables from the drill holes back to the surface. I could only take one cable at a time to ensure I did not cause a spark between the cable's ends. This operation took four days to complete. It had been agreed upon with the local authorities to carry out the planned detonation of the explosions on Wednesday, October 8, 1980.

I was disappointed that no cameras were allowed on the site due to security restrictions, as it would have made for a great picture, given that we had placed nearly 250 kilogrammes of explosives into the coral reef. The operation site had been cleared of all non-essential personnel, but no one informed the senior Saudi personnel that they were not permitted to be there. On the morning of October 8, 1980, all the explosives had been double-checked in the water and on the surface to ensure they were ready for detonation. We had to wait for the local authorities to permit the explosives engineers to ingrate the explosives.

Still, they would not give it until the senior members of the local chiefs were present, as they wanted to see the big explosion.

All safety distances had been marked out to prevent personnel from being exposed to any debris that may fall after the explosion. As the large limousines drove down, the safety barriers were lifted, and the local chiefs' vehicles drove underneath them, as they wanted to be close to witness the explosions. No one dared tell them it was unsafe to be that close, and the order was given to press the buttons to set off the explosion. The button was pressed, and the explosives went off; well, the surge of water upwards was 20/30 feet tall, the coral was blasted over 100 feet away, and the rocks from the coral seabed face rained down on everybody. Everyone was running for cover, and coral rocks were falling on top of everybody. People were diving for cover wherever they could find; what the fxxk were my words? Once the stones had stopped falling, we all lifted our heads to see what had happened. I could not stop laughing as all the local chiefs' limousines were beaten to a pulp due to the amount of rock that had fallen on them. All of them were hiding underneath their cars. Everywhere was a mess. What the fxxk happened was the big question!

After an investigation, the explosives engineers were given the wrong information. They were informed that the divers would set the drilling machine in 50 feet of water and drill down to 30 feet. In some ways, this was correct; we were diving into 50 feet of water. However, the engineers did not consider that the first drill holes were located 15 feet underwater, and we made our way down the coral face to 50 feet underwater. The engineers had determined that a cushion of 50 feet of water above the explosives would reduce the amount of rocks hitting the surface. In theory, it did, but we had drilled holes filled with explosives, ranging from 15 feet to 50 feet below the surface of the seawater. The shallow explosions at 15 feet threw rocks all over the area.

Luckily, no one was hurt. Only pride hurt, but it made me laugh. We continued drilling more holes and filling them with more explosives for the next few days. The idea behind the explosions was to loosen all the coral reefs in front of the sheet piles, which ran directly across the seawater intakes. The coral reef in front of the sheet piles was protecting them, and the coral reef, which the explosions had loosened, was to remain in place to protect the sheet piles. The sheet piles were over 80 feet in depth. They were 20 feet deep into the seabed and another 60 feet high above the seabed.

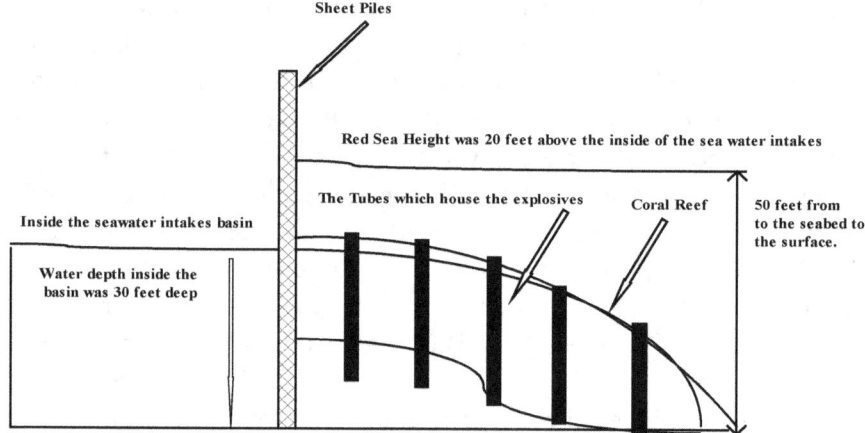

On October 8th, the last of the controlled explosives were completed with no further incidents. The operational plan was then to leave the coral reef for a couple of days to allow the loose rock to settle; while that was happening, I continued jackhammering inside the seawater intake basin. The jackhammering continued for two weeks; we also had to carry out extensive airlifting to remove all the loose rock and soft sand from the areas affected by the jackhammering. We had to get the seabed to a certain level before fitting the concrete support frames. Once levelled, these would be filled in with concrete to form a concrete base, where we would then install 50-ton concrete blocks, creating the support structure for the 16-foot-diameter glass fibre pipes.

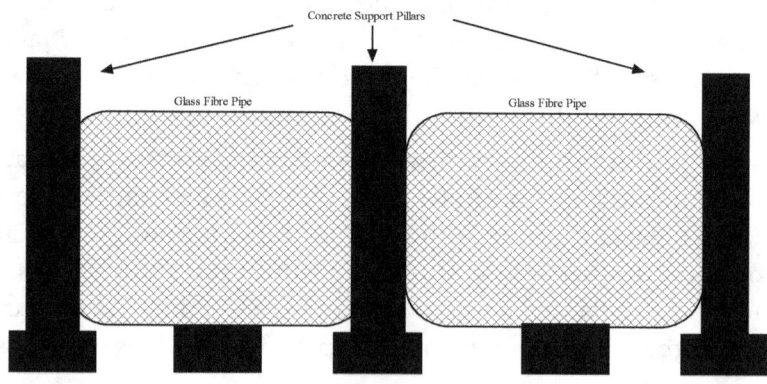

Into the Blue and Beneath The Waves

On November 2nd, we completed all the jackhammering and airlifting and started placing the concrete support beams on the base of the seawater basin. Once all the base supports were in place, they were concreted to prevent movement. After they solidified, we began installing the 16-foot-diameter glass-fibre pipes. The support beams were installed nonstop for the next four weeks, and the glass-fibre pipes were concreted and fitted. Then we had to fit chloride pipes inside them, which ran along the inside of the glass fibre seawater intake pipes.

Everything was going well. The progress was up to date, and from what I could gather, all the project managers were pleased with the underwater operation's progress. But what happened next was a complete disaster. We arrived at work one morning to find our diving superintendent, Dave Speller, shouting at the project engineers. The other divers and I were wondering why he was yelling at them to stop what they were doing. All I could see was a large crane at the end of the seawater intake basin grabbing all the loose rock in front of the sheet piles.

"What are you doing?" Dave was shouting. "Stop what you are doing," he was screaming. "Stop removing all the loose rocks. It's the only protection the sheet piles have in front of them; if you remove the loose rock, they will be exposed to the Red Sea, and 60 feet of sheet piles will be exposed with only 20-foot piles into the seabed. If a storm comes, it will rip the sheet piles to bits." The project engineers would not listen to Dave and told him not to worry. We don't get bad storms in the Red Sea. Well, that night, a storm hit Jeddah, and the Red Sea roared up and ripped right through the unprotected sheet piles. A 20/25-foot-high wall of seawater ripped through the sheet piles like a big piece of paper just waving in the wind. The seawater intake basin was approximately 20 to 25 feet lower than the Red Sea, measuring over 100 feet in width. A massive seawater rush poured in, pushing everything into the seawater basin and loosening rocks, scaffolding, platforms, machinery, and everything and anything in this tidal wave. The rush of water carried up to the power station, which was a quarter of a mile away. No one could do anything until the seawater rush stopped pouring into the seawater basin, and no one could do anything to stop the Red Sea from pouring in. It took about four days for the seawater to settle down. The water was just a very dark, muddy brown colour, so there was no point diving, as you could not see anything until the seawater cleared up. On December 13th, we began our underwater survey to assess the damage. The five 16-foot-diameter pipes were filled with loose rocks from the coral reef, along with tons of sand; the height of the stones and sand reached the top of the seawater intake pipes. It was a complete mess.

Before we could inspect the damage to the glass fibre pipes, we had to initiate a large airlifting operation using the largest airlift I had ever encountered. It was 3.5 feet in diameter and powered by two 800-HP diesel engines; it was over 60 feet tall and had an end tail about 15 feet long, which would throw all the debris away from the working area. All the rock and sand covering the front of the five 16-foot-diameter pipes had to be removed before we could enter the pipes to see how much rock and sand had been pushed up inside the glass-fibre pipes.

The front of the Glass Fibre Pipes was completely blocked with rocks.

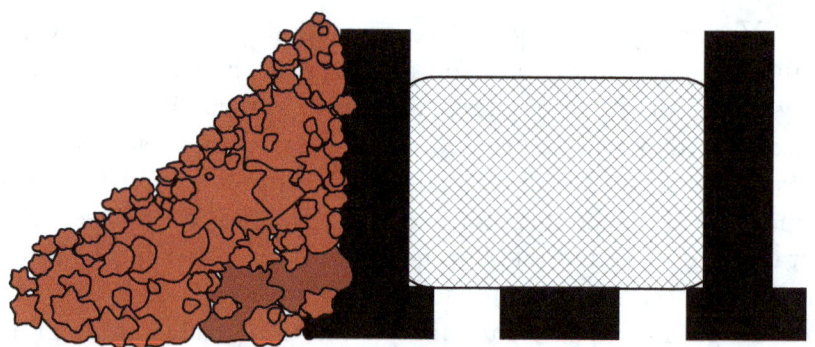

It was now a big clearing-up operation that was nonstop night and day. We slept and ate on site. We never left the site at all, but we were getting double rates on our day shift and triple rates on our night shift. The giant airlift we were using was very powerful. It could lift the big rocks from the sea bed and blow them over 10/15 feet away from our working area. The airlift was blowing all the rocks back towards the Red Sea so they would not fall back into the areas we were clearing. It was a big operation clearing out all the rocks and sand, but you had to be very careful that you kept your diving umbilical out of the suction at the mouth of the airlift. It was very powerful, and you had to avoid the suction. Additionally, the only way we could manoeuvre the airlift on the seabed was by attaching winches to it from the surface, as it was too heavy to move manually.

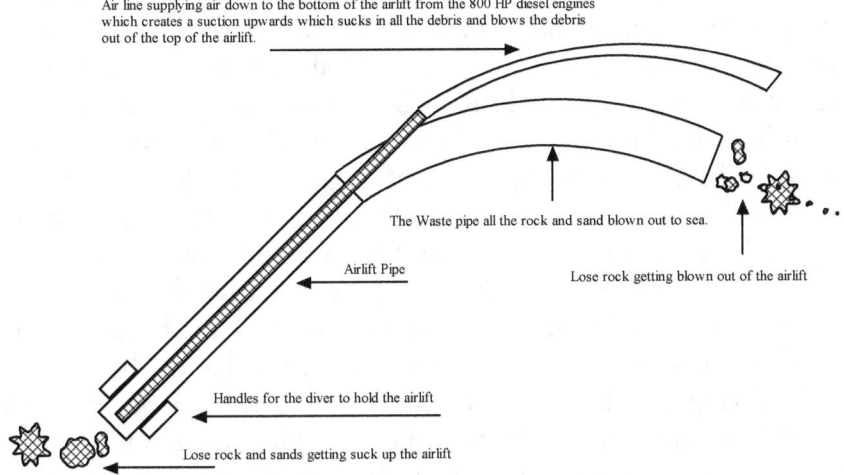

As we were that busy, our diving superintendent, Dave Speller, also gave everyone a break by doing some diving, which allowed us to rest between dives. It was decided that we would use the local Indian labourers as our tenders. Dave, the superintendent, watched over them as they learnt how to be diver tenders. They were taught how to dress the divers and be divers' linesmen by playing out the diver's umbilical and bringing it in when it felt slack. It was going very well; the diving supervisor would sit by the diver's radio, and the Indian tender would play out and take in the diver's umbilical slack. However, a nasty incident occurred during one particular dive, although it did seem hilarious afterwards. Our diving superintendent Dave Speller had somehow got sucked underneath the big airlift. Due to the roar over the diver's radio from the airlift, the diving supervisor could not hear anything except the Indian tender saying, "Mister Dave wants a lot of the diving umbilical." Sitting by the divers' radio, Bob Rumble just said, "OK, give him more umbilical." Then, the Indian tender said in his pidgin English, "But he has taken it all with him, and left me with the end of the umbilical." Now, Mr Dave is out in the Red Sea waving, "What the fxxk says, Bob, are you saying?"

The Indian tender is holding the end of a ripped diving umbilical in front of Bob and says, "Mr Dave has broken the umbilical and is now waving at us from the Red Sea." Bob looks at the ripped diving umbilical, totally confused, and then he turns around and sees Dave waving at him, drifting out into the Red Sea. "What the fxxk!" says a very confused Bob Rumble. Quickly, a Zodiac is sent out to pick up a very exhausted and badly bruised Dave. Once he was picked up, he was rushed to the hospital as he looked in a terrible state; he was lucky that he had not been diving for very long in 50 feet of water before he got sucked up the airlift. After Dave had been released from the hospital, he met up with everyone at the campsite and told us what had happened. He had been working away with the airlift when a couple of rocks got stuck inside the airlift. As he tried to free the big stones, his diving umbilical got sucked up inside the airlift. He reached over to pull his diving umbilical out of the airlift before he knew he was inside the airlift getting beaten with rocks and sand. He could not move as his diving umbilical was being held by the Indian tender, who was holding onto the umbilical on the surface. While he was inside the airlift, he could feel his diving hat being sucked off, but he couldn't do anything as he couldn't lift his arms due to the airlift's confines.

All he knew was that his head was getting smashed with rocks when, all of a sudden, he shot upwards and was thrown out to sea. Luckily for him, his diving umbilical had been ripped apart, but now he was drifting out to sea with just his bail-out bottle giving him air. He could see the Indian tender waving at him back at the work site and hoped the Indian tender could get help. He said it felt like a lifetime when he saw a Zodiac coming to rescue him, as he was exhausted by now. At first, we were all in shock, but by now, we had all been drinking homemade beer and could not stop laughing.

Even Dave could not stop laughing now, though his ribs and face were sore. I continued airlifting day and night until December 21, 1980, earning a good amount of money. On December 22, I flew home for Christmas to rest before heading back for my next adventure in the Middle East.

I went home for Christmas, which was a fantastic experience; getting home a couple of days before Christmas is something that cannot be put into words. It's a buzz you'll never know unless you've been away for a long time; it's just magical.

Chris and I were together at Christmas 1980.

But at the same time, for the first time, I noticed something different, not from the family, but from people I grew up with and played football with. People who didn't like me as I was a pain in the backside, (which I was), who just because I was earning and making good money expected me to pay for everything if they saw me in the local pub. Growing up in Gateacre, I would visit the Lee Park Hotel, my local pub, where I played most of my football for the local team. One comment summed it up for me. Peter was his name, and he said to me, "Ah, a lad, you travel the world now; all I need my passport for is proof of who I am to cash in my dole money, whereas you, lad, cross borders."

The other thing I noticed was that my life was changing. The more I travelled, the more my education changed. I was beginning to become different from the person who started my journey in diving work in 1975. The more I travelled, the more I came to let home life move in a different direction. Rose and her mum got used to life together while I was away. Rose's mum and dad moved in while I was away for 90 days each time. I became a visitor for 30 days every three months, and every time I came home, after a couple of days Rose's mum and dad would be on the doorstep, but as they had looked after and made sure Rose and Chris were fine while I was away, I had no problems with that. Still, it would have been nice to have time to ourselves when I got home.

I flew back to Abu Dhabi on February 2, 1981. As soon as I landed, I was sent to an operation on Zirku Island to begin building a seawater intake structure that would supply water to the island. The island had been converted into an oil refinery to offload oil onto oil tankers offshore via an SBM (Single Buoy Mooring). The Island needed water for all the accommodation/working facilities required for an oil installation to supply oil to the tankers. I could not believe it. As soon as I arrived on the island, I was picked up and taken straight to the operation, where I started diving to inspect a pipeline that might have been in the way of our main operation. The dive lasted about 60 minutes in ten feet of water. The dive was because they were expecting bad weather on the island and wanted that pipeline survey completed. After that dive, I had about eight days before I needed to dive again. For a few days, I was able to explore the island, which was a bird sanctuary. However, the island was covered in bird droppings everywhere, and it had to be cleaned up, and it was not a very healthy place to be.

The island, as I understood it, was bombed with chemical bombs to try and kill any diseases that might have been on the island from the bird excrement. Until 1978, Zirku Island was a refuge for cormorants and other birds, but it began to undergo development for oil processing.

The island had been bombed for three weeks before it was safe for humans to stay there. The bombing also scared away many birds, who flew to nearby islands. Amenities were scarce; my room was just a portacabin with nothing but a bed, chair, wardrobe, and a shared bathroom. There was a big messroom for all the workers on the island, a games room, and a TV room—that was it. However, I was not bothered, as I was working a 12-hour shift, then eating, and sleeping.

On February 12, I started my second dive. It was airlifting, not a giant airlift as on my last operation, but airlifting for two hours non-stop in 12 feet of water, and this went on for over three weeks before we had cleared enough of the seabed to start placing big support pods called gabions which were oversized wire mesh frames filled with big stones which would act as support bases for the oversized metal frames that we would place over a 40-foot square area. The idea was that these gabion wire mesh frames would support the frames that would be concreted in, eventually supporting 500-ton concrete caisson blocks. On March 5th, we cleared an area where we could start placing the gabion wire mesh frames into position. Once the surveyors had checked the levels of the wire mesh gabions, we would begin lowering the large support frames into the wire mesh frames of the gabions.

I was the diver who fitted the first frame. It took around two hours to lower the frame into position and level it to the surveyors' specifications using their theodolites, which were fixed to the frame. The frame had lifting jacks fitted underneath the base supports, which were designed to lift the frame up or down to achieve a level position. But every time you operated the jackhammer, it pushed down onto the wire mesh frames. We then had to fit small concrete blocks under the jacks to stop them from pushing down. Eventually, I got the frame to a level the surveyors would accept. On March 12th, once the frame had been allowed to settle, another survey was carried out, and the go-ahead was given to start pouring concrete inside the framework, which involved continuous concrete pouring for over two hours. At long last, the first frame was in position and concreted. We continued the same work for over two months, airlifting and placing the gabion wire mesh frame, followed by the main frame, the central support base, and finally, the concrete. At long last, the first 500-ton concrete caisson blocks were ready to be fitted into place. The large concrete block had to be lowered down a slipway on railway tracks, as it was situated on old railway frames. It slowly slipped down the railway tracks on the slipway into the water. As the concrete block reached a certain water depth, two giant flotation tanks were brought alongside it, and the flotation tanks were secured to the sides of the concrete block with large steel H-beams running through them.

Gabions wire mesh frames filled with rocks. A support frame is on top of the wire mesh.

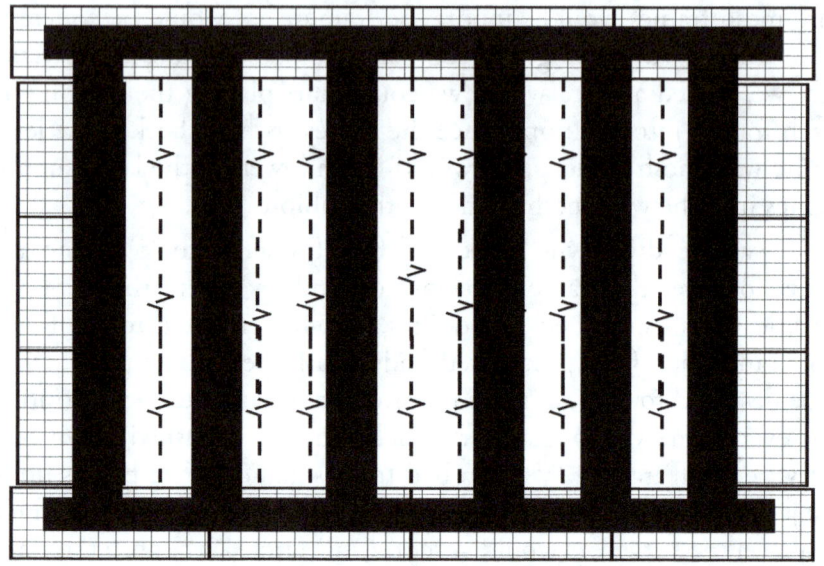

The inside of the frame was filled with concrete.

Plan View

H-Beams

Floatation tanks

Air Vents

H-Beams going through the 500-eon caisson blocks, resting on top of the flotation tanks which had hydraulic valves to allow seawater into the tanks and vents to pump the seawater out to control the lifting and lowering of the floatation tanks onto the base frames.

Side View of the Caisson Blocks as it was lowered onto the support base frame.

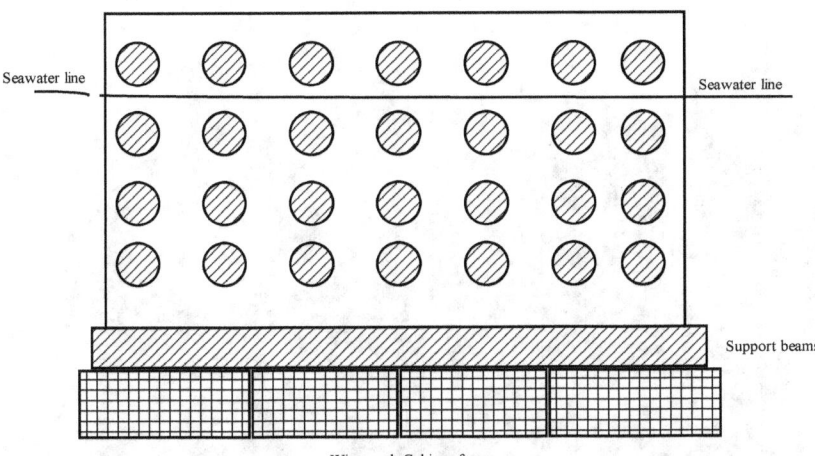

I was on the Island for just over three months, during which I was involved in the daily routine of airlifting, placing various base supports, concreting, and assisting in the placement of the 500-ton concrete blocks. The length of the seawater intake was around a quarter of a mile from the island. My last dive was on May 15th, and I continued with topside work before returning home on May 25th, 1981. By then, I was looking forward to going home.

I returned just three weeks later. I was not ready to return to work, but I would not have considered turning down work in those days. But now, when I look back, I see that I should have spent more time on my home life and family instead of just working and working for very long periods. Once I was back on the island, I continued the same diving work until the first week of July 1981. I was pleased that this operation had ended, as I was ready for a change of routine after nearly 6 months working on Zirku Island.

I arrived in Abu Dhabi in the first week of August 1981, where I joined a vessel called the Grey Fend, which carried out anchor surveys for the NPCC 648 pipeline lay barge. On the 12th of August, I was transferred from the Grey Fend to work on the NPCC 648 lay barge.

That's the NPCC 648 lay barge in the background, and that's me on the left-hand side.

I had never worked on a pipelay barge, so it was a new diving experience. I was on the day shift, which was from midday to midnight. My first dive was to survey a damaged pipeline and photograph the damage. In the middle of the above photo, there is a fantastic character called Davie Bruce in the background. I spent only a few weeks on the NPCC 648, carrying out pipeline surveys to ensure that no damage had occurred as the pipeline was lowered down the stinger on the barge's stern to the seabed and that the pipeline crossed the crossover points correctly.

Cross-over points were areas where one pipeline crossed over another, and concrete frames on the seabed allowed the pipelines to overlap.

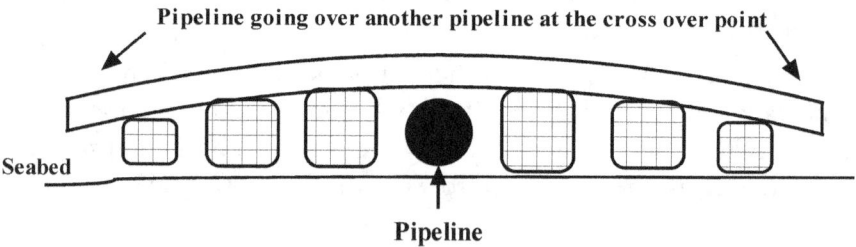

I continued taking numerous photos of the pipelines to demonstrate that there was minimal damage. Meanwhile, I also captured many pictures of the divers on the deck of the NPCC 648 lay barge. I often wondered what use the Lloyd's inspection course I had done back in Falmouth in March 1979 would be to me. But it has kept me employed in many ways, as many diving operations needed someone to take underwater photos. Now I realise just what lovely memories these black-and-white photos evoke as I recall my past. I have found many black-and-white pictures from my time on the NPCC 648 that tell stories that need to be enjoyed simply by looking at them, without requiring a narrative to explain what the divers and I were doing on the seabed. So, enjoy the black-and-white photos below that I took and had to develop, and get other divers to take pictures for me to create. This is a copy of the one above, but I got the Filipino diver to lift his head this time. That's me on the left, Davie Bruce, and Ossie on the right, but I cannot remember the Filipino diver's name.

***That's me after my dive and helping the other divers to get in the Zodiac after
our pipeline inspections.***

That's me on the right, taking the other diver's air bottle into the zodiac.

I only spent ten days on the NPCC 648 before being transferred to the Antares drilling rig. For the first time, I was the diving supervisor for a six-man diving team.

All the other divers worked for a diving company called Binali Diving from Bahrain, but the client, ADMA, insisted on a diving supervisor from CCCUE, and I was selected. Two of the divers, Steven Hardy and Mike Lee, were involved in a tragic incident many years later in Hong Kong. Both were hilarious men and an absolute pleasure to work with. Another diver was Tug Wilson, with whom I have worked frequently since this operation. Our diving operation involved removing large manifolds, commonly referred to as Christmas trees, from the seabed. These manifolds are the operating units that allow oil to flow from the seabed to the surface.

Our working hours were 24 hours a day, seven days a week. We could be called at any time, so we slept and ate when we could. As the diving supervisor, I was still expected to participate in diving. On August 25, 1981, I made the first dive to survey the Christmas tree. It was a ten-minute dive in 64 feet of water, during which I secured a downline, checked for any fishing nets entangled around the Christmas tree, and assessed the amount of marine growth covering it.

On the morning of August 26, 1981, we began removing all marine growth from the Christmas tree before commencing underwater oxy/arc cutting. This was necessary to remove the protective frame surrounding the Christmas tree. Once we had cut the protective frame away from the seabed, we would remove the Christmas tree from the seabed after shutting down all the required valves on the Christmas tree.

On August 27th, at 3:47 a.m., we began our underwater oxy/arc cutting of the protection frame. Everything went very well, and we were now ready to begin shutting down all the operating valves on the Christmas tree. We completed everything around 10:00 a.m. and were exhausted after a long, early morning operation. As you can see from the photo, I looked exhausted, and I was wearing all the best safety gear. No one back then asked divers to wear safety gear; we just walked around the oil rig in flip-flops and shorts.

That's me in my best safety clothes and the picture of the Xmas tree coming out of the water.

After the Christmas tree had been lifted and the wellhead capped off, the oil rig moved to a new location in deeper water, where the Christmas tree was much larger to work on. We didn't have any underwater cutting on this Christmas tree. We used many hydraulic impact wrenches to remove all the tension bolts connecting it to the main manifold block. As we were in deeper water, we had to use in-water decompression stops, diving to a depth of 75 feet.

Our first few days involved releasing the tension bolts around the main manifold block between 02:00 and 07:30. On some days, we started as early as 07:30. We worked nonstop for the next four days, removing all the tension bolts. However, the hydraulic unit broke down, and we did not have a spare on the oil rig. So now we had to resort to hard labour with big hammers and wrenches, which was difficult. Those tension bolts were tight, but we had no choice, as we couldn't get a replacement hydraulic unit out for at least four days.

One of the divers with a big wrench is trying to remove the tension bolts.

After four long days, we removed many bolts around the main manifold block just as the replacement hydraulic unit arrived. We fitted the hydraulic unit for the last ten bolts, and finally, we removed all the tension bolts; the Christmas tree was ready to be lifted to the oil rig's deck. Over the next two weeks, we had to remove another three Christmas trees, and I got to know Mike Lee and Steven Hardy well. They were a couple of excellent divers and two hilarious guys. It was very sad to read about Steven Hardy years later in a disaster off Hong Kong, when the derrick barge they were working on sank during a typhoon, with Steven still inside the saturation system.

On September 20th, we finished removing the Christmas trees, and I enjoyed my first experience as the diving supervisor. I said my goodbyes to the divers from Binali Diving as they flew back to Abu Dhabi on the helicopter. For me, I was picked up by a crew boat and sent back as a diver to a barge called the NPCC WB1. There were better barges to work on than the WB1.

The accommodation was a tiny cabin with four beds and no cupboards to store most of your clothes, so you had to keep most of your belongings in your travel bag. You had to share the toilets and showers with the rig labours, who were mainly from India and Pakistan but were not used to western toilets and would shit anywhere and over everything. So, we had some sorting out over that issue, which we did, but it still was not very nice; as I was told, "That's offshore life. Get on with it."

The operation on the WB1 involved riser setting, where we would connect the oil pipeline laid by the NPCC 648 to the offshore oil rig jacks or platforms. My first couple of dives were to survey the pipelines and ensure there was no damage anywhere. The next few weeks were a bit of a blur, as I had been offshore for up to four months and had had enough. I could not keep going. I just wanted to go home. But I was trying to stay on the operation to make sure that when I did go home, I would be home for Christmas. On October 26th, the WB1 had to go into Abu Dhabi for some repairs, and all the divers had a terrific run ashore. We all shot off to the Ally Pally bar, which was in the Ali Ain Place Hotel, but anyone in Abu Dhabi always called it the Ally Pally Hotel. Getting ashore, having drinks, and shopping for a few days was great. When it was time to go back offshore, I could not face it. I had had enough, so I contacted the CCCUE operations manager and told them I wanted to take a break. They could not say no to anything as I had done over three months. The operations manager said, "Fine, no problem." You have done your time. We will make arrangements for you to go home. On October 28, 1981, I flew home for an excellent two-month break, deciding not to return until after Christmas and the New Year.

I had a tremendous two-month break; it was nice not to think about anything work-related. It allowed me to have some home time and not have Rose's mum around all the time. It gave both of us time for ourselves and time for young Chris, which, until then, we had not had the chance to do, as I had always been away working. We had a great time, and at long last, we could enjoy some of the money we had worked hard for and saved up after all these long trips away. After the New Year, I received a phone call to see if I was ready to return to Abu

Dhabi. They had another diving operation for me to join, working on a French barge called Derrick Barge E.T.P.M. 202, where I conducted pipeline surveys for a few weeks. On January 3, 1982, I flew back to Abu Dhabi for another three-month offshore diving operation. After security clearance, on January 13, I joined the Derrick Barge E.T.P.M. 202. I spent the next four weeks scuba diving to carry out pipeline surveys until the first week of February, when I was transferred back to the NPCC 648 lay barge. I was on the day shift on the NPCC 648. I carried out my first dive on the 9th of February when I had to connect the hook-up line to the end of the pipeline from the 648 so the pipeline could be picked up from the seabed and brought up to the end of the pipeline stinger, as the pipeline had been laid down onto the seabed due to bad weather. I have been on the day shift for a couple of weeks now on the NPCC 648, and I enjoyed the other divers' work and company. My supervisor for the first couple of weeks was Bill Lawson, who suddenly left and was replaced by a quiet and friendly guy named Simon Hamblin. Simon Hamblin became well-known in the diving world over the following years.

The diving work was just a steady routine. The first dive at the start of each shift involved swimming along the stinger to ensure no damage was being done to the pipeline as it descended the stinger. It was also a bit of fun. We had a winch wire going down the side of the stinger, and when we reached the end of the stinger, we had a signal line back to the barge. When we pulled the signal line, a winch operator would engage the winch, pulling us back to the end of the barge, as the stinger was very long. It was great as I would fly back to the barge through the water. We would also record the depths of specific points on the stinger to ensure they were manageable and shallow. We would report the depth reading to the dive supervisor, who would pass on the information to the surveyors. Often, they would ask the divers to go to specific points on the stinger and inflate or fill the air tanks with water to adjust the stinger's depth and height, ensuring it remained at the correct angle as it was laid down on the seabed.

We would often have to go ahead of the lay barge to carry out 50-meter circular searches on the seabed to ensure there would be no debris in the way of the pipeline as it was laid down. It was a varied operation for the divers, which I enjoyed, as there was always something different. I had been on board for a couple of weeks now, and I had gotten used to the daily routine of the day shift. On this particular day, bad weather was approaching quickly. We had to get out onto the zodiac soon and release the pipeline from the lay barge as promptly as possible to ensure the pipeline was released from the barge; the barge superintendent wanted photographic proof that the anchor wire, which was used to lower the pipeline, had been released. So, on my dive, the diver photographer dived with me.

I'm getting my dive gear ready and getting into the Zodiac. That's me standing up in the front.

That's me next to the laydown head on my right-hand side of the pipeline, with me hitting the large shackle with a massive lump hammer to remove the laydown head winch wire.

I enjoyed working on the pipeline barge. It was varied and always busy, with fun moments. The weather in the Arabian Gulf during winter can deteriorate rapidly, and we were constantly connecting and disconnecting the winch wire.

I was becoming very skilled at swimming down to the lay-down head, disconnecting the winch wire, and heading back to the surface. One day, the diving superintendent announced that if anyone could disconnect the winch wire in under 5 minutes, he would reward the winner with a large box of chocolates. It might not sound like much, but the only treat we had offshore was sweets. On February 25th, we experienced adverse weather conditions, and we had to disconnect the winch wire from the lay-down. It was my turn to dive. I left the surface in scuba at 15:26 to dive to 80 feet of water to disconnect the winch wire, and I returned to the surface at 15:29. My dive supervisor, Mr. Simon Hamblin, verified this.

I must admit that I wasn't feeling great after that dive, and I felt very odd for a few days, but nothing happened. It may seem silly in retrospect, but no one else managed to do it any faster during the rest of February, and I won the big box of chocolates.

That's me looking all cocky after my swift dive to 80 feet.

Not long after that dive, Simon went home on leave, and a wonderful character named Davie Bruce took over as our supervisor; anyone who worked for CCCUE back then knew what a great guy Davie Bruce was. The diving work continued as usual now that I had been on the lay barge for three months. It was beginning to get to the point that I needed to go home for a break, as three months offshore is a long time. I still had a couple more weeks before going home, and the work had been nonstop. As I was coming to the end of my trip, the Diving Superintendent, Mr Harry King, decided it was time to get my box of chocolates, and he brought out his colour camera to get a picture of me and the rest of the diving team on the day shift. One of the divers, whom I had beaten by 30 seconds, was very happy for me, as you can see from his hands being raised in the air.

That's me in the red wetsuit with a Filipino diver, an Egyptian diver, and a Lebanese diver.

At long last, after a hectic few months, I was going home on March 24, 1982. I left the NPCC 648 lay barge and headed to Abu Dhabi. On March 26, 1982, I flew home for at least six weeks' rest and looked forward to returning home. By now, Chris was five years old. He was my best mate, which is strange to say about your son, but I loved spending time with him and bringing him home presents. One we both loved was a small Pac-Man game. We would spend hours together on it, killing aliens. Chris was a natural at it, and I guess from an early age, Chris just loved anything to do with computer games.

On May 6, 1982, I flew back to Abu Dhabi to join a joint venture operation with Mutawa Marine and CCCUE on an M.V. Oceane vessel. This vessel was a big surprise. It was a pleasure motor yacht; I do not know how it was accepted as an offshore DSV. This was unreal after some of the barges I had been used to working from; the toilets even had padded seats. The Oceane came from the south of France. From what I could gather, some backhanders had gone on, but why should I be concerned? If I were to spend some time offshore, why not spend it on a motor yacht? To top it all off, we had to visit Abu Dhabi's free port every 7 to 10 days due to its size. I could not have been happier.

Our diving supervisor was a man named Fred Hussy, who was a genuinely lovely person. The diving work involved swimming along pipelines, and if we found any gaps, we would mark off the areas with marker buoys. We would then return to the vessel, where the captain would manoeuvre the boat close to the marker buoy, and we would push all these sandbags on the deck into the water. Once that had occurred, the vessel would proceed to an anchor location, and we would initiate our diving operation, all conducted in scuba gear, placing sandbags under the gaps along the pipeline. The quicker we got rid of all the sandbags, the less time we spent offshore, as we would need to head back into Abu Dhabi's free port to pick up more bags, which generally took 24 hours to load all the material.

What a lovely job it was! When we weren't swimming pipelines, we would remove debris from around the free-standing, well-head jackets, but even that was great. As soon as the vessel's deck was full of debris, we would head into Abu Dhabi's free port. What was lovely about the operation was that it gave me plenty of time to see Abu Dhabi. I usually fly in, then join a barge for three months, and then fly home. This operation allowed me to spend some time in Abu Dhabi, which I enjoyed. I found it to be a great place, and I ended up spending many happy years working there. It was one of the nicest operations I had ever been on, and I spent a fantastic three months working on this particular diving operation, if you could call it work. I carried out my last dive on July 21, 1982, at a depth of 75 feet to survey some riser clamps and remove previous debris before heading back to Abu Dhabi. I flew home on July 28th for a lovely four-week leave.

By now, I had learned to become part of the furniture when I arrived home, as Rose had her routine around the house, and Rose and Chris had grown accustomed to having her mum around all the time. I felt like a guest until I had been home for a few days, but that was to be expected. You cannot just go away for months and expect everyone to change their routine just because you have come home. So, I would try to blend in until it felt normal for everyone to have me around the house.

I would start taking Chris out on my own to visit my parents and take him to the park. Still, each time I got home, Rose's mum was there all the time, but it was difficult to say or do anything, as each time I would go away, Rose's mum was there, everywhere. However, Rose was happy with that, so what could I do? Nothing, really, so I just got on with everything the way it was.

I flew back to Abu Dhabi on August 25, 1982, to join a Dive Support vessel called the Franklin, with a dive supervisor named Ian Larkin, also known as Nakin Larkin. I don't understand why he was called Nakin Larkin, but I found him to be a nice guy. However, it didn't matter much, as after a few days, I was transferred to a vessel called the MV Attyah.

On September 26th, I carried out my first dive on the M.V. Attyah. My diving supervisor was a Scottish guy named Louie Fox from a well-known diving company in Scotland called Fox Diving. He was a lovely guy and very popular wherever he went. He was fantastic on the guitar. He was so good on the guitar that the personnel ashore would try to find out when our ship was coming in, and they would arrange to meet him in the local bars to hear him play and sing all his favourite Scottish folk songs.

Our offshore diving operation consisted of seabed surveys around free-standing wellheads and positioning Deadman anchors for supply ships to anchor to. It was an excellent diving operation, one that I enjoyed with an excellent diving supervisor, and also a very entertaining guy to run ashore with. I flew home at the end of November to spend a lovely Christmas with Rose and Chris. I flew to Saudi Arabia in the first week of January 1983 to rejoin the NPCC 648 lay barge, but we were not laying pipelines this time. The diving operation was working in very deep water for an air diving operation, and we were diving to a depth of 166 feet on air. The operation involved replacing old pipeline spool sections with new 16-inch spool pieces, hydro-tightening flange bolts, and underwater oxy arc cutting.

I was on the day shift, and our supervisor was Keith Davis, or as many people knew him, "Scouse Davis". I first met Keith in Liverpool in 1978 while working for a diving company called Manor Divers. Manor Divers was a civil engineering diving company that mainly worked in and around the docks in Liverpool. I remembered Keith because he visited Manor Divers one day to greet the owner, Mark Berry, whose real name was Stan Berry, but that name did not have a good business look, so he called himself Mark. I always remember Keith visiting Mark and our senior diver, Sam Musket. Keith drove up one day in his yellow Lotus, threw me the keys, and said, "Look after my car, lad, while I speak to Mark."

I never saw Keith again until I joined the NPCC 648-lay barge. He never remembered me, but I never forgot him or his yellow Lotus. On our first day shift, I met him and asked if he still had that yellow Lotus; he looked at me, surprised, and asked how I knew about it. He couldn't stop laughing when I told him I was the one he had thrown his keys to and asked to look after them while he saw Mark. It was I who covered the top of his Lotus with thick grease. We hit it off right away. He knew where I had started my diving career, in and around Liverpool's docks. We were both on the day shift, and it was my turn to dive.

My dive took place at 19:50 hours on January 14, 1983, in the evening, at a depth of 166 feet in the Arabian Gulf of Saudi Arabia, and I was diving on air. The operation was oxyarc cutting, which means cutting with an oxygen mix. I was cutting into an old pipeline, which had to be removed. As I was cutting, I must have hit a gas pocket, which caused a giant explosive backlash that hit my diving hat; all I could remember was a big, bright light and me flying backwards, a voice shouting "free flow, free flow, free flow," continuously. I automatically activated my free-flow air supply on the side of the diving helmet, which blew all the water out of it and provided me with air. The free flow system was a backup on your diving helmet to keep any water out of your hat if the demand valve (which was the primary control of the air you were breathing) on your diving helmet failed. Water was rushing into my diving helmet as my demand valve had been blown inwards. The free-flow system, which I had switched on, kept most of the water at bay as Keith kept shouting, "Free-flow/free-flow." I was over a hundred feet from the dive basket, and my hat's underwater lights had gone off. My underwater comms was ineffective due to the noise from my free-flow system, and the guys up top were unaware of what was happening.

I could feel my diving umbilical, which was going through the dive basket, being pulled backwards towards it. This gave me a straight line to follow to return to the dive basket. Keith kept shouting "free flow" while trying to figure out how to rescue me. At last, I reached the dive basket, but they could not raise it unless I could speak to the surface. I had no choice but to switch off the free flow, which was keeping back the water to allow me to breathe. Once I switched off the free flow, I started shouting, "Lift the basket," but I wasn't sure if Keith could understand me. I had to switch the free flow back on to keep the water out of my diving hat. But then I felt the dive basket moving upwards. I have never felt so good knowing I was returning to the surface. As I was so deep, I had to carry out in-water decompression before I could go into the decompression chamber.

I reached my first in-water decompression stop, the standby diver waited for me to check if everything was okay. I was delighted to see him and gave him the thumbs-up. I completed my in-water decompression stops, and once on the surface, I could finish the rest of my decompression in the comfort of a decompression chamber. I have always been grateful for Scouse Davis's calm and professionalism in keeping the guy alive who covered his yellow Lotus with thick grease.

I kept in touch with Scouse Davis until he sadly passed away a few years ago. Keith went on leave after a few more days, and I was very grateful he was around when I needed a calm head. For that, I will always be thankful. Keith was replaced by another very experienced supervisor, John Parrot, who was much quieter than Keith had been. The diving work continued for another few weeks underwater in 166 feet of water without any further issues, and I went home on leave on February 6, 1983.

By now, I had grown accustomed to going home and blending into whatever Rose and Chris were doing, but I was still unhappy with the amount of time Rose's mum was always around. What could I do or say? Rose's mum would be there as soon as I was gone, but it just became the usual way of life for all of us. I would go away, and Rose's mum would move in, and when I came home, I would be the visitor. Now, when I look back, perhaps I should have said more or even taken a diving job back in the UK, but I enjoyed my working life in the Middle East; being there was my education in life, and it changed me as a person. Without realising it, I was changing from the person I was to a different, more educated person due to travelling and meeting people from various walks of life.

I flew back to the Middle East around February 18, 1983, so I didn't have much leave. In many ways, my working life kept me away from home, so when I look back, why should Rose and Chris change what they were doing? I was not there to be a real husband or dad. On February 20, 1983, I joined a brand-new vessel called MV Barracuda. I did not know how long I would be associated with the ship, as I was still on board over twenty years later when I redesigned and certified the vessel's new diving system.

The diving operation was an SBM (Single Buoy Mooring) maintenance project. It was my first time working on an SBM, and 20+ years later, it became my most crucial diving operation. My diving supervisor was David Leigh, who worked for the Abu Dhabi National Oil Company (ADNOC). He was a fully employed diving supervisor on a salary that I had never encountered before, as everyone I had worked with was a day-rate diver or diving supervisor.

I was being cross-hired from CCCUE as ADPPOC, but for now, ADPPOC did not have any divers, as the diving section of ADPPOC had not been set up for long. The Dive Support Vessel DSV Barracuda was a purpose-built SBM diving vessel, and everything was brand new. It had two Decompression Chambers, with 50-litre air quads that filled automatically when the air pressure dropped below 1500 PSI. However, what amazed me was that, despite being a brand-new diving vessel equipped with two DDC air quads, etc., it still lacked a dive control station on the deck. We used a suitcase diving panel to which the diving umbilicals would be connected to a manifold block inside the suitcase.

I did not mind any of it, as it was a new experience working on SBMS. My first few dives were all scuba, and I was conducting configuration checks on the underwater SBM hoses, as each flange area had to be at a specific depth to maintain the hoses' shape. I would measure the distance from the hose flange to a plumb line that went down the SBM's centre from the surface. The illustration below shows the layout of an SBM, as well as the shape of the SBM hoses underwater. The SBM hose has flotation buoys to maintain the correct angle of the SBM hose.

The SBM and the SBM hoses.

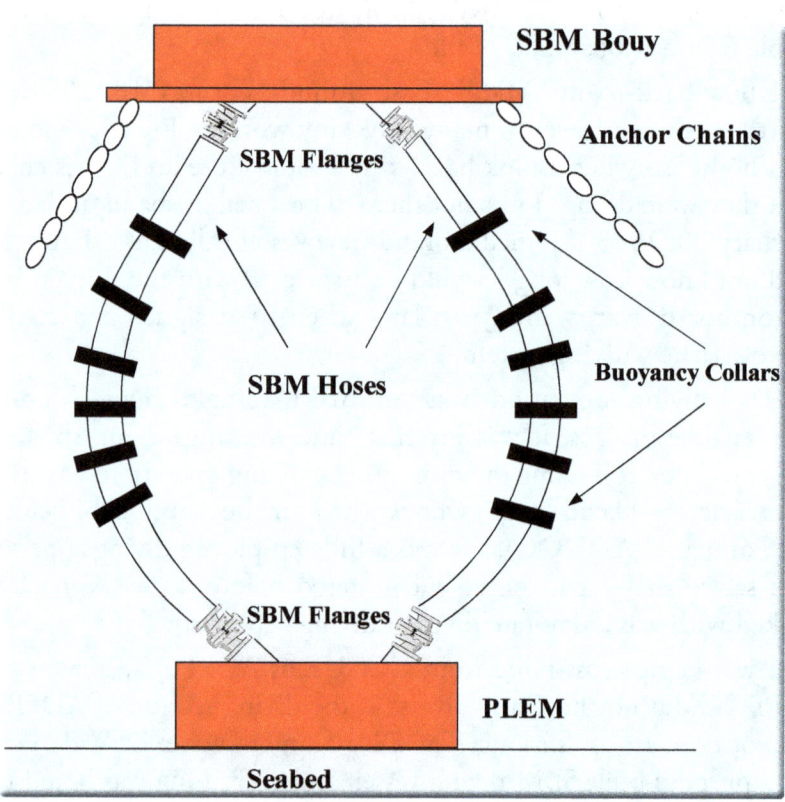

The arrows point to the SBM flotation buoys, which I would have to take a depth reading of to check the angle of the SBM hoses. Then, from the flange of the underwater SBM hose, I would take a distance measurement to the centre of the plumb line, which is lowered down the middle of the SBM, indicating that the SBM was in the correct position. I enjoyed my time on the Barracuda, a lovely new vessel to work on. Still, it was odd at the same time, as I was back working on Zirku Island, where I had been part of the dive team that installed the seawater intakes a few years ago, which now supply water to the Island and all its facilities. And what a change! The island now boasts all the modern conveniences and new accommodations for the oil workers. I continued working on the Barracuda diving operation on the SBM for another three weeks before being transferred back onto the NPCC 648 pipeline lay barge.

Once more, my dive supervisor was Davie Bruce, who had been my diving supervisor on many projects and would no longer wonder if I could be trusted to conduct an underwater diving operation. On one of my last dives on this extended trip, I was lucky to have a diver photographer in the water as I guided the pipeline to its connection point on one of the free-standing wellheads. It was in colour.

That's me guiding down the pipeline with its connection frame on the NPCC 648 to a free-standing wellhead.

My last dive was on March 21st, 1983, and I flew home on March 25th, 1983. The more I travelled, the more I changed. The more different people I met, the more comfortable I felt talking to others, mainly because I used to speak in a dialect of English that slowed down my Scouse accent. I was becoming different from the one who first started diving in 1975. Plus, no one looked at me as a coloured person anymore, as everyone was coloured overseas, and everyone would try to get a good tan before they went home on leave. I had a long break and returned on June 9th, 1983. Some people may wonder where I got all these dates as I write this information. I have managed to keep all my old passports, as they contained a working visa, so when I had to renew my passport, my old one was stapled onto my new one.

Chapter Fifteen

My Many Stamps, NPCC WB1 & 1000.

Below are some of the stamps on my passport. I must admit that I missed getting stamps when we joined the European Union. I am fortunate to have kept my old passports, as they have greatly assisted me in piecing together my life, story, and book.

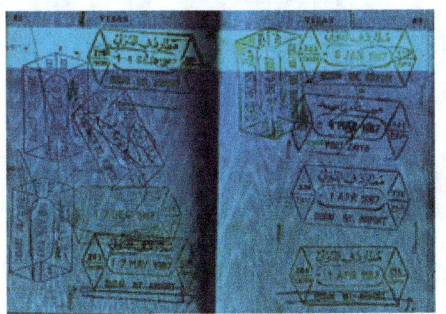 

Also, my passport caused me problems, or my passport photo did when I worked offshore in Kuwait, but that story comes later. I re-joined the barge, the NPCC WB1, and it must have been the worst barge I had worked on. Everything about it was primitive. I had worked on this barge before and hoped the vessel had improved, but it had worsened. The only positive aspect of the operation was the dive supervisor, a lovely individual named Jeff Chaganis, who was a very calm and easy-going person who could not wait to leave the offshore diving world. Our operation on the NPCC WB1 was installing a pipeline raiser, which was very interesting. The operation involved connecting approximately 6 to 12 davits, each fitted with winches to assist in lifting and lowering the pipeline, depending on the water depth and the number of davits used. The shallower the water, the fewer davits needed to be fitted onto the pipeline we were lifting to the surface. Once the pipeline was lifted to the surface, we would get a break from diving as the welders had to weld on the riser to the end of the pipeline.

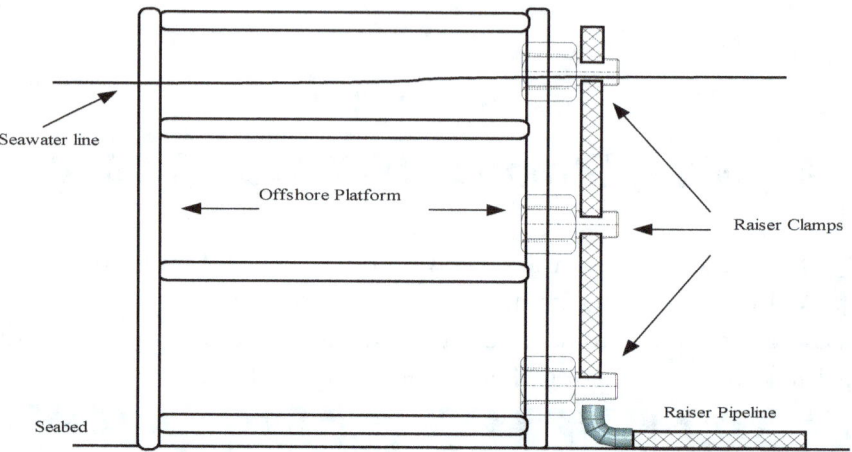

This particular operation lasted around five weeks, and on July 18, 1983, I was transferred to another diving operation on the dive vessel MV Cecile Tide. By then, I had worked on numerous diving operations offshore for CCCUE, and the company had come to trust me more. On the MV Cecile Tide I was assigned as a relief diving supervisor and had to conduct a handover for a few days before assuming the role.

The diving operation I was taking over was to conduct all the underwater inspections for the operation I had been on, which seemed odd. The client on board the vessel was also a diver who enjoyed diving and would check our inspections. At the same time, he would go spearfishing, but hey, he was the client, and he could do what he liked. His name was David McCredie; he had been in the Middle East for years, and I had the opportunity to get to know him well during my time there. I still hear about him from time to time. The diving operation went very well, and I enjoyed my time as the diving supervisor. However, I knew that after this operation, I would be heading home, and when I returned for my next trip, I would be back as a diver. I had no problems with that, as that's how things worked back then. I flew home on August 16, 1983, for a lovely four weeks at home, and as usual, I blended into home life, having grown accustomed to long trips away and the occasional four-week break.

I flew back to Abu Dhabi on September 11, 1983, which I didn't mind, as it meant I would be home for Christmas, my favourite time of year. The next few months passed quickly, and to my surprise, I was appointed as the diving supervisor on an underwater inspection operation. Everything went well, and I also earned some extra money as the supervisor, which was very handy with Christmas coming up.

I was a diver on a diving operation aboard the MV Super Tide, supervised by Dave Abbott, a highly experienced diving supervisor, during a pipeline repair operation. The pipeline we were inspecting was from an Island called Mubarass, which was looking to reopen some old pipelines. During our diving inspection of the pipeline, we found that large areas of the weight coat, which was designed to protect it, were missing; as a result, the pipeline was exposed to seawater and was rusting away. The pipeline was so thin that I could put my diving knife through it, which was supposed to withstand up to a couple of thousand pounds of testing pressure, but this was just not possible due to the pipeline's extreme thinness. A decision was made to relocate the diving operation to a work barge called the M/B Carol to carry out the repairs, and CCCUE determined that I would serve as the diving supervisor on the night shift. This did not go well with Dave Abbott, who wanted his mate, Louie Fox, as the night shift supervisor. However, CCCUE overruled him, and Dave told me he was unhappy and would be watching me closely. Additionally, he assigned Louie to my shift, which was great for me, as Dave did not know me. Louie and I got along well, and he was happy to be working with me as a diver. Plus, he was not interested in being a supervisor; he was just happy being a diver.

The diving operation started on my night shift due to how long it took for the barge to get set up, and in our first 12-hour shift, not only had we started to remove a lot of the damaged weight coat which covered the pipeline, but we had also installed three Pimlico sleeves over the damaged areas. They were ready to be pressure tested, which our client was pleased about. Dave could not say anything any more about not having his mate as the diving supervisor, but Louie just laughed about it all when I told him what had gone on with Dave, and he told Dave to piss off as he was happy as a diver and Dave, in the end, found it all very funny. Additionally, it was beneficial for me to serve as the diving supervisor again, which meant CCCUE was increasingly trusting me. I was constantly learning about the various offshore diving operations. I enjoyed my three months of diving operations, working as both a diver and a diving supervisor. I went home for Christmas on December 4, 1983, and I was looking forward to putting up the Christmas decorations and tree. Chris, who was young at the time, was also looking forward to Christmas and all the trimmings that came with it. Life felt good, and I knew I had another diving operation to go back to after Christmas, so it was a great time to enjoy the time at home and some of the money I had earned.

I flew back to Abu Dhabi on January 1, 1984, to join a new barge called NPCC 1000. Jeff Chaganis was my diving supervisor, and Pete was the diving superintendent. I had never met or spoken to Pete, but I had heard a great deal about him and looked forward to the opportunity to meet him. I was on the main deck of the barge with Jeff, setting up the diving equipment, when Pete walked down the deck to say hello, or so I thought. He approached Jeff, who I was standing next to, and shook hands with him, introducing himself. I then extended my hand to say hello, but he completely ignored me and walked away, leaving me surprised. Jeff asked what I had done to him; I shrugged and said I didn't know, as I had never met him before.

Perhaps he didn't see my hand and was busy, but that's not the case. He told Jeff to keep me out of his way. Jeff said I must have done something to him. No, I told Jeff I had never worked with him or met him, so Jeff and I were wondering what was going on with him concerning me. Jeff told me not to worry; maybe he had mixed me up with someone else. "Okay, Jeff," I said, "you're probably right." But no, for whatever reason, Pete had it in for me, and I never knew why for years and years. My first scuba dive was on January 26th. I had to fit a hydraulic hose connection to the lifting jacks under the support members of the wellhead jacket that had been installed; they were not level, and our diving operation was to fit the lifting jacks under them so the wellhead platforms could be lifted into the correct position. Once the platform was level, our diving operation involved fitting sandbags under the support members to help keep the platform in position in case any lifting jacks moved. The platform had four legs, and sandbags were placed around each leg and under the support members. Once the platform was level, concrete was poured down the inside of the legs, which had caisson piles inside them, to a depth of around 25 metres into the seabed. We would then fit small cofferdams around the platform legs, which would help contain the concrete from the seabed. Our diving operation monitored the seabed areas around the platform legs and informed the diving supervisor on the surface once the concrete started coming over the cofferdams. The concrete engineers would determine when to stop pouring the concrete. Once that decision had been made, we would wait for the concrete to set. After the concrete had been set, we were required to take underwater photos of the cofferdams to show that the concrete had covered them before we were allowed to remove the sandbags under the support members.

My problems with Pete became evident during the following diving operation. Jeff had known me on many diving operations and, by now, was familiar with my capabilities. One of the diving operations I could perform was underwater photography, and he knew I had been a photo technician and could develop the photos. The client wanted a photo survey, and the images were produced before we left the site to move to a new well-head jacket. As I was getting ready to dive, Pete came down and told Jeff that I was not to take any photos under any circumstances, and that another diver would take them instead. Jeff was not happy with this and told Pete to piss off and not to interfere with Jeff's shift. Jeff had been around a long time in the diving world and was not going to take any shit from anyone. Pete was unhappy with this and started arguing with Jeff when the client appeared and asked what was going on. Pete informed the rep of his decision on who should dive; the rep said, "I don't give a fxxk. Chris is ready to dive, and we don't have any time to waste, so let's get on with the dive." Pete walked away, saying he would sort this out later. Jeff turned around and told me to get in, take the photos, and not let him down. I took over 40 black-and-white pictures, ten on each leg at different lengths and angles, with a Nikon Mark 5. Once out of the water, I began developing the photos. Halfway through my shift, the client came down and asked if any pictures were ready for him to look at. Jeff gave the client a choice of what photos he wanted and what size picture he wanted. Pete came down to the dive control later and started to shout at 'what a fxxk up' I had made of the photos. He had picked up a few and said what a load of shit they were when all of a sudden the client appeared and asked what was going on. Pete apologised for the state of the photos, but the client said they were not the photos Chris had taken. They were samples of pictures of the shit he did not want, and the images I took were perfect.

Did anything improve after that for me with Pete? No, it never did, and for years, he would do anything he could to stop me from participating in his operations. I never did find out what his problem was and every time I met him, I was always polite, but it never made any difference. Whatever his problem with me never improved which in the end became very funny for a lot of the regular divers I worked with over the years, and they always made jokes about it. The diving operation on the DLB 1000 was completed on February 20, 1984. I was then transferred to another barge with Jeff to the 'Construction Barge' 111 or CB111 as it was known, afterwards I discovered that Pete had informed CCCUE that I was never to work on any of his diving operations while he was working for CCCUE. Why I never knew as I had never worked with him before the DLB 1000. I know I can be a pain in the arse we are not all perfect, and I had never met Pete before. In the end, I got my own back before I finished working for CCCUE, but that comes later.

For the following six weeks, I worked as a diver on the CB 111, installing risers onto the wellhead platforms, without any further issues with the diving superintendent, and the subsequent operation went very smoothly. I continued to work on that operation with Jeff Chaganis and another diving supervisor called Mel Beilenson, a great guy with whom I had worked a few times before. I went home on leave on July 2, 1984; I did go home a bit confused about Pete's attitude towards me, but I thought, 'Forget it, go home and enjoy my leave.' I had a lovely time at home, and I had gotten used to blending in without disturbing anyone's routine, as it was their routine. I had to get used to it. Now, I look back and see I was away too much, but I was enjoying my work and all the travelling. When you're that young, you don't know what's ahead and what issues it can create in the long term. I flew back to Abu Dhabi on August 12, where I was to join the NPCC 648 again for a couple of months. I would work in depths of up to 167 feet, performing pipeline repairs, photography, and installing new pipeline risers. By now, I had become accustomed to all the offshore underwater work and was developing into a highly experienced offshore diver.

My diving supervisor at the time was Peter Taylor, a skilled instructor with a great attitude and easy to work with. I got on well with Peter, which was just as well, as he was moving to another diving operation on a work barge called the 'Instant Mariner' and asked me if I wanted to go on his next operation as one of his diving supervisors, which I was pleased to do. It turned out the operation was to carry out repairs on the seawater intakes on Zirku Island, which I had been a part of many years previously. The concrete base had started to break up as the sea began to erode the seabed, causing the base to crack. I was happy to head back to Zirku Island, and being one of the diving supervisors was a good experience. But what a difference it was! I had left the 648 working in 167 feet of water to work in 20 feet of water, but I did not mind. The operation involved carrying out concrete repairs underneath the seawater intakes and placing large 10-15-ton boulders around the base of the seawater intake. The operation went well, and it was nice to see how much Zirku Island had changed since I had left; it was an up-to-date Island with excellent accommodations and facilities for its workers. I worked there until the end of October, but this time, I had decided to spend around six to seven weeks at home, as I needed to be there more than just being a visitor. I flew back to Abu Dhabi on January 9, 1985, and Rose was one month pregnant. We were looking forward to another baby, and hopefully, Rose would not have the same postnatal issues as our first child.

I joined a barge called ETPM 801 as an inspector diver for Dubai Petroleum on a pipeline inspection operation. The operation was to be conducted in very deep water. Our diving inspections were to be carried out in scuba from a Zodiac. The leading diving company was Oceaneering, which was carrying out the pipelaying work and repairs, as well as all riser installation, using air/mixed gas surface-supplied diving equipment and Saturation diving.

Our diving supervisor was a Scotsman named Ian Bruce. My first dive was 152 feet in scuba to survey a 42-inch pipeline for damage, which was not a good way to build up any resistance to nitrogen narcosis, which leaves you feeling a bit light-headed and drunk, but it was okay. I was expecting it to happen, so I was ready for the drunk feeling.

My first dive on January 12th lasted only 15 minutes, and my decompression table was USN 160/15 minutes, which required two water stops for a total of 5 minutes. I would have preferred to have been on a deeper table, but Ian was the dive supervisor. My next dive was over 6 hours later, again on scuba, back to the same depth of 152 feet with a 4-minute penalty, so I only dived for 10 minutes along the pipeline. My dive buddy and I had to swim quickly to carry out the inspections, and again, we used the USN 160/15-minute table; everything went well. Each day, I dived to different depths in scuba and built up a resistance to nitrogen narcosis. Plus, I was getting quicker at swimming the pipelines. There were always two of us diving together. One of us would conduct the inspection, and the other diver would pull a rope connected to a marker buoy on the surface, allowing the crew in the zodiac to follow us and know where to wait for us as we surfaced after our dive.

Wherever we finished our dive, we would tie the marker buoy onto the pipeline so we always knew where to start again for our next dive. We carried out two dives daily, one in the morning and one in the afternoon. Over the next couple of weeks, we began inspecting the support sleepers that the pipeline used, to cross other pipelines. However, we are now entering extremely deep water for scuba diving, and I was diving over 167 feet of water using a twinset. I will never forget this particular dive. My dive buddy John Magine and I were swimming along the pipeline when we noticed the saturation diving bell ahead of us, and we saw the two saturation divers working on the pipeline; as we got close to them, we tapped them on top of their diving helmets and gave them a big thumbs up, they looked entirely startled seeing two guys in scuba in 167 foot of water waving at them and giving a thumbs up, and then we made our way along the pipeline again. Once we had finished our dive, and completed our decompression, and were back in the Zodiac, we noticed a lot of activity on the barge next to ours, and we wondered what was going on. We later heard that the saturation supervisor had asked what the saturation divers were shouting about, and it concerned two scuba divers waving at the saturation divers and giving them a thumbs-up sign.

The saturation supervisor thought something was wrong with his divers, so he aborted their dive. Our supervisor could not stop laughing when we told him it was us and told us not to tell anyone what we had done. Our dives are getting deeper and deeper for air diving. We started diving in scuba gear to 175 feet for 13 minutes, taking photos of the pipeline, but our diving tables were still very tight. Our diving supervisor kept us on USN 180 for 15 minutes, and I performed repetitive dives to the same depth in the afternoon. But everything was going well; no one had problems with the deep air dives. The next day, I reached 181 feet for 13 minutes on air, and in scuba, our dive tables only went up to 190 feet, which we had now started using. I was now on a USN dive table at 190 feet for 15 minutes, and our total decompression time was only 11 minutes. I was beginning to wonder how much longer we could continue diving to this depth without experiencing any decompression illness. Still, so far, nothing had gone wrong, and we continued diving deep.

On February 16, 1985, I dived into 192 feet of water on air and in a scuba twinset. No one had realised that the end of the pipeline would be that deep. Our diving tables stopped at 190 feet, and now my dive buddy and I had dived beyond our decompression tables. We both looked at each other and thought, "O fxxk." Now, what do we do? We headed for the surface with our decompression tables at 190 feet, but we had dived to 192 feet.

We added a couple of minutes to each decompression stop, starting with our first one at 30 feet and then at 20 feet. When we reached 10 feet, we stayed there until our air supply ran out, and then we headed to the surface. The divers in the zodiac were wondering what on earth we were doing and why we were taking so long to complete our decompression. Once we returned to the Zodiac, we informed the supervisor that we had reached a water depth of 192 feet. "Holy fxxk," he said, "the pipeline was not meant to be that deep." The diving supervisor decided that we should not dive again for a while, so we were to be monitored in case we developed any decompression illness. A few days of bad weather had affected our operation, and for the next week, no diving took place due to a terrible storm. My dive buddy and I did not develop any decompression illness, and we were put back into diving operations as and when required. The following two weeks passed very well. We had not been diving as deep as we had, but we were still diving over 160 feet. But then it happened: I had a decompression hit, and I had to be put on a USN table 5 as I had had a hit in my right arm joint. It was excruciating, but I guess it had to happen sometime; we could not carry on diving that deep in the air in scuba and not have any decompression illness.

The decompression treatment went well, with no significant issues. I then had a few days of no diving, but it wasn't long before I was diving again. My first dive was at 131 feet, and I still used scuba gear, but I had no further problems. Additionally, we had been transferred to the ETPM 401, where my oldest brother, Roger, was a diver on this work barge, and I had to inspect his work. My oldest brother was a new diver who only got into diving because he had seen me doing well. He also became a diver because he wanted to try something new. I was able to assist him and provide tips on the work he was doing, as he needed help understanding how to work on pipelines, raise settings, and connect the lifting davits that were being lowered from the deck of the work barge to the seabed.

The diving inspection work was still conducted in very deep water. By now, I had become so accustomed to diving deep in scuba that I could descend to 165 feet, complete my inspection, and exit the water in under 15 minutes. My last deep dive on scuba was on April 4, at a depth of 161 feet. Overall, it had been a fantastic experience diving that deep in scuba, but also, looking back on that time, I remember how crazy it was to be diving that deep on air with just a twinset.

I flew home on April 10, 1985, and was looking forward to a long break. I had planned to take Rose and Chris away for a holiday in, of all places, Torquay. I don't know why I chose Torquay; it seemed like a good idea at the time. Rose was now five months pregnant, and it seemed like a good opportunity to escape while we could.

Chris and I are on holiday and playing crazy golf.

Overall, we had a good time. Rose did not want to do much, as she was five months pregnant, which was understandable. We went home after a week. We had a good time, but once we got back home, Rose's mum was just too much; she wanted to control everything Rose was doing, but I did not want to cause much fuss, as I had already received a phone call to head back to Abu Dhabi. Rose seemed more at ease with her mum than with me, as she was pregnant. I just let them get on with things.

I flew back to Abu Dhabi on May 11, 1985, and the next time I went home, we would have our second child. On May 12, 1985, I joined the Japanese oil tanker Echo Maru, a permanent oil tanker connected to an SBM. The tanker circled in the Total Al Bukosh oil field, where I would live and work for the next eight weeks. The diving work involved carrying out oilfield maintenance and SBM maintenance for Total ABK Oil Company, which spanned a long and successful period in my diving career, as I worked with Total Oil for many years.

Chapter Sixteen
TOTAL ABK

I am by the SBM with the Echo Maru in the background.

The diving operation was exciting and varied. We worked in scuba up to over 45 metres of water, conducting numerous seabed surveys and platform maintenance. We also looked after the SBM, as we received many tankers each month that came alongside the Echo Maru to remove all the oil pumped into the tankers from the oil field.

When any tankers came alongside, we would get a couple of days off, as the operation would require our diving vessel for the mooring operation and to be on standby in case the tankers needed to be separated in a hurry due to any emergencies.

A visiting Tanker would come alongside the Echo Maru to load up with oil.

It was great for the divers, as we had nothing to do besides using the tankers' swimming pool and having a few beers. The tanker had drinks on board, and the crew would have a BBQ on the tanker, so it was a great few days of chilling out and having a couple of beers.

I am in the Tanker's pool, having a cold beer while the two tankers are together.

With two oil tankers together, the Echo Maru transfers the oil onto the other tanker.

Once the two tankers are together, the lead tanker pilot leaves the tanker. The loading master stayed on the Echo Maru to oversee the oil transfer from tanker to tanker, which usually took up to three or four days. This was great for me, as my hobby was making ships in a bottle. There was an excellent woodworking room on the Echo Maru, so I would take myself off and work on my ship in a bottle. I would also run around the tanker to keep fit, making it a great, relaxing, and varied diving operation. One of my first dives after the loading tanker had left was to swim along the pipeline from the SBM towards a wellhead platform to carry out two diving operations. One was to inspect the pipeline for any damage that may have occurred if anchor blocks had been dropped into position for the tugboats to tie up overnight. The other operation was to collect any golf balls that had come to rest along the pipelines that had been hit out to sea from the oil tanker by the ship's crew.

The captain, the loading master, and I after the other tanker had left.

I know! Diving for golf balls offshore? During downtime, the Japanese crew would go to the tanker's stern, to the golf net by the tanker's swimming pool, and just hit golf balls after golf balls into the practice net. But after a few beers, they would get bored of hitting golf balls into the practice net. When the tankers were in the correct position, the tankers would go around in circles as they were tied up to the SBM. They would remove the practice net and keep hitting golf balls out to sea, knowing the tide would take the golf balls back alongside the pipeline. We had to swim along and inspect each pipeline after each tanker moved off. What was good for the divers was that the more golf balls they brought back, the more beer and whiskey they would receive from the tanker crew.

Little did the crew know that we always kept a spare bag of golf balls handy. If we didn't come across any golf balls as we swam along the pipeline, we would use our spare bag of golf balls to give back to the crew, as we frequently found golf balls along the many other pipelines.

The diving operation was a great job. It was also the first time I encountered Comex diving tables, which differed significantly from the USN diving tables I had used previously. I found them to be excellent and straightforward to use. Approximately 90% of our diving was conducted using scuba gear, reaching depths of up to 45 metres.

We would dive twice daily, inspecting the pipelines and carrying out seabed surveys around the wellheads to ensure the seabed was clear of debris before any oil rigs came alongside the wellhead platforms. Our diving supervisor was a great guy named Bob Precious. He was easy-going and worked directly for Comex. I was hired from CCCUE along with another diver named Sean Cunningham, who was a fascinating guy. He used to be a glassmaker for Waterstones Crystals in Ireland.

Sean and one of the Filipino divers.

Sean was a great guy, and we both had a good time working from the Echo Maru, doing a lot of diving work on and around the SBM together.

I'm on top of the SBM.

Before diving down the SBM hoses, I had to perform topside maintenance to check that none of the flotation buoys attached to them had moved or broken off. I enjoyed my time on the Echo Maru, but it was time for me to return home and prepare for our second child. I flew home on July 31, 1985. The next part of my book is about my breakup with Rose. It is only my view about the breakup, how I saw the breakup, and how I walked away from my family, which at the time seemed the correct thing to do to stop all the arguments and fighting, and it will be challenging to write about, but it is part of my life story, and I have to include it in the book; otherwise, it's not my story, my book, or my life. I am happy that Rose and I are getting on well now, but it does not alter the fact that I walked away and never gave my kids the dad they should have had. I cannot change those years, but Rose did a fantastic job of raising the kids to be well-mannered and very well-educated, and for that, I cannot thank Rose enough.

Chapter Seventeen

Our home life and problems.

I cannot believe my daughter is approaching her 40th birthday, and how well Grace has done. I must thank her mum, Rose, as I was never there for her or Chris. Chris was always used to me being away, but Grace never got a chance to understand why I was away. When Grace was born, home life for her, Chris, and Rose would never be the same as it had been over the early years. When Grace was born, it was a great day for us all, and after all the problems with post-natal depression Rose had with Chris, I did not think for one minute Rose would go through the same thing again.

Rose seemed fine when we took Grace home, but foolishly, I let Rose's mum take over, and she did. I thought I was doing the correct thing by letting Rose's mum help out with Grace. Rose went to her mum for help. In a way, Chris was pushed to one side, and he did not understand why all the attention was on Grace, which is only natural as he had been used to all the attention, but now he had a baby sister. All seemed fine, and I received a call to see if I was ready to return to work. By now, I had been home for nearly eight weeks and thought returning to work would be okay. If I went now, I would be home for Christmas. So, in early September 1985, I returned to work, thinking everything was great, but it wasn't. I was the day shift diving supervisor on a Barge called the WB1. The diving operation involved pipeline surveys and the installation of pipeline risers to wellhead platforms in the Arabian Gulf, which was progressing very well.

After two months, I received an urgent phone call from our project manager in Abu Dhabi, who informed me that my wife was not feeling well and that I needed to return home immediately. On November 5th, I flew home to what I did not know, but I soon found out. Rose was in an awful state with post-natal depression, and the doctors had recommended that Rose be put on Valium, which I was not made aware of. Rose's mum would keep putting Valium in everything Rose drank. I found out that if Rose wanted a cup of tea, her mum would rush out to make it and add Valium to the tea, which I was not aware of at the time. However, I was not happy once I discovered this.

I tried to stop Rose from receiving all this Valium, but it caused all sorts of arguments in the house, affecting Chris and Grace. Rose leant more toward her mum than me, and I felt utterly useless, no matter what I tried to do. So, to stop all the arguments, I backed off and let Rose's mum take over; life was never the same again. However, after a while, things began to settle down, life returned, and things started to pick up again. I thought life at home was finally settling back into normalcy. I stayed home until after Christmas. On December 29, 1985, I flew back to Abu Dhabi to re-join the Echo Maru oil tanker, but I didn't mind, as I thought everything at home would be okay now. How wrong I was and naive to think that. Once I was away from home, Rose's mum took over Rose's life again. I did not know it then, but it marked the beginning of something from which we would never recover. If I had been home more often instead of being away all the time, I might have been a better husband and father to Rose and the kids.

I joined the supply boat on December 30, 1985, to transport me to the Total ABK oilfield complex, and then joined the Echo Maru on January 1, 1986. I wondered what 1986 would bring, as the ship horns bellowed out at midnight to welcome in the new year. During my first few days back working on the Echo Maru, I was disconnecting strops from piggyback anchor buoys at a depth of 42 metres using scuba, which, by now, I had grown accustomed to. It was nice to be away from all the arguments at home, but my mind was always on home. How were Rose and the kids doing? No messages came from home, so I guessed and hoped everything was fine. Everything went well with my diving operation on the Echo Maru; no emergency calls came from home, which was a great relief. I flew home on April 6th, hoping to have a settled life with Rose and the kids, but Rose was no better, and her mum had kept all the problems from me. I asked Rose's mum to leave us for a while so I could attend to everything with Rose and the kids.

However, that plan did not work, as Rose wanted her mum, and I didn't know what to do about it. Some days were lovely, but most were full of arguments, which were unsettling for the kids by now. So, I took a step back and let Rose be with her mum. It made life easy, I guess.

Grace and I in happier times.

These are just a couple of pictures I have of Grace and me in happier times, but they were few and far between. I could have and should have done more to help out, but I suppose I took the easy route and let Rose's mum handle everything, which was poor of me. I began to find I was happier away from home, away from all the continuous arguments and fighting. Chris did not understand what was going on; why should he? At his age, I would take him to school when I was home, but it was clear he didn't understand all the problems at home.

I flew back to Abu Dhabi on May 8, 1986, and was working on a barge called the DLB 1000 with Keith Davis as my supervisor on a large underwater oxy-acetylene arc-cutting operation. It was good being away, which it should not have been, with everything going on at home, and was very poor for me to think like that.

Chapter Eighteen
Mixed gas diving off Sharjah and to Oman and PDO SBM maintenance.

The underwater cutting operation went very well and lasted for a couple of weeks before I was transferred to a few smaller diving operations while I waited to join the NPCC 648 on a deep mixed gas diving operation, diving to 64 metres using Comex mixed gas diving tables. My diving supervisor was Brian MacMillian, also known as 'Shades', because he always had sunglasses on, whether inside or outside the barge. My first dive to 64 metres was in a diving basket, and my task was to disconnect some lifting davits that were lowered from the barge. The dive lasted 24 minutes on a Heliox mix of 82/18, 66/30-minute Comex in-water decompression table. The in-water decompression lasted for over 2 hours while sitting in a diving basket, which is very dull; you can only keep looking at the fish for so long.

There was a wet diving bell, but if that was in use, we had to use the diving basket. The operation was 24 hours round the clock; the diving bell was at the stern of the barge, and the diving basket was around the middle of the barge. It was a non-stop diving operation, but due to the time spent underwater, the changeover took too long for the barge superintendent. So, another dive basket was brought out with the idea that it would hang off a crane. Once we had reached our in-water decompression stop at 40 feet, the divers would leave the one dive basket and swim over to the other dive basket hanging off the crane, freeing up the main dive basket, so no dive time was wasted, as the barge superintendent put it.

I must say that it worked, but you wouldn't get away with doing stunts like that nowadays. But it was horrible in the dive basket hanging off the crane while you were carrying out your in-water decompressions. I was not too fond of it when the 10-foot decompression level was reached, as the crane would go up and down with the swell, and I had never been so uncomfortable. I felt seasick in the dive basket, and it was the only time I was close to saying that I was coming up and stuff, the decompression. I had never been so close to ripping off my diving helmet. I was so uncomfortable that I had to fight myself from doing so. I was happy once my long in-water decompression in that dive basket was over. The deep diving operation went well, and I was lucky not to have to hang off the dive basket at the end of a crane anymore. On June 14, 1986, we completed the diving operation, and I was transferred to a diving operation in Oman, which changed my life and that of my family.

I landed in Oman on June 21, 1986, to join a diving operation conducting SBM (Single Buoy Mooring) underwater maintenance. Oil tankers used the SBM to load oil from the oil refinery. I must admit I did not get off to a great start. I was pretty tipsy from having a few beers before boarding the plane to Oman. At the airport in Oman, I missed my pick-up driver and booked a room at the Gulf Hotel in Mina Qaboos, outside Muscat. When I woke up the following morning, I called CCCUE to report my location. In those days, everything was still done using a landline phone, and I did not have a contact number for our project manager in Oman. The project manager in Abu Dhabi was not amused, and I had to cover the cost of the hotel room and food, but that was fine, as I had earned extra money from the mixed gas diving operation.

I was picked up by the CCCUE driver, who took me to the white camp, as it was known, which belonged to the construction side of CCCUE, where I met the Oman project manager, Mr Mike Warner, who was a great guy and one of the best managers I had the pleasure of working with. I met up with the other divers and knew a couple of them. I met a couple of divers for the first time, but there was a great atmosphere among the guys; they were friendly and an amusing group. Our diving supervisor was Stuart Gibbons. The other divers were

Simon Weiss, a Welsh-American guy I had known for a while; Frank Neil; Tommy Smith, one of the funniest guys anyone could work with; and Graham Watts. Our lead diver was an Indian guy, Arul Dhairyam.

After being on the mixed gas diving operation, this operation was a complete change. The job was daytime, and we lived ashore in Oman, a fascinating country. As we worked ashore with Fridays off, I had the chance to explore some of Oman, which I hadn't done the last time I worked there. For the first time in a long time, I felt happy and relaxed, which was unusual, as I had been feeling stressed and uptight due to the problems at home. That was no one's fault apart from my own. I could have done more at home, but I didn't. I just let things happen and hoped it would all settle down, but when I look back, I see that I didn't do enough to help Rose and the kids. I also began to enjoy life away from home, and the more I moved around, working with different people and visiting other countries, the more I changed. I was no longer nervous about meeting or talking to people; I felt confident about myself. My accent had slowed down, and people were no longer asking me to speak slower so they could understand me. Oman was about to change my life and that of my family. I will not write about who did this and who said that; I walked away. Rose never asked me to leave our family; that was my choice, not anyone else's.

There were three SBMs at different depths, plus two bitumen hoses were laid on the seabed. The shallowest depth was 80 feet, and the deepest was 165 feet. I enjoyed diving in the Arabian Sea, which most people would think is part of the Indian Ocean, but in a way, it is, as there is no land between Oman and India. The barge's backdrop was the mountains of Oman, which were fascinating to see from the barge. My first dive on the SBM was from a small work barge called the PDO 1. It had an A-frame on the bow, diving equipment on the stern, and diving hoses running down the vessel's side away from the work deck. I dived to 78 feet to inspect the condition of the SBM hoses. The water was clear, and the fish life was colourful and big. I loved it.

PDO 1 Work barge

The SBM in Oman in the Indian Ocean.

I enjoyed everything about this operation, usually, as a diver, you don't get to see or enjoy the expat life in the Middle East as you are primarily offshore, unlike here, we were part of the expat life, and we got invited to parties and days out; our operations manager was a great guy called Mike Warner, who was the life and soul of everything we did, he made sure we went out to some of the parties he was invited to. It was at one such party that I first met a lady called Dee. It was a party with the British Ambassador, and we were told to behave ourselves and dress smartly or casually, but we never wore smart or casual clothes –

just jeans and T-shirts. So off we went to this party where everyone, apart from us, was bright and tidy. Most of the men wore bow ties and striped jackets with straw hats, and the ladies wore long dresses; this was a genuine formal party, one I had never attended before. What was this? I thought to myself and the other divers, we all looked at ourselves and thought bollocks to this, let's take the piss out of them.

Mike Warner is wearing a straw hat, and some people are at the party.

I decided to wear a plastic parrot on my shoulder just for a bit of fun. When people asked me what I was doing at the party with a plastic parrot on my shoulder, I told them the parrot was my good luck charm as I was cycling around the world to raise some funds for Live Aid. Unbeknown to me, they believed my story and started a whip-round to raise money for me when, all of a sudden, my supervisor, Stuart Gibson, asked me if I could do him a favour and go help out a lady on the dance floor that some plonker in a striped jacket and a straw hat was pestering and needed rescuing from. "Ok," I said, me and my plastic parrot, shot over to the dance floor, tapped this guy on the shoulder, and said, "O mate, move on, give someone else a chance to dance with her," and nudged him out of the way. Much to her horror, she was now staring at a guy in jeans and a t-shirt dancing with a plastic parrot on his shoulder. "It's okay, love," I said. "I was asked to get you away from that plonker." She just looked at me and asked why I had a plastic parrot on my shoulder. I said, "I am cycling worldwide for Live Aid, and the plastic parrot is my good luck charm."

When I asked her what she was doing here in Oman, she told me she was a veterinary surgeon and a marine biologist. I thought I was in over my head here, so I asked her name. She told me her name was Dee Freke, and she asked me to tell her my name. I said it was de Beaufort. Now, we both thought someone was taking the mickey. I then told her my first name was Chris, and my surname was de Beaufort, but by now, we were both not believing anything the other told us. "How did you get into this party?" she asked me, as I didn't look like the usual guys here, all dressed in ties and striped jackets. "Oh," I said, "I was with the divers, they found me on the side of the road with a puncture on one of my wheels, and they offered to help and look after me until my bike was fixed." Now, she was getting annoyed with me, and she then asked, "So, how do you pass the time when your bike is broken down on the side of a road? I make ships in a bottle," I told her. "Right?" she said, "I have always fancied a four-masted in a bottle." But she didn't; she was just fed up with my stories and asked for a four-masted schooner just to shut me up. Suddenly, one of the people at the party asked me if I was the guy cycling around the world for Live Aid, that they had raised a lot of money for me, and who should they give it to.

Much to my horror and fun, I noticed my boss, Mike Warner, was with the British Ambassador, and I said to the guy, "Do you see that guy with the white hair talking to the British ambassador? Well, he is looking after me, so could you give it to him, that would be fine." Well, the look on his face when he was handed all this money, for the guy he was looking after who was cycling around the world for Live Aid, he looked down and saw me and the other divers waving at him. It was priceless. "Right," said Stuart, our supervisor, "it's time to get out of here before Mike gets any more questions about the guy he is looking after while he waits to get his bike fixed before setting off around the world for Live Aid."

We drove away, laughing at the evening entertainment after taking the mickey out of everyone at that party, we never expected to be invited back to any more parties in and around Oman again. For the next few days, we continued diving on the SBMs, carrying out inspection work and fitting hydraulic clamps onto the SBM hoses. This was necessary to replace the existing hydraulic hoses from the SBM to the PLEM

(Pipeline & Manifold) on the seabed. I was enjoying myself and had not been so relaxed for a long time; the work, diving and the country were remarkable. One day, one of the divers came onto the barge and asked us if we fancied going ice skating with some of the people from the party, as they enjoyed our company and thought we were just a bunch of guys having a good time.

Ice skating in the Middle East in Oman, we thought, he's taking the piss, or someone is. So, we all agreed to go ice skating, thinking it was set up, but it wasn't, it was a real ice-skating ring and one of our guys, Simon Weiss, was good at ice-skating as he was brought up in America, where he played a lot of ice hockey and boy did he show off, but he was excellent. We then noticed some of the people from the party, and I saw Dee was there. We got talking, but this time, we spoke without all the mickey taking. Dee was not a veterinarian, surgeon, or a marine biologist, and she realised I was not cycling around the world for Live Aid. Dee was a keen sports diver eager to discuss professional diving, so we sat down, ordered a couple of coffees, and joined a few other people there. Dee was a second lieutenant orthopaedic nurse for the Oman military hospitals. She enjoyed her work, her life, and Oman. She was not looking for anything or anyone apart from enjoying life. Dee had been married and did not want to go down that path again. We just talked about anything and enjoyed each other's company. Was I thinking of home? No, I should have been, but I was enjoying myself. Dee asked if I made ships in a bottle, or was that just a load of bullshit as well? No, I laughed and said that was the only part of the story that was true. Dee said, "I wouldn't mind a four-masted schooner in a bottle." I said, "No problem, but I don't have any bottles." "Don't worry," she said, "I'll get you a bottle." "Okay, that would be great." Not long after that, we finished our ice skating and headed off to our campsites.

Tommy Smith (Smithy) and I are outside the ice-skating rink in an area called Mina Qabos near Muscat.

Tommy Smith was a great lad and very funny; he has to be one of the funniest and nicest guys I have ever encountered, but he was hopeless at ice-skating and football; I think Tommy had three left feet, not two like everyone else. Word was getting around about what a fun bunch of guys we were, but it was beginning to annoy a few construction workers at our campsite. We were getting invited everywhere, and the construction guys at our campsite were unhappy. After an evening of drinking and socialising in the camp bar, they challenged us to a game of footie on the local rock/sand football pitch by our campsite, the White Camp. Our boss, Mike Warner, was looking forward to this challenge, and he knew it would be great fun. The word got around that the divers had a football team and would take on the construction workers. People started to arrive from all over the place to watch our game of footie. As the crowd approached the football pitch, the spectators noticed some players on the pitch warming up and looking good in their football kits. The more they looked, the spectators from the hospital and the PDO worksite, did not recognise any of the guys on the football pitch and asked where the divers were. "Still in the bar, drinking and smoking," came the answer. It was then that our boss Mike Warner said, "Come on, lads, out we go, and let's have our photo taken before we start our match. When we went outside, there were loads of people who had come to watch the game, and have a good time and watch the divers get beaten before heading back to the bar for a few more beers. Everybody had a great day; even the construction guys had a good laugh, and they put out an invitation for a revenge match for later in the month, as they had got beaten which we happily agreed to as we had had a fantastic time.

The CCCUE divers' football team is coming straight out of the bar.

Mike Warner, Stuart Gibbons-Frank, Frank Neil, Simon Weiss, Tommy Smith-A, a guy with no t-shirt who just wanted to be in the photo with the divers, Arul Dhairyam, Graham Watts, and me.

What a line-up in our best footie kit with big CCCUE stickers, fags hanging out of some of the guy's mouths, and most of us half-pissed. Well, everyone watching knew it was going to be a fun day, and it was, we won 4-0; as much as most of us were half pissed, we were fit, and what the opposition did not know, was we could play football and we could run around, and no one was going to beat the divers. We had a great day; the spectators could not stop laughing at the state of the divers' football team. Dee was there with some of the hospital staff who had come to watch us. Although she did not like football, she had a great day, much to her surprise. After the game, everyone returned to our bar for a good drink and a sing-along. A few days after that, we received more invitations to parties, as everyone knew that having the divers at their parties would ensure a great time, since all we wanted to do was drink, laugh, and have fun.

Our diving team and some of the spectators after the match.

Our diving work was going well; we would turn up in the morning, and as long as we did five dives a day, as Shell, who controlled all the work on the SBM, did not allow any repeat diving, we would return to our campsite. We were now diving to 130 feet and fitting the last of the hydraulic hoses to the PLEM, which was a significant operation. We now had a couple of days off due to bad weather, and we were informed to come in once the weather improved.

Paddy Saunders, on the far right, never made our footie team but made the drinking team.

It was great having a few days off, and I wondered what I would do with myself during that time. I remembered that Dee had given me a bottle for the four-masted schooner she wanted, but by now, she had forgotten about it. So, I got my ship-building tools out and set about making her the four-masted schooner, which helped pass the time and kept me busy during the day instead of just sleeping and drinking, which was not a bad way to spend the day, at long last I finished the four-masted schooner in a bottle for Dee, which she still has after all these years.

The bad weather did not let up, so we were instructed to go down to the barge for a couple of hours to ensure all the diving equipment was safe and secure. Dee heard that I had had a few more days off and asked me if I would like to see some of the old parts of Oman. Yes,

I said I would love to see parts of old Oman. So, we went off to see an old town called Nizwa. It was in the northern Oman mountains. It was about an hour's drive, but it was well worth it. The drive itself was fascinating, and driving through the mountains was something I usually would not get the chance to do. As we got to Nizwa, we could see the old fort and the freshwater streams. Nizwa was the last town to fall during the Forgotten War in the late 1960s, 1970s, and early 1980s. The British army fought to remove the old ruler, Sultan Qaboos, and install his son as the new Sultan of Oman. In one diving operation, the British military flew me to Salalah in Oman, as it was the only way to get around. I loved Oman, its people, and its history. I loved Nizwa. It was a fantastic place with its old fort and old ways. Later on, I managed to get some photos of the locals and the freshwater streams. I was outside the old fort of Nizwa, taking pictures of locals who didn't mind being photographed in their traditional attire and wearing khanjars.

I just loved being there. It was a million miles from my everyday life. I was changing so much that I loved everything I did on my boy's adventure. I was no longer thinking about the real world. If only Tom Hooper, my old foreman, could see me now, miles away from the white walls and the lathe machine, staring at the same wall for 40 years, I was now surrounded by real living history in Oman. What an adventure I was on, and I loved it! It was a fantastic day out, and I could not wait for the next foul-weather day off, but I had to return to the real world somewhere along the way.

I was at the freshwater streams that ran through Nizwa.

I was not expecting to find this area so beautiful. It was real Beau Geste stuff, freshwater streams in the mountains of northern Oman.

Into the Blue and Beneath The Waves

Outside Nizwa Castle and with the local sheep herders.

It was fascinating for me to walk around these old forts and see the locals still living as they had been for many thousands of years; the locals loved their way of life and were not bothered by living in modern houses or apartments. They were happy with their simple way of life, but changes were coming as the younger generation was being educated more. However, the youngsters respected their old way of living and culture, and their old ways would always be respected as the country transitioned to a modern way of life.

I am outside the old fort with an original cannon by the fort's main gates.

It was time to head back to my camp, but what a few hours I had touring around Nizwa! I loved every minute of seeing old parts of Oman. It was an excellent opportunity to see parts of a country I would typically never have seen, as I was usually on a work barge or a diving vessel. It was time to return and start work again, but I felt great and enjoyed myself.

On June 28th, we resumed diving on the SBM hoses to a depth of 135 feet, connecting hydraulic hoses to clamps along the SBM hoses and down to the PLEM. This was an enjoyable diving operation that took us about five days to complete. One day, we were told that if we wanted to, we could bring people offshore on Friday onto our work barge for an open day so people could see how we worked and dived. Our boss thought this was a great idea and asked us to find out who was eager to come out for the open work day on our work barge.

We asked around and got to know a few of the nurses, including a Welsh scaffolder and a keen amateur diver who couldn't wait to go out for the open day with us. What we didn't realise until our guests arrived was that they had brought a fantastic box full of beer, soft drinks, cheese, crackers, fruit, and bread and asked us if this was okay. We just laughed and said it was fine. It was great. The weather was perfect, and after we had completed a few dives, our guests asked if they could go diving in our professional diving equipment. We looked at our supervisor, who says, "Yes, why not? Great, let's go for it." We did check that they had diving certificates, and they all had PADI dive certificates and medicals; in those days, that was enough. You can see in the pictures below that the Walsh scaffolder is getting ready to dive, with the nurses assisting with all the diving equipment.

Graham Watts, Tommy Smith, the Walsh Scaffolder, Stewart Gibbons, our supervisor, Dee, and Victoria, the SBM, will be diving in.

What a fantastic day it was for all of us! When do you get a chance to bring guests out to go diving on an SBM with a cooler box of food and drinks? Even the local fishermen came out to see if we wanted to buy some fish from them. It was an experience that is generally not encountered in professional diving. Our guests had a great day out, as we did, and it was a moment that has stayed with me for years.

It was time to return to the real world, as the operation was nearing its close. I did not want it to end, but it had to, and now I had to face going home to Rose and the kids. I left Oman and flew home on July 31, 1986. I thought it would be okay once I got home; life would be fine, and I would move on, as Dee had done. She was off to tour Peru on a train, and we would forget about each other. However, it never worked out that way for either of us. We both couldn't stop thinking of each other. In time, we thought our feelings would pass; however, they never did. We had a fantastic experience together in Oman, one that cannot be put aside, as I was married with two kids. I was no longer sure what to do, apart from waiting for the next phone call to return to the Middle East.

Chapter Nineteen
Away from Home, French Royalty and being exoceted.

Where do I begin? I won't be writing about who did this and who said that. I take full responsibility for giving everyone a horrible time while I was home. My mind was still away in Oman, not in Liverpool, and as much as I tried to forget everything about Oman and Dee, I couldn't. Rose was still not well, and her mother was attending to everything, but I was not giving my full attention to Rose or the kids; I was selfish, as I wanted the new life I had found. I wanted to be single again and start living a life which I never thought possible; I wanted to travel and have an adventure, and the more I thought about it, the more I was pushing everyone away: Rose, Chris and Grace, who was very young and did not know anything as Grace had not spent much time at all with me as I was always away and now I look back I was not a great father to them at all.

In September 1986, the Vice President of CCCUE, Dave Penson, called me to ask if I could fly out to supervise a diving inspection operation for Total Abu Al Bakhoosh from the vessel Conoco 111. "Yes," I said. I was happy to be away from all the problems I had created. But then he said to me that he was not pleased to be told who would supervise the inspection operation. He was only asking me to be the diving supervisor, as I had been requested by Total Abu Al Bakhoosh; he had no say in the matter. He said he would sort me out once I was out in Abu Dhabi, about me pulling strings to get the job, but I told him I didn't know what he was on about, as I had not pulled any strings to get the job. Dave was not having any of it, and he would see me once I was in Abu Dhabi.

I flew out on September 8, 1986, and was taken directly to the vessel in Abu Dhabi's freeport from the airport once I had landed, along with the rest of the dive team. After a night's rest and getting to meet the other divers, I received a phone call from Dave telling me to get the vessel clean and tidy as the president of Total Middle East was coming to meet with all the other senior people of Total Middle East. Dave said to me he didn't know what strings I was pulling. Still, he was unhappy and warned me about pulling strings.

Eventually, the president of Total and his entourage arrived on the jetty where our vessel was moored and asked if he could meet the 'French' royal family member of the dive crew, Mr de Beaufort. I shouted back, "Hi, wack, that is me; what can I do for you?" in my Scouse accent. "No, no," he said, "I want to meet the royal Frenchman, Mr de Beaufort." (My surname is from one of the royal French families from when France had royal families.) "No, that is me. I am from Liverpool; my dad was an Indian Frenchman from the royal side of France a time long ago." "You are not French; no." I said, "I am from Liverpool." "Liverpool," he said. "Yes, I told him, the home of the Beatles." "The Beatles," he said in his French accent. "Yes, the Beatles," I said. "I love the Beatles," he said, "my favourite band, my favourite music. I love this man from Liverpool. He is a royal Frenchman from the home of my favourite band, the Beatles." Then, he turned around, jumped back into his limousine with his entourage and left.

The CCCUE VP, Mr Dave Penson, looked down at me and said, "We got this job because the president of Total thought you were a member of a French royal family." "Yes, Dave," I said, "it looked that way." Dave could not stop laughing and realised that I had not been pulling any strings. It was just my surname that got me the diving supervisor position. He then told me to take all the divers out for a meal and drinks at the company's expense and have a great evening. We all headed to the local bar, the Ally Pally, which is on Abu Dhabi's Cornish seafront and was the central drinking hub for all the divers that came in and out of Abu Dhabi. The other divers were Boyd Starzynski, Graham Watts, R Gill, and the youngest diver, Paul Bromfield.

They were all great guys who underwent a horrific experience later on in the diving operation when the oil rig we were alongside got hit with three Exocet missiles. Our main diving operation was to inspect all the oil rig platforms and pipelines. It was an incredible operation with a great bunch of guys on the vessel. It was one of the best diving operations I had ever been on. The evenings were also great. We had some drinks offshore, and we would have a BBQ most evenings after work. Some of the guys would also go windsurfing when we went to anchor up for the evening. The client would retrieve his golf clubs, practise his golf swing, and hit golf balls out to sea, which we would look for when we went on pipeline swims. It was a great operation. We were always laughing; we even had a lucky mascot with us, whom we would put on the diving panel and get dressed up in diving gear.

That's Paul Bromfield, a crew member, the bear and me.

Bear on the diving panel, all ready for action.

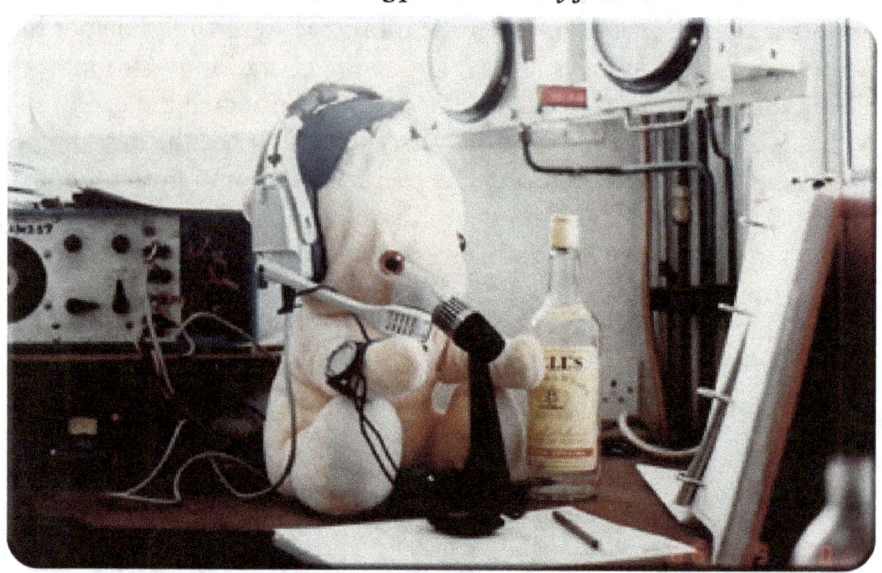

 We all had a great time. Diving started at 07:00 hours daily, with coffee breaks, an hour off for lunch, and work always finished at 17:00 hours. One of our jobs was to remove any debris from around the platforms, and if we came across any fishing nets that had broken free that had drifted to the platforms, we would recover them to the vessel and either free the fish if they could not be eaten or keep the fish, crabs and lobsters we came across for our BBQs which made the crew happy, plus if we had recovered a lot of fish we would gut them, freeze them and take some ashore to sell if we could, which would give us some beer money while we were ashore as we would go into Abu Dhabi every few weeks for supplies.

 I enjoyed the operation, but the problems I had created back home were always on my mind. I was unsure of what I was doing in my private life. Still, I had to ensure I kept my work separate from my problems, as I was running 02 diving operations using the Comex in-water 02 diving tables, which I found to be excellent diving tables; not everyone liked the Comex in-water 02 tables, but we never had any problems, and the divers got used to Comex dive tables. I sometimes pretended to have issues with the 02 in-water tables and put the headphones over my face whenever the client walked past the dive control room, which always made the client laugh. I also did my fair share of diving, as I enjoyed exploring the oil rig platforms, where the fish life was beautiful and very colourful.

I'm in the dive control room and getting ready to carry out an inspection dive.

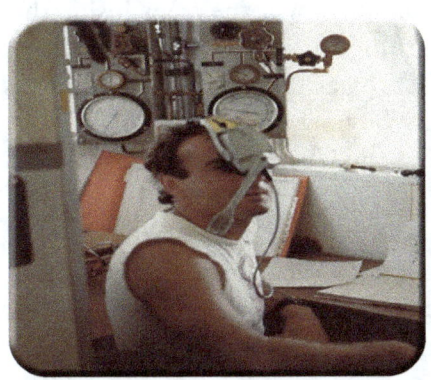

Everything was going great; the divers were having a good time; the client was pleased with the progress of the inspection operation, but little did we know what was coming. Not far away from us was an Iranian oil field complex. It was very similar to our oilfield complex but did not cause anyone any problems. We had the local UAE Navy in the area due to the issues with Iran and Iraq, but no one had any issue with the UAE, so we never felt in any danger. We had grown accustomed to the military jets flying overhead, checking the area as the UAE sought to ensure its oilfields were safe and protected.

But then, one day, all hell broke loose. During lunch, while the divers were sleeping, I was in the dive control room preparing the photo equipment for the afternoon dives. Suddenly, I heard jets flying overhead at some speed; I then noticed the ship's sides were coming towards me as if they were being squeezed inwards, which was a very odd experience. This was followed by two big explosions sending the boat sideways with such force that it broke all the mooring lines on the ship's port side, and then all the port hole windows/doors in the dive control room blew inwards due to the force of the explosions. Luckily for me, the force knocked me down before all the glass flew across the dive control room. As I ran outside, more jets flew over us. We were alongside a Maersk oil rig, which was hit with three Exocet Missiles. Two of them went off. The third kept going round and round on the oil rig deck, at the same time, all the divers/crew came running up from their cabins shouting what the fxxk happened; it was then we realised the ship was drifting away from the rig's boat platform and all the ship's power had gone off.

We noticed the oil rig workers coming down the steps inside the rig platform, trying to escape the burning rig. I ran up to the bridge to get the captain and the Ch-engineer to get the ship's engine up and running so we could return alongside the boat landing to pick up the rig workers. I then saw the captain and the Ch-engineer were lying on the deck covered in glass as most of the windows on the bridge had been blown out, and they were in shock. As I had been on the ship for a long time the captain sometimes let me control the boat, which now came in handy. I went onto the bridge as the second engineer started up an engine and electrical power; I then took the vessel back alongside the boat landing to pick up the rig workers that were coming down the inside of the platform rig. 90 of the oil rig workers came down and onto the boat plus there were a couple of dead oil rig workers. Our ship was only designed to house 28 people, but now we had 90 oil rig workers onboard, so we had 118 people on the vessel, plus the two dead guys on the deck. We did not have any air conditioning as that had been damaged, and there were no portholes as they had been blown out, so it was roasting on the ship, and this was the height of summer in the Middle East. After we had got everyone on board, the senior rig supervisor carried out a head check to see if anyone was left on the oil rig; after he had completed his head check, we pulled away to escape the burning oil rig when the local UAE navy opened fire on us as they did not know what was going on. They just started shooting at anything that moved. We managed to hide behind the burning oil rig, and the Navy stopped firing at us as more jets appeared and began firing missiles at the main oil complex. The Navy then left us to proceed towards the main complex, providing some protection and attempting to safeguard the Echo Maru oil tanker.

The oil rig is ablaze after the missile attack.

We did not know what to do, as the ship's radios were going mad, and all the other vessels in the area asked for instructions. They were unsure what to do: move away or hide, or would they also become targets? It was a frightening experience for everyone, and no one was in control; all you could hear was screaming over the ship's radios with military jets flying overhead. It was horrible not knowing what to do. It took us 12 hours to get permission from the UAE Navy to leave the area and sail to Sharjah on one engine. Before we did that, we had to offload the dead oil rig workers onto the Echo Maru oil tanker so the bodies could be taken ashore by helicopter. It took us over 15 hours to sail to the opening of the Sharjah Creek, where the Danish ambassador met us to remove all the Danish oil rig workers.

Our ship then continued its journey into Sharjah, where CCCUE had their own harbour; the CONOCO 111 looked like a complete mess with blown-out port holes, no cabin doors, and gunshot holes; the vessel was damaged everywhere, with no AC, no port holes, no doors, or windows, the ship was a mess, our company VP, Mr Dave Penson, met us at the CCCUE base and looked at me, smiled and said, "de Beaufort, what the fxxk have you done to my ship?" It was a great comment and made us all laugh. Dave then gave me a load of money.

He said, take all the divers to the Hyatt Regency Hotel in Dubai, where rooms, food, etc. had been booked for us and just get everyone drunk, and when the money runs out, let him know as he would send us more money until a decision was made about what to do with the inspection operation and repairs to the vessel had been carried out.

We all set off to Dubai to check into the hotel, and then we hit the bar; we were having a great time, having plenty of drinks and food, when all of a sudden, a young blond lady tapped me on the shoulder and said, "Are you the supervisor of these guys?" The young man standing next to her which was Paul Bromfield. I said, "I was. Has Paul been telling you that three Exocets had hit us and we had rescued 90 oil field workers, been machine-gunned, and had to sail for 15 hours on one engine to Sharjah, and then been given a load of money to come into Dubai and get drunk and have a great time until we go back offshore." "Yes," she said. I told her that Paul tells that story to every girl whenever we come to Dubai, as it's his chat-up line. She then turns around, throws her drink all over Paul, and walks out. Paul is standing there soaking wet and asks me why did I tell her that it was his chat-up line. I said to him, "Look, young man, if we aren't getting lucky tonight with a bird, neither are you." Then we all started laughing and carried on drinking and having a great time for the next few days.

After about five days, we got a call to head back to the head office as a decision had been made about our operation, that after all the repairs to the vessel had been completed, we were to head back out to Total ABK oilfield to continue with the underwater inspections on the oil rig jackets that the Exocets had not hit. We were told to stay away from the damaged oil rig and main complex as no one was sure if there had been any unexploded Exocets in those areas. We headed back out and saw some of the damage to the main complex. It didn't look very good from a distance. We also heard that it was the Iraqi Air Force that had mistaken the TOTAL ABK oilfield complex for the Iranian complex, which was close by, which is why they knew how many Exocets had been fired. These Exocets had to be accounted for before anyone could make the area around the central complex safe.

The right-hand picture shows some of the damage to the main complex, with the pipes hanging in the water and a hole in the top section of an office.

I didn't realise it then, as there was no internet or mobile phones, and the news channels were not great, but the attack was mentioned in many international newspapers. I don't know if it was heard at home, as I never contacted anyone about it. I wrote Dee a letter, as we were still in contact, but we didn't know if we would see each other again, since working away from home is never easy. Dee did get back from Peru, but she found it difficult touring as she was still thinking of me and how I was coping with everything, so it was unknown to us what would happen. I finished running the last dive on November 8, 1986, and we sailed into the CCCUE base in Sharjah to offload all the equipment, complete the diving inspection reports, and catch up on some mail that Dee had sent me about her trip to Peru.

Dee had had a wonderful time, but I had to head home to check on everything. It was not good; nothing had improved; it was a horrible time for the kids, for Rose, and no matter what, it was all down to me, and it was the worst Christmas I could ever remember. Everything was affecting the kids, and I just wanted to be away, as being there was causing too many problems. I flew back to Abu Dhabi on January 6, 1987, to return to Total ABK, as everywhere had been declared safe. They wanted us to conduct underwater inspections on all the platforms that had been attacked to check for any damage underwater. I was also assigned to a larger dive team, as Total ABK required more dives throughout the day, given that we worked from 06:00 hours to 18:00 hours each day.

I noticed this time that my mind was on home a lot more, and I had to make sure I was concentrating on the operation at hand, as we would also be using Comex in-water O2 repetitive diving tables, which I had used many times. Still, it was new for some of my extra divers on this operation. They were a bit concerned about using in-water O2 repetitive dive tables, so I ensured that the divers who had used them before were the first to use them, allowing the new divers to see that these Comex in-water O2 dive tables were suitable. Our first few days were taken by surprise as we could now see the full extent of the damage to the main complex and the surrounding platforms.

It was not until we saw the damage up close that we realised what the workers on the platform had gone through; it must have been horrendous. One of the first operations was to inspect all the platform support beams and the main complex legs for any damage, in case the missing Exocets had struck the primary structure of each oil rig support member. We also had to swim around the seabed and recover any work boots or clothing that was on the seabed into bags, in case any body parts were in them. Hence, we treated that part of the recovery thoughtfully and respectfully, as some workers still needed to be accounted for.

We also had to inspect all the pipelines, from the seabed to the surface, to check if any missiles had struck them. It was a vast underwater inspection operation, and we were very busy. Due to the nature of the operation, it was all carried out in a relaxed atmosphere. Every evening, we would go out to anchor after work and have a BBQ and a few drinks with all the guys and the client, who was still practising his golf swing. We even built him a driving range mat on the upper deck where he could hit as many golf balls as he wanted out to sea. We would recover them during pipeline inspections.

There was no time limit on this operation as TOTAL wanted everything inspected before they would commence an oilfield operation. They had numerous repairs to be carried out on the main complex and wanted to ensure that everything, from top to bottom, was safe to operate.

The guys and I enjoy our BBQ and a few drinks after work. That's me in the yellow top and blue trousers.

The Maersk oil rig that we were next to when it got hit with the Exocets was still in position as the oil rig legs had been damaged, and the rig could not be lowered to the surface of the water for it to be towed away so they had to bring in a big floating ship which would fit under the oil rig. It was a complex operation to lower the oil rig onto the floating boat, which could be flooded and then pumped dry to raise and lower the boat. Still, we were told to keep a distance as it was hectic around the recovery of that oil rig. We were also asked if we could bring any fresh fish to the main complex that we caught of an evening at anchor; we would go fishing as there were plenty of fish in the area as the locals were not allowed back into the area yet. A few guys had a fishing licence so of an evening while having a BBQ we would fish from the side of the ship. One day, we were allowed onto the main complex to look around as we dropped some fresh fish for them. It was quite a sight to see all the damage up close and to see how far some of the shrapnel had travelled through the complex. You could see through some of the damaged areas to where the shrapnel ended up. It was unbelievable, and it gave us an insight into the terrible day for the guys working at the main complex, as you can see from the pictures below.

That's me about to dive onto one of the structures for an underwater inspection before a missile hit it, as shown in the photo below.

The main complex below is part of the main complex hit by a missile.

It was unbelievable to think that I had dived close to the main complex before it was hit and then come back and see the damage caused by the missile attack. We were allowed to walk around the complex, but we were not allowed to enter any areas that were roped off. Many stairways had been badly damaged and needed replacing, and the other regions had big holes in the decking that had to be repaired or renewed, as you will see from the photos below.

You can see the pipeline hanging in the water as there used to be a bridge across the two structures, but it was hit with a missile and is now lying on the seabed.

In this picture, you can see more pipelines hanging down, as the bridge supporting them was located on the seabed. Additionally, a large hole is visible in the top of the central complex.

Wandering around was a humbling experience for us all, as it made us realise just what those guys had gone through on the day of the attack. Although we had gone through a significant attack, it was because we were next to an oil rig, no one was looking to target our vessel. Unlike our boat, the main complex and the oil rig were deliberate and planned targets, which happened to be in the wrong spot at the wrong time.

As I walked around, I could see the damage; numerous holes were visible where metal fragments had pierced areas of the main complex after the missiles struck. It was unbelievable to see the extent of the damage around the complex. No wonder there were so many injuries.

The damage was unbelievable. Walking around the complex, I saw all the metal twisted and ripped apart like a lump of cheese. It must have been frightening for the oil rig workers.

After dropping off the fresh fish, I returned to CONOCO 111 to continue our underwater inspection of all the structures' main supports and sea-bed surveys to ensure that no Exocet missile was lying on the sea bed around the complex or wellhead platforms. On February 16, 1987, I finished the last dive and inspection on the TOTAL ABK oil complexes. Apart from the damage to the main complex, we found no evidence of damage to the underwater structures caused by the missiles. The complex was given the all-clear to resume the topside remedial work, and all the underwater pipelines were also given the all-clear to start pumping oil again. My dive team and I were then transferred to another diving operation off Dubai on the 23rd of February, a vessel called MT Norris Tide, to carry out an underwater grouting and sandbagging operation in 130 feet of water, which was not as exciting as looking for lost Exocets, but at least it was another job. At the time, I did not realise it was getting harder and harder for CCCUE to find much diving work, which hit home in a couple of months when I had to start selling my blood to survive. Still, it was no one's fault apart from my own.

Chapter Twenty
Selling my Blood, getting banned from Kuwait to Thailand, Penang, India and Saudi Arabia.

After completing the short grouting operation, I was transferred to a large vessel called the NPCC HLS 2000 to begin installing large offshore platforms in 65 feet of water. The operation was fascinating as it was the largest offshore vessel I had ever worked on. The main crane could lift 2000 tonnes, the diving operation of installing these offshore jackets was the same: making sure the seabed was clear of any debris before positioning the offshore jacket onto the seabed, then supporting the prominent members with sandbags and mud mat lifting frames which you could alter the height of, using hydraulic jacks to level the platform before any drilling would be started inside the legs of the platform so that Caisson pipes could be fitted inside the legs, then grouting would be pumped inside the Caisson legs until it came to the top and over the seabed. The grout would be allowed to harden which secured the platform to the seabed.

The vessel and crane hook were enormous, and they needed to be if they were to lift 2000 tons.

The 2000-ton crane lifts significant offshore platforms into position.

The operation went on for a couple of weeks. I enjoyed my time on the vessel, as there was plenty of space, reasonable accommodation, and food, but my personal life was always on my mind. I found it was affecting my work, as I could think of nothing else as each job ended, and I had to take some leave.

Throughout the early period of 1987, I found everyone at home and work was troubled by my concerns. I loved my kids, but I was not a good dad, as I was always away. I was not a good husband to Rose, who was severely affected by my selfish attitude of finding a new life, which I was enjoying while working away but not enjoying at home, which was always causing arguments. The kids were disturbed, and deep down, I knew I would leave as I was no good to anyone staying at home. I decided to pay off the mortgage and leave all our money in our joint bank account for Rose. In early 1987, after another big argument, I packed my bags and went on a return air ticket to Dubai from CCCUE from my last operation thinking that I would not worry, I would get a job with CCCUE and keep sending money home for Rose and the kids. Everything would be all right, and I will start a new life with Dee. Life is not that simple, which I was about to find out. I did not think it all through or consider the hurt I would leave behind, so what happened in the following months was all my fault.

Upon arrival in Dubai, I made my way to Sharjah and booked the Sharjah Beach Hotel for a couple of days, as I thought I would pick up some work with CCCUE in no time at all, which was not going to be the case as it was very quiet offshore in the Gulf throughout 1987. I got a couple of days of work on a jack-up barge called the SEP 250; I booked myself back into the Sharjah Beach Hotel and thought I would hang around, and something would come up. I let CCCUE know I was available for anything at any time. "Okay," they said, "but there's nothing, so there are no problems." I thought everything would be ok. Dee knew I was in Sharjah, but she had her job to concentrate on. I did not realise how bad things were regarding work, and there was just nothing out there. I had no money coming in, and I had to pay for the hotel room, which was now mounting up on my credit cards. As I had three of them, I was using all three, thinking it would be okay in the end. I had stopped eating breakfast and had nothing for lunch. In the evening, I would have some soup and bread, but even that was using money I didn't have. I kept believing that work would soon come in, and to pass the time, I would walk around Sharjah each day on my own. Dee would call, but I never told her how bad it was; she offered me some money to get by, but it never felt right to take money from her. She never knew how bad it was.

During my walks around Sharjah, I came across local blood banks, and I would often see people waiting outside to be called in to donate their blood. It was a common thing in the UAE to sell your blood for around 200 dirhams, which was about £40. I knew a lot of the divers used to sell their blood in Abu Dhabi to cover their drinks when they had a run ashore. I knew that no checks were carried out, and anyone could sell their blood; I was beginning to think I should start doing that if things just carried on as they were. One week later, I had no choice; I had no money coming in, and bills were coming in, so I decided I would start selling my blood to get some money, as I had stopped eating daily and could only eat every few days. I was living rough, and the hotel had started inquiring with CCCUE about who was paying for the hotel room, as my visa was with them. CCCUE then asked me what was going on. I told them not to worry and that I would sort everything out, so I maxed out one of my credit cards without paying it off and checked out of the hotel. I slept on the beach hammocks and used the local washrooms, which were not great, but what else could I do?

I went to the first blood bank, signed in, gave a pint of blood, and received 200 dirhams in cash. It seemed like a million pounds, but it meant I could eat something that night, but I did not know how long the money would last me. I had a bowl of soup and some local bread on the beach; while on the beach, I noticed a guy from the blood bank and said 'hello' and got talking to him; he was giving blood three times a week at different blood banks, and each one gave you cash and told me that local taxis would ferry people around once they had six customers in the taxi. The cab would not move onto a blood bank until he had six guys, and it would only cost 5 dirhams about (50 p) for each trip, so in a week, I could get 600 dirhams, which was around £140, and would cover me for food and the odd night or two in the beach hotel. So that's what I started to do. It was the only way of getting money to survive until work began to come in.

Little did I know that work was not forthcoming, so I had to find different blood banks around Sharjah, Ajman and Dubai, anywhere really that I could sell my blood. I was beginning to look like a pincushion. Dee knew I was struggling to pass the time as nothing happened daily, and Dee offered me money to help. I would not take any money from her. She had a few days off, so she decided to fly to Sharjah to see me and help out, which was a great relief. We stayed in the Sharjah Beach Hotel while Dee was there, but Dee could tell I was struggling to cope. Seeing her gave me some hope that things would improve, hopefully very soon. After Dee flew back to Oman,

I returned to sell more blood. Money was money, and I had given up caring where I got money from. At long last, I heard that a job might be available on the HLS 2000 in Kuwait if I were interested. If I were interested!? I jumped at the opportunity to do some work and even volunteered to help mobilise the job, which included food and a cabin to sleep in on the vessel. CCCUE accepted my offer to mobilise for the job and paid me $50 a day, which was a fortune, and I could stop selling my blood. God knows how many pints of blood I sold, but I did not blame anyone, as it was all my making. I had hoped this would be the turning point.

The operation in Kuwait was not a long diving operation for me, just around four weeks at $130 a day, but it was a job. I heard that other jobs were starting to come in, so I was feeling more confident that I could begin paying off my debts on the credit cards I had run up overseas and at home. If any jobs were available, I was ready to take them on. The operation in Kuwait was installing a boat landing in 40 feet of water. We had two shifts, working 12 hours a day, 7 days a week, but I didn't mind, as I was working, sleeping, eating, and earning money. The operation went well, and along with mobilisation and sailing to Kuwait on the vessel, I earned around six weeks' worth of funds, approximately $5,000 US dollars. So, I was delighted, but then I got into trouble when I went ashore in Kuwait. As I had sailed into Kuwait on my Seaman's book, I should never have left the vessel. I should have stayed on the ship and sailed back with the boat. So now the Kuwait authorities held me in their holding pen as an illegal immigrant as I did not have an entry stamp on my passport. The authorities informed me that a request would be made to the British council to tell them that the Kuwait authorities have a British subject in their holding pen. I could not believe it. Just when I thought everything was going well, I get put into a holding pen. Luckily for me, the captain of the HLS 2000 heard about my problems and contacted the shipping agent for the HLS 2000 in Kuwait to see if he could use his contacts to help me leave the country. The shipping agent came back to me looking very worried as now the Kuwait authorities were asking questions concerning the photos in my passport and my Seaman's book. As far as the Kuwait authorities were concerned, they were two different people, and as from the pictures below I could see why they would think that.

I could not believe my luck or bad luck. After a lot of back and forth in which money was exchanged, I was informed that I would be kicked out of Kuwait and would never be allowed back, and I was escorted out of the country. I was taken to the airport, where I was stamped into Kuwait, then stamped out immediately and sent to Dubai. From there, I went to the British Embassy in Oman to obtain a new passport photo.

Seaman's Book Photo, Old Passport Photo, New Passport Photo

I was now back in Oman, living in Dee's accommodation in an area called Al Khoud, which was a great help while I was waiting on more work, which was still slow coming, but every little bit was helpful and kept me going, and I was able to continue to pay off my credit cards. Plus, I did not have to sell my blood anymore, and my arms stopped looking like a pincushion. With the few jobs I was getting from CCCUE, I had saved enough money to travel to Thailand with Dee for a couple of weeks. Additionally, CCCUE covered the air ticket costs, as I had completed enough jobs to offset the expenses.

We travelled as cheaply as we could around Thailand. We spent a few days in Bangkok before travelling north to Chiang Mai on the local bus, which took hours and hours. It was amazing to see the countryside along the way before arriving in Chiang Mai, where we would spend two weeks touring around Chiang Mai and Chiang Rai on a Honda 50, but I changed it to a Honda 250 motorbike after a few days. We stayed wherever we could as long as it was not too expensive, the cheaper, the better. We had a great time on the motorbike, even if Dee did fall off the motorbike, as we went up a hill to see the elephants. I never realised Dee had fallen off the motorbike until I got to the top of the mountain and turned around to speak to her only to find she was not there, but when I looked down, she was walking up the hill looking not too amused but laughing at the same time. We had a great time in Chiang Mai, and got to know each other much better; we loved travelling and living cheaply, which was easy in Thailand, and accommodation was very cheap in and around Chiang Rai. We travelled to Chiang Rai to have a look around when on the way we noticed all these cottages with thatched roofs. We wondered what they were when we came across an entrance to these cottages and saw it was a national park with a coffee shop and a reception area, so we decided to stop and have something to eat, drink, and look around.

We discovered that an old tea clipper captain who had bought some of the land and built cottages was from Cornwall, missed home, but loved the area. When he died, he passed the land on to the local rulers, who eventually handed over all the land and dwellings to the Thai National Parks. Then we found out that we could rent any of the cottages, which were relatively inexpensive. Additionally, all the local food was sourced directly from the park, making it very affordable. We decided to spend a couple of nights there and have a look at the area, which we found out was very close to the Golden Triangle, which was a name given to the region by America due to the location being well-known for its heroin and other drugs. We checked in and started to explore the area, which was terrific. Besides the fantastic countryside, the area was also famous for its redwood furniture, which was produced in small warehouses along the roadside. If you stopped to look around, you could get a free beer with the hope that you would buy some of the stuff they were making, and I have to say it was terrific.

One of the roadside warehouses where they made the redwood furniture.

We travelled a lot around the countryside of Chiang Rai. We saw many interesting items, but suddenly came across working elephants, not just the ones in special areas for viewing elephants. It was fantastic to see working elephants up close in the countryside. We came across this by accident, and it made our trip out in the countryside well worth it.

We decided to head back to our accommodation to get some rest and something to eat as we were planning to travel to the tip of the Golden Triangle the following morning to say we had been there and seen the three countries that make up the Golden Triangle which are Thailand, Myanmar or Burma and Laos, when we got back, Dee had eaten something that did not agree with her. She spent the night rushing back and forth to the toilet, and the following day, Dee was not feeling very well and had to spend the day in bed but told me to go out and see the Golden Triangle, so I set off on our motorbike on my own and went to the tip of the Golden Triangle to say I been there. Still, you were looking across a vast range of countryside, but I had done it. I returned to our accommodation, and when I got back, Dee was much better. Whatever food bug hit her had cleared up, so we decided to walk around the National Park and its thatched cottages before heading back to Chiang Mai.

Our Cornish Cottage in Chiang Rai National Park.

Our first motorbike, and feeding the elephants in Chiang Mai.

We had a great time and got on well, but it was time to head back to the Middle East. We hoped to return to Thailand to explore more of it and see more of Bangkok. I returned to Sharjah after hearing some work was coming up, and Dee returned to Oman. I picked up a few small jobs. Then, at long last, I got a diving job for a few months that would take me up to the middle of December 1987. In those days, we did not have the internet or mobile phones, but I could communicate by writing letters, which I hated because I couldn't write or spell very well. I did receive mail now and then, mainly bills from home, which was fine, as I still had responsibilities, even if I had walked away from Rose and the kids. This was not Rose's fault or the kids' fault; it was mine. I have to accept what I did, which, looking back, was not great – just jumping onto a plane and going. However, that's what I did, and I had to move on. Nevertheless, it never stopped me from thinking about the kids all the time.

At the beginning of October 1987, I had to mobilise the Conoco 111 once more for the annual underwater inspection of the ABK oil field with the same team of divers from the previous operations at ABK. It was great to meet all the guys again. The diving operation once more utilised Comex in water at O2 stops, but by now, the guys had grown accustomed to them and were very happy to continue using them. One of the guys had brought a spear gun, as there were loads of fish around the platforms, especially tuna, which was a mighty fish, as I discovered to my horror. I was sitting on a member of the platform in about 20 feet of water in scuba when a few tuna were going past me, and I shot one of the tuna with the spear gun; what happened next still makes me shiver; the tuna shot towards me and went around the back of my head, and the wire on the spear also went around the back of my head and started to pull the mouthpiece of my diving bottles and then the fish shot to the seabed which was about 100 feet deep. I could do nothing as I was pulled down to the seabed with the wire around my neck and face, and I could not slacken the wire. As we hit the seabed, the spear broke loose from the tuna, and the strain on the wire stopped. I never felt such relief as at that moment, and I gathered myself together and swam back to the surface after a short decompression stop. I never went spearfishing again after that.

The diving operation proceeded smoothly, with no further incidents. On December 7th, we completed our last dive of 1987. After completing all the paperwork for the operation and attending to the mail and bills that had accumulated, I set off to Oman for Christmas with Dee. After Christmas, we headed to Thailand for a diving holiday to Phuket via Bangkok; it would be like a busman's holiday for me to go diving. Dee was a very keen sports diver, and it was an adventure for us both as we stopped off in Bangkok for a few days, then headed on to Phuket and finished up in Penang, Malaysia. One thing that did come up from Dee was, after reading the letters I had sent her, Dee realised I was dyslexic, which at the time meant nothing to me apart from I must be thick, which I had always thought as I hated writing letters and filling in reports. I used to get the guys to double-check them for me before I would submit them to any client.

Dee was surprised that I could remember details and books from years back, or recall a conversation from months ago. I was reluctant to talk about it as I did not fully understand anything about being dyslexic, and at that time, there was no Google to look up. I hated studying stuff about anything unless I had to, but Dee was not letting it go, so I thought it best if I listened to what she was trying to explain to me. I could see a lot of what Dee was explaining, and I could recall small details and technical information from years past, so maybe I wasn't thick. Perhaps I could learn about dyslexia if it was to help me get on in life. I began to notice that more and more clients were asking for specific diving certificates, not just my HSE Part 1 diving certificate, and if I wanted to continue diving, maybe I would need to start going on different diving courses in the future. But first things first, we went on a diving holiday to Thailand.

We flew to Bangkok on January 7, 1988, and landed on January 8. We stayed in a pre-booked hotel for a few days until we figured out how to get a hotel at a low price. I discovered that you can secure a nice room at any hotel by booking through the travel agent located at every hotel office, rather than booking directly at the hotel reception. This seemed odd at first, but it worked, and once settled, we went out and explored Bangkok, which is fantastic. The first thing we did was visit the Oriental Hotel in Bangkok, where Dee wanted to have their famous English tea, which was all we could afford. The tea and cakes were excellent, and everything else was just classy all over the hotel, wherever we looked. Dee could not wait to get a photo of her going up the steps at the hotel, and afterwards, we headed to the Marble Palace, which was unbelievable.

Into the Blue and Beneath The Waves

The stairs in the Oriental Hotel, and we're going for afternoon tea and temples in the Royal Palace.

This time in Bangkok, we arranged for a local guide to show us the sights instead of just wandering around. Her name was Charlie. She was fun and a good tour guide. We had never seen anything like the royal palace or the marble palace, which was known to be unreal. We enjoyed exploring the palace grounds and having Charlie show us around. She took us to the golden Buddha, which was 5 tons of gold and was only found to be of gold when the concrete cover started to fall off as it was being transported many, many years ago to hide it from the Burmese troops and once it was safe, it was put on display for all to see. We also had a good laugh with Charlie as I asked her if she could see the 80 ft concrete Buddha; she said no concrete 80-foot Buddha in Bangkok; we said, but our book says there is one, she said if we find 80-foot concrete Buddha, I buy you a case of beer if no 80-foot concrete Buddha we double her pay for the day. "Ok, deal," I said, so Charlie took us to where our travel book said there was an 80-foot concrete Buddha. Well, I won the bet, got a case of beer, and she asked for our travel book, as she had never seen the 80-foot concrete Buddha. So, we gave Charlie our travel book, as she was so kind.

Charlie, Dee, myself and the Golden Buddha.

The 80-foot concrete Buddha that won me a case of beer from Charlie.

Into the Blue and Beneath The Waves

The whole experience was terrific, but it was time to move on to Phuket for our diving holiday. We flew to Phuket on January 24th, but we had not yet arranged any accommodation. We just thought we could get something once we were there, as there were plenty of places around the beach. I told Dee to wait while I walked along the coast. There were plenty of small beach huts for hire, and I just marched along, looking at places on my own. The Thai girls who rented the beach huts would shout, "Hay Johnny, you come here, I'll give you a good price and will look after you," "Come look at my beach hut." A few huts I looked at were ok, but in the end, I got one with an A/C and toilet at a reasonable price as the Thai girl thought I was on my own. After I paid for the beach hut, I waved to Dee to come and rest in our beach hut. The girl laughed and said, "You are a naughty boy. I offered you a reasonable price since you're single, but if you have a girlfriend, there's no business for me at night."

After we checked into our accommodation, we went to find the diving company to register for our diving trip around the nine Similan tropical Islands. One island has a national park building, but the rest are uninhabited. The Komodo Dragons roam those remaining islands. We were allowed on the islands, but we had to watch out for the Komodo Dragons, and there were big lizards. We registered with the diving company and, after presenting our diving qualifications, we were informed that we could join the yacht the following day, once all the other divers had signed in. We could see the yacht offshore from the beach. The yacht was called the Andaman Explorer and was run by a diving company called Fantasea Divers, Phuket.

We were both very excited and looking forward to sailing and diving around these islands. The following morning, after a night out in Phuket, we loaded all our diving equipment and meagre clothing onto a small Zodiac, as there was limited storage space on the yacht. We would be in a tiny two-man cabin. There were eight divers, two non-divers and the five-man crew. On the first day on the boat, we got to know the other divers and the safety drills for the vessel. We did a few dives before we set off so the captain/owner, who was also a diver, could see each other's level of diving ability and if the owner needed to pair any divers off who were not so proficient in diving and who would do the deeper dives and who would do the shallow water dives. Once the owner was satisfied with everything and understood what people were looking for regarding the dives, we prepared the vessel for sailing. We would sail through the night so that we could arrive at the Similan Islands as the sun rose. Once the yacht was ready to set sail, we had dinner. Jan, the captain, told us what he would do once we reached the Islands. As he would be up most of the night sailing the vessel, his lead diver would take us ashore in the Zodiac or if we wanted to, we could jump off the yacht and swim ashore onto one of the islands as they charged up all the air cylinders. We could chill out on the island, and he would call us back once lunch was ready and he had had some sleep.

The Andaman Explorer is the black yacht on the right.

Dee and I are on the bow as we sail to the Similan Islands.

We arrived as the sun was rising. It looked amazing as we sailed towards the island. The water was crystal clear, and the island was beautiful. The crew dropped anchor, and the yacht settled. I was having a coffee as the sun started to rise, and saw the different colours in the sky as the sun came through a gap in the rocks.

I was up early because I was used to sleeping on vessels, whereas Dee did not get much sleep. After all, she was not used to sleeping on a boat. Eventually, she woke up and joined me on the deck for a coffee and her first look at our location, which she loved. The sea was calm, and the first island was very close, so we decided to swim to the island after breakfast. Apart from Jan, the captain, and the other divers, all the crew were awake by now. We gave the crew a hand in setting up the table for breakfast, but most of us decided to have breakfast on the deck and enjoy the view. Breakfast typically consists of fresh fruit, cereals, toast, eggs, ham, cheese, croissants, coffee, and fresh fruit juices. Sitting on the deck was lovely, as was watching the sun rise and shine down onto the sea, which was so clear that you could see the fish swimming around the yacht. It was not very deep where we had anchored about 10 feet, but it felt like we were floating on air. The water was that clear. Once we had helped clear up all the breakfast utensils, Dee and I got ready to dive overboard and swim to the island, which was uninhabited apart from Komodo dragons, which we were told to stay away from, but also, they very rarely come down to the beach area when there are tourists on the Islands.

From the picture below, you can see how close we were to the island, so Dee and I decided to swim to the beach; a few others waited for the Zodiac to come and pick them up. We took our underwater camera with us so we could take pictures of the island, and you can see just how clear the water is, as the local boats appear to be floating on air. It was just beautiful. The whole experience of being on this island is mind-blowing.

The water was so clear that you could see the shadows of the small boats on the seabed; we couldn't wait to start diving, later in the day. I never thought I would be this excited in looking forward to diving, but it was very different diving to what I was usually used to as it was for pure pleasure; so far from thinking this was going to be like a busman's holiday for me I was enjoying myself in the different environment of being on holiday on a yacht, diving for fun and exploring the islands of which we had time to visit, and dive on and around them, plus I enjoyed helping out on the yacht as part of the crew with putting up the sails etc. It was a wonderful experience. We had only just started our first day.

Jan, the captain and diving supervisor, said we would be using microbubble decompression gauges, which I had never encountered or heard of before. After he explained how they worked, I became very interested in how they functioned. At the same time, I would have an underwater USN dive table with me to double-check what we were diving with, as I had learned over the years not to trust anything that was told to me without verification. The microbubbles worked from a dive gauge that, as you dive deeper, the bubbles would go past a marker line on the indicator, which then would show that you needed to decompress on the way up; as you went up slowly, the bubbles would reduce, and as they reduced, they would go into a safe decompression mode which meant you were ok to continue upwards. I would compare them to my USN dive tables for Dee's safety and mine, but they were new. They worked very well, and in the end, I began to trust them. They were straightforward, and as you went deeper, you could see the decompression bubbles move towards a decompression line; as long as the bubbles did not pass the decompression line, you were ok to continue diving; once the bubbles went past the decompression line, you knew you had to wait for the bubbles to reduce back past the decompression line and you could continue to head upwards to the surface.

Our first dive was jumping in the water off the yacht to have a swim around the bottom of the shallow water and to see the marine life at around 10 to 15 feet; it was fantastic; the water was warm, crystal clear and filled with fish life everywhere. I could not believe just how much I was enjoying the whole experience. Dee had opened up a whole new life for me that I could not have imagined all those years ago when Tom Hooper said to me, "One-day Lad, all of this will be Yours." I never thought that as I was going down to any blood bank, to sell my blood to eat, that I would be in a place like this; my life had changed an unbelievable expanse. My life had become an adventure, from flying over the mountains of Iran and the revolution, to diving in the clear waters of the Similan Islands of Thailand.

That's Dee, a guy from Germany and I getting ready for our first dive off the side of the yacht.

It was just a shallow dive, about 10 feet in warm, blue water, with plenty of beautiful, petite, and very colourful fish. It was a great way to finish our first day on the Similan Islands; we looked forward to the evening meal, a BBQ on the yacht's stern, accompanied by drinks and listening to Chris Rea's music tape, 'On the Beach'.

The following morning, we awoke early to have coffee on the deck and watch the sunrise before having breakfast. This morning, we would go a little deeper, around 40 feet, to see more of the coral. Plus, it was planned that after lunch, we would be diving again, which was Jan's plan to dive shallow in the morning and a bit deeper each afternoon so we could get two dives in each day if we wanted to; some did some didn't, but Dee and I were looking forward to two dives each day, and I would partner Dee in each dive not just because we were together but as a safety buddy when we went deeper. I would keep an eye on Dee to make sure she never got into any difficulties. We would load up all our diving equipment into the Zodiac and set off to a floating buoy that had been dropped into the sea that we would go down on to start our dive; the idea was to dive down to the seabed and swim no farther than 40 foot away from the marker-buoy and keep it in sight at all times – a safety measure, as Jan did not want to lose any divers or divers popping up all over the place.

Dee and I are on the left in the Zodiac, I in red, and Dee on my left, starting our first dive from the zodiac.

Our dive to 40 feet was fantastic. You could see forever, and the coral was incredibly colourful, with lots of vibrant fish everywhere. The water was lovely and warm, with just a slight tide, but nothing too much. We were informed that the tide could get very strong on some islands quickly, so keep an eye for any strong tides. However, Jan hoped all his plans for where and when to dive would go very smoothly. I loved it and was beginning to enjoy this busman's holiday. After we had completed our dive time, Jan instructed everyone on how long to dive before heading back to the marker buoy, so we would all arrive around the same time. That way, he could tell if anyone had drifted off. But everyone arrived safely within a few minutes of each other, and once back on board the Zodiac, our diving equipment was stored, and everyone started talking about their sights of the fish life and the coral. I was not used to this, as it's usually just about pipelines or wellheads, so it was lovely to hear how much these divers enjoyed their underwater experiences. I was smiling as it was nice. Seeing another side of diving was an excellent experience, bringing pure joy to these divers.

I was laughing to myself when Dee asked me what I was laughing about when I explained to her the different stories from sports divers to professional divers after they had been underwater; she also started laughing as she had not thought about the differences. The sports divers looked at everything underwater whereas the professional divers just looked at the job in hand and got on with it. We very rarely stopped and had a look around. It was get in and get the job done, not waste time looking around the seabed.

As you can imagine, with all the diving, washing, cooking and having showers with all those people on the yacht, fresh water had to be looked after; otherwise, we would run out of water very quickly, so everyone was conscious of the need to look after the water supply, but then one morning Jan took us to one of the Islands where you could get fresh water and the best shower in the world. Now, we were all looking to see what was in store for us, and as you can see from the pictures below, it was a neutral spring water shower with the water flowing down from the hills. It was an amazing experience.

Dee was on the stern as we sailed to the island, and many people were coming ashore for a freshwater shower, to wash some clothes, and so on.

We had a freshwater shower, and we could wash our clothes in a big bucket beside me.

It was great having a shower right off the hills. As you can see, the sea was a beautiful blue with a white sandy beach. We had a walk and some lunch, consisting of just fresh fruit, which perfectly suited the whole experience on this beautiful island. After we had all finished having a shower, washing our clothes, and filling up some water cans, we set off back to the yacht, all feeling very clean and refreshed due to the cold-water shower. Everyone was thrilled and loved the whole experience of diving on and around this deserted island apart from one but how could you not love this busman's diving holiday. It certainly was different to any other diving I had done. Perhaps I have been converted to understanding why amateur divers love to go on diving holidays, given that this is what they do while on holiday.

We had a few days left, and the dives were getting a little deeper to around 100 feet; a couple of the divers decided to give those dives a miss as they wanted to go snorkelling around the island, but I was happy to dive that deep to see what the coral was like at that depth. It was amazing. Some of the clamshells were so big that you could sit in them. I had never seen clamshells like that, and the water was crystal clear even at that depth. Dee and I headed back to the surface as the micro-bubbles on our depth gauges had passed the decompression line. We headed up slowly until the micro-bubbles reached the non-decompression line. It amazed me – this depth decompression gauge. It worked well, but I still double-checked the USN decompression table card. The micro-gauge worked well. Once we reached the surface, we climbed onboard the Zodiac and returned to the yacht with the other divers to store all our diving gear and prepare for dinner.

The following day was our last full day around the islands, so we would dive from the yacht while the crew prepared the boat for sailing that evening, as Jan wanted to get back to Phuket the following morning. After the last of our dives, everything stored, and dinner finished, Jan told us to watch the front of the yacht as we sailed away, and it could not have ended any better; as we sailed away from the islands, the dolphins started jumping up at the bow of the yacht, it was a great way of ending the fantastic visit to the Similan Islands.

Below are the dolphins following us as we left the Similan Islands. It was the perfect way to leave the islands.

As we sailed away, Jan again played Chris Rea's 'On the Beach'. It was just the right music to listen to while drinking under the stars and with the sails up as we headed to Phuket. We had one night to spend in Phuket before we headed to Penang, Malaysia. The following morning, as we approached Phuket, we could see a large American Naval ship anchored outside the port. Jan told us the navy ships came to Phuket for Rest & Recuperation or RR from the Arabian Gulf. The evening in Phuket when the navy was in town would be very lively as the navy guys would be chasing all bar girls as would be the single guys on holiday so expect fireworks he told us as they usually all got drunk and would end up fighting for the bar girls. Jan was not wrong at all; as we approached Phuket, we could see all the bars putting up loads of welcome signs to welcome the USN to Phuket, and as we went ashore, we could see all these small navy boats heading ashore with all their Yankee dollars to spend in the bars and on the bar girls. After checking into our accommodation for the night, Dee and I decided to stay away from the main area that evening. In the morning, I headed to the central part of the beach and bar area. It was a sight to behold with all the navy lads heading back to their ship with the bar girls hanging onto them, shouting, "I love you, Johnny, don't leave me," with quite a few in handcuffs as they had been fighting with the single guys on holiday over the bar girls. What a way to finish our trip to Phuket!

On January 17th, 1988, we landed in Penang for a week to tour the island. We were unsure what to find, so we booked a hotel called

Into the Blue and Beneath The Waves

One Pine Tree. As we were taken to the hotel by taxi, we could have a good look at the surrounding areas and houses, which we found very odd as it was like being in an area of Surbiton in London, which the taxi driver told us was from the time when the British ruled the island in the colonial period. The houses had stood the test of time and were sought after by the well-off. When we reached the hotel, we could see why it was called the One Pine Tree Hotel, as it had one pine tree in the driveway. After checking in, we met with our tour guide to discuss our upcoming jungle trek the following morning. We needed to find out where to meet, which was very easy, as the trek would start outside our hotel. We walked into town to have a drink, but we found out there were no bars. If you wanted a drink, you had to go to a restaurant for a meal and a drink, as it was a Muslim country, but that was fine. We had no issues with that, as we wanted some food anyway. The following morning, we woke up early, had breakfast, and prepared a packed lunch to take with us.

We were looking forward to the tour of the local jungle, as we were unsure what we would see or hear, or how many people would also be on the trek. When we all met up, there were about 20 people from all over the world. It was nice, and our tour guide gave a small speech about what we could expect to see and hear. So, we set off into the jungle, which was very humid, but we didn't mind, we were accustomed to the humidity. As we entered the jungle, we heard all these birds singing away. The tour guide would point out to us where the bird songs were coming from and the names of the birds which was very helpful if we wanted to take pictures of the birds when all of a sudden he stopped and looked around as he had come across a bird song he had never heard in the jungle before. He stopped everyone and kept looking up and down at the trees as we all did to try and follow the bird song as it was a new experience for him. He thought he had come across a new species when all of a sudden he looked at me and said the song was coming from me which confused me somewhat, when Dee said it was from my Casio watch and asked if I switched the alarm off this morning. The bird song was the alarm call I had set but forgot to switch off; at least everyone had a good laugh including the tour guide. The tour was fantastic, as we saw a wide variety of birds and butterflies everywhere. However, we were told that upon reaching the top of the mountain, we would come to a waterfall where we could spot turtles, take a break, and stop for lunch.

Our Tour Guide and the Waterfalls at the top of the mountain.

Dee is having a break by the waterfall and the turtles below.

After a rest and lunch, we set off to see the turtles, which live in the mountains but are very popular. As we walked further up the hill, we could see loads of people through the trees, all heading up to the turtles, a big attraction on the island. They were worth the trek up to see them eventually, as they were native to the mountains.

We were told not to feed them or get too close to touch them, as the park rangers that looked after them wanted them to stay as natural to the mountains as possible. After we had seen them, we headed back down the hill and got a chance to talk to some of the other people about the sites to see on the island. One of the sites we were told to visit was the snake temple; at this time of year, all the snakes would head to the temple to hibernate until it was warm enough for them to return to the jungle. Additionally, we discovered that the roads were very safe, and the best way to get around was to hire a motorbike. Therefore, once again, we decided to hire a Honda 50 to tour the island, hoping that Dee would not fall off again.

That's me on our motorbike on our tour of Penang Island.

We set off on our tour to find the snake temple; the roads were excellent to drive around and very safe; the funny thing was that the local policemen also moved around on Honda 50; the only difference was they kept the handguns in a shopping basket in the front of their Honda 50 which we noticed when we pulled up at some traffic lights. Dee tapped me on the shoulder and told me to look at the motorbike next to us, it was the local policeman on his bike in all his uniform with his gun in the shopping basket. We both smiled as it was not what you would expect to see. We drove around the island and found it lovely; the countryside was nice and very dense in many areas, as it was a jungle. Eventually, we found the Bayan Lepas Snake Temple, also known as the Temple of the Azure. In the same area was the Kek Lok Si Buddhist Temple, so we decided to make a full day of touring, which we were both looking forward to. As we entered, we were told to give our eyes time to adjust as it was very smoky inside due to all the incense that was used to keep the snakes calm and quiet; once we entered, at first, we could not see much but as our eyes adjusted all you could see was the walls and ceiling moving very slowly which seemed odd until we realised it was not the walls and ceiling moving, it was the snakes moving very slowly. It was like a big jelly just wobbling from side to side. Then we could see loads of snakes everywhere. We just looked at each other and thought about what we had entered, but as we stood very still, we slowly grew accustomed to watching the snakes, which were very sleepy due to the incense that had been circulating. Still, it was amazing to see, and we were pleased once we had gone back outside. It was a sight to see all those snakes lying there, very happy inside the temple. Some of the snakes in the temple were amazing to be that close to, but at the same time, we were not sorry to go outside. Once we realised what we had been up close to, we shivered.

Some of the snakes in the Bayan Lepas Snake Temple.

After some lunch, we were back on the road heading to the Kek Lok Si Temple, which was a big temple, not hard to find, and it was quite a sight; as we got closer to it, the first thing we noticed was a big white temple with a golden dome. The entrance was very big, it's the largest temple in Malaysia, and it brings in visitors from all over Asia. It was built in 1891 and is known as the Temple of Supreme Bliss. We were both looking forward to exploring and not having to watch out for any snakes lying around. Once inside, we found some big golden Buddha statues; one must have been around 15 feet tall and was surrounded by many smaller orange Buddha statues. The main temple was over 30 metres tall, and the architectural style comprised three sections: the base was Chinese, the middle section was Thai, and the top section was Burmese. It was an awe-inspiring sight; the area was approximately 30 acres, so we wouldn't be able to see it all, but we were happy to walk around the main temples and explore the numerous shops in the area.

We enjoyed our visit to the temple and the history associated with the entire site. Dee particularly enjoyed seeing all the different flowers in the gardens surrounding the temples and ponds. Additionally, we were informed that after the Chinese New Year, the temple remains open late into the night, with thousands of lights illuminating the area to create a stunning light display for 30 days. Once or twice a year, hundreds of monks come from Thailand to what is known as the Long March festival. It was a great day of touring to see the Snake Temple and the Kek Lok Si Temple, and Dee never fell off the bike once.

Some of the golden Buddhas at Kek Lok Si Temple.

We had a great day touring around; we only had a couple of days left before we had to head back to the Middle East to start work again. Dee was going back to Oman and I heard I would be going to India with CCCUE. We spent our last few days walking around the town where we were staying. We went to the local park, and as we had heard, you can feed the local friendly monkeys, so we decided to go and look. They were numerous, but all were very friendly and accustomed to being fed by humans. We obtained some local food that they were eating and started to feed them. It was a lovely way to finish off our tour of Asia.

On January 27, we left Thailand and landed in Dubai. Dee flew back to Oman, and I spent a few days in Sharjah before flying to India on February 5. I flew to Bombay to join the NNPPC PLB 648 work barge, which involved air diving and saturation diving work, laying new pipelines for ONGC, the leading company in charge of the oilfields around India. I had a few days in Bombay before joining a supply boat to sail out to the 648, so I took the opportunity to explore Bombay. I was told many things about Bombay before I arrived. There were only two ways of living in India: you were a rich Indian, or you were a poor Indian, and if you were poor, you had nothing apart from begging for anything you could get. First, I was shocked to see all these people sleeping in anything they could get to sleep in, many people were missing limbs be it legs or arms, and they would be out in the streets with postcards in their mouths as they had no arms to hold them, but I was warned whatever you do, don't get out any money to give to them as you would get surrounded by hordes of people all wanting cash off you. I soon learnt not to withdraw any money after a large crowd of beggars surrounded me. After a few days, I learnt to ignore the beggars. Plus, I had now grown accustomed to the smell, as there were open-running sewers everywhere, and most people who lived on the streets would simply go anywhere to use the toilet, without bothering to find a designated spot. They would do their business anywhere, in full view of anyone.

You soon learn to ignore it, but you have to keep an eye on where you are walking, as nothing gets cleaned up. I was staying in a hotel called Fariyas, in Colaba, located very close to the Gateway of India which was a monument dedicated to Queen Victoria, even though she never visited India. I had seen it many times on TV and in newspapers, but I wasn't going to miss out the chance to visit, and it was great to see it up close and walk around it. Slowly, I was beginning to enjoy my time in India, as my dad was originally from India, and he would be happy knowing I was in his homeland. They never knew where I was at any time as I was always travelling around, so I made sure I sent them a postcard from India. I spent much of my free time walking around Bombay; it was a fantastic city, so I made the most of my few days there before joining the supply boat to sail out into the Indian Ocean to join the NPPC 648 as an air diver, and we were expected to work with the saturation system as helpers.

Me at the Gateway to India.

Into the Blue and Beneath The Waves

I am heading from the Gateway of India to my hotel Fariyas, Colaba

I enjoyed seeing the sights of Bombay, but the poverty was unreal; families would sleep in large drainage pipes, make a home out of anything they could find if there was a free space, and then move in. It was just the way they lived in Bombay, and everyone seemed to accept that was their way of life. The people came to find work, and until they found employment, they would be begging on the streets. It's now called Mumbai, and I'm not sure if it's still the same, but hopefully, it's changed for the better. Below are some more photos of Bombay, but one picture is shocking as it says, 'Mass Rape by Bihar Cops'. Whether that's just the way of English or it means something else, I was not sure, but it certainly surprised me.

The Sign at the top of the picture that Surprised Me

I just loved this picture; the guy was not a beggar but a friendly Indian who wanted to welcome me to India. I found out that if he ever sees any visitors, he likes to go and say hello and welcome, so from mass rape by Bihar cops advert to hello and welcome to India.

My few days in Bombay were over. I joined the supply boat with about another 12 guys, some divers, and some crew members for the NPCC 648. We sailed overnight, but typically, there were no beds for everyone, and I ended up sleeping on top of all the luggage bags for about 8 hours; so now I was back in the real world of offshore life in Asia, but I was used to it all by now, and I just got on with things as they were, no point in complaining as our supervisor Sean Company was also sleeping on a load of bags for 8 hours. After a 12-hour sail, we eventually arrived at the NPCC 648, and our superintendent was there to meet us off the supply boat. He was a very well-known superintendent in and around India, Mr Jock Foot, who called everyone 'Chuck'. On his left hand, he had a tattoo that said, 'Thank You'. I think it was his joke when he got paid in cash.

I landed on the NPCC 648 in the early morning of February 9, 1988, and by 15:04, I had begun my first dive to 85 feet for 19 minutes, conducting a stinger check to re-establish my shift pattern. I was on the day shift, which started at midday and ended at midnight, as it was just a quick inspection of the pipeline stinger. It also allowed me to examine the saturation system we were expected to maintain. The saturation system had one diving bell, one accommodation chamber and one transfer chamber, which the diving bell would sit on before and after each saturation dive; we also found out the system would be used for mixed gas bounce dives, which was to save money. I think whoever went into saturation would be paid a lot more than the air/mixed gas bounce divers. What amazed me was that the diving bell umbilical, which was about 6 to 8 inches in diameter, had to be manually lowered into the water, which was fine. It had to be pulled up after each dive, which wasn't easy as it was cumbersome. We had to lay the umbilical down in a figure of eight; it was heavy but also it was not very safe to me. The other guys inside the umbilical basket would be in much trouble if the bell had a problem and fell back into the water. The diving umbilical did go over a big wheel; it was not hydraulically driven, so we had to lower the umbilical into the water as the diving bell descended and ascended.

The pipeline lay barge had around 8 to 10 anchor blocks, four on the bow and four on the stern, with a few spare anchor blocks. A few small tugboats would move the anchor blocks into position, winch wires would be run out from the barge to the anchor blocks, which were connected to the winch wires, and the lay barge would pull up the slack, which helped the barge move forward, sideways, or astern, anyway the barge wanted to move, to lower the pipeline into the correct position. The tug boats also had surveyors onboard their vessel who plotted the dropping locations so no anchor blocks were dropped onto any other piles on the seabed.

I dived every day for nine days, checking the stinger from depths ranging from 70 feet to 124 feet for around 5 to 10 minutes, depending on what I had to check on the stinger and pipeline as it left the stinger. One thing with our superintendent Jock Foot was that he did not like us sitting around on our 12 hours shift; he would make us paint everything continuously, even if it did not need painting; it was this painting that I must admit was a pain, this non-stop painting but in the end, CCCUE stopped all the painting as they received a significant invoice from NPCC for all the paint we were using from the barge's paint store, which made us laugh but then he just got us brushing up all the time after our dives. At long last, the diving bell was brought into action for a short saturation dive, which stopped us from cleaning up everything, and I was on umbilical duty as the diving bell was being lowered into the water. When the diving bell reached a depth of around 70 feet, it dropped about 10 feet. The hydraulics that lowered the bell had a problem, as it stopped, the diving bell umbilical was pulled down, just as I stepped out of the middle of the umbilical in the diving basket. The extra umbilical that got pulled down landed on the diving bell.

Before any further movements were planned, Jock decided it would be quicker if I got into the air diving equipment, as the diving bell was only about 70 feet down. I got ready to dive and jumped into the water, as Jock wanted to make sure the umbilical was not wrapped around the diving bell's guide wires.

I checked the guide wires on my way down to the diving bell, and I could see the umbilical had got caught up about 10 feet from the diving bell in the guide wires. It did not take me long to free everything, and I headed back to the surface. Once I got out of the water and out of my diving gear, Jock said, "Well done, Chuck! Now get back into the umbilical basket and don't drop the bloody umbilical next time," with a smile. I will say that some of the biggest fish I have ever seen were in the Indian Ocean, especially barracudas. They used to hide inside the pipeline stinger; they never bothered me, but they would look at you with menacing eyes. They hid inside the stinger, as smaller fish would also hide there, and they would be easy pickings for the barracudas, which I did not mind, as it meant they stayed away from me.

I was never selected to participate in saturation or mixed-gas diving jobs, as some divers held saturation certificates, so I continued to work on most of the air diving assignments. On March 13, 1988, I completed my last dive in the Indian Ocean and flew back to Dubai on March 16, from where I travelled to Saudi Arabia. I had a few days in Sharjah before arriving on the IMS P280 work barge on March 20, 1988, to perform pipeline repairs and install new pipeline risers on offshore platforms. It was a mixed gas and air diving operation. I was put on the night shift, and my diving supervisor and a Middle East legend, Taff Williams, whom I had worked with a few times. He was a great character and well-known around the Middle East. Another great guy on the night shift was Dave Ferrar, a fantastic man with a great sense of humour. I have always enjoyed working with Dave and Taff or Bubbles, as he was known to some divers. Sadly, both divers have passed away, and I will always have fond memories of them. The work barge was not built for comfort; it was designed for working offshore, featuring a restroom, but no facilities for watching movies, tiny four-man cabins with limited space for luggage, and shared toilets. My first dive was at 00:35, diving from the wet bell using helium/oxygen mixed gas in the morning in 83 feet of water, placing grout bags under a pipeline and fitting a grout hose to the bags to start filling up the grout bags with cement to give some support to the pipeline as it was not sitting on the seabed. I spent 140 minutes in the water, and everything went smoothly; I then completed my decompression in the decompression chamber. I had not yet met the superintendent, as he had been working from 6:00 a.m. to 6:00 p.m. He was new to working with CCCUE, so I guessed I would meet him in the morning, which I did. He introduced himself as Duchy Holland. I never really got his first name. Because of his surname, he liked being called Duchy. Some people are like that; they want to be called by their nicknames. The work was interesting as we used hydro-tightening equipment on pipeline spool pieces, which I always enjoyed working with. We were carrying out this work on-air as Duchy wanted to save as much helium/oxygen as possible for the deeper dives, since it was not easy to get a supply of the gas mix for the dives. The client, Aramco, wanted the divers to spend longer on the seabed, as they were paying for a mixed gas diving operation. They also wanted a mixed gas diving operation because we had many 12-inch pipeline spool pieces to install.

<small>12 inch spool piece pipeline with flanges that are bolted together with a hydraulic bolt tightening system which is connected to the bolts on each side and pressure is applied which tightens the bolts to the flange and pulls the flangers together</small>

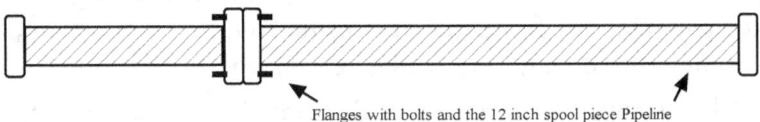

Flanges with bolts and the 12 inch spool piece Pipeline

We began conducting more helium/oxygen dives from the wet bell, which was satisfactory. I had no problems with that, as Taff knew what he was doing. Plus, we got an extra $30 on our day rate if we used mixed gas. It's not great, but it's better than nothing. By now, I had spent a considerable amount of time offshore, and I felt very confident in knowing right from wrong in the offshore diving world.

Many diving supervisors loved to push diving to the limits, disregarding consequences; they thought they were gods and believed no one would question their actions. It was always a case of doing what I told you or you're off my job. On this particular night, I was woken up early to be ready as the first diver on our night shift. I went onto the deck to see what I was to do, but could not find Taff anywhere. The superintendent, Duchy Holland, told me to prepare to dive, as they needed a diver in the water immediately. I said I was almost ready, but he kept asking me to get moving. Just as I was about to put the diving hat on, one of the day shift divers said, "You do realise the last four divers on mixed gas have all been bent, and one is still in the chamber." The superintendent says, "Get in the water now! And stop wasting time." To which I replied, "You can fxxk off; I am not diving on mixed gas as four divers have got decompression illness." ('Bent', as we call it in the diving world).

I said I would dive on air, "and if you put me on mixed gas while I'm in the water, I would come back up, as I'm not going to get bent out of shape for you." This did not go down well with the diving superintendent, who wanted me off the barge immediately. The decompression chamber door opens, and out climbs Taff. Much to my surprise, the diving superintendent said to Taff, as he was getting out of the chamber, "I want this guy gone now, as he's refusing to dive on mixed gas." Taff then grabs Duchy by the throat and pins him against the chamber, and says, "The only guy going off the barge and over the side is you, you wanker; if I had known what was going on, I would never have got into the water on mixed gas." Taff was the fourth diver to get bent. Taff told Duchy to fxxk off with the mixed gas until the mixed gas is tested. Taff then turns to me and says, "Now you, tosser, get in the water on air," and winked at me with a Taff smile.

What I always enjoyed with Taff was, he would never take any crap from anyone, including Duchy Holland, who was still trying to use mixed gas for diving regardless of the four-decompression illness or the bends, as we called it. As I was the diver who said I was not using the mixed gas for diving, I was the one who caused the dives to be on air, not mixed gas, but I could not give a fxxk, nor could Taff or Dave Ferrar, who also said, "Fxxk the mixed gas." Eventually, Taff got all the newly supplied mixed gas quads checked along with the O2 analysers and found out the O2 analysers were not reading the O2 content correctly; hence the divers were on the wrong USN mixed gas dive tables for the depth of water we were working in, all for an extra $30 a mixed gas dive. In the end, thanks to Taff we were now on heliox mixed of 81/19% USN 160-feet/for 60 minutes without any more problems but Duchy Holland never forgave me, the wanker. He could never fault my work, as I was also an underwater photographer. He needed me more than I needed him, which made Taff laugh, as I always had to wait for pictures of the finished diving work before it was approved to move on to the following location. I finished the last dive of the operation on the 14th of April 1988 by de-rigging the hydro-tightening equipment with the last of the photography pictures of the operation in a depth of 132 feet on air, as we had run out of mixed gas, which made Taff and Dave Ferrar laugh as I had completed the last dive on air in 35 minutes, then after my decompression completed the development of the pictures for the client, all to the dislike of Duchy Holland who made a complaint to the CCCUE project manager about my refusal to use mixed gas. He came to me about the complaint and said to me, "Fxxk him," as I had been with CCCUE long enough for them to know what I could do as a diver/supervisor.

We set sail from Saudi Arabia and arrived in Abu Dhabi. I then took a flight to Oman on April 24, 1988. I had not stopped travelling all over the Middle East and Asia for months and was looking forward to a break. CCCUE conducted another diving operation in Oman for me, and I am now back working at PDO on the SBM, which is excellent for me, as Oman has become my home. I could not wait to explore more of Oman; by now, I had learnt to get around by learning some basic Arabic. The other divers were living in the CCCUE camp, called the White Camp.

I lived in Dee's accommodation in Al Khoud. I would get the local taxi, where I would wait for at least four locals to hop on board a pickup truck before it would take us to where we wanted to go at the cost of about 10 pence or 1 Omani riyal, I would get the local taxi to the white camp to meet up with the other divers and get a lift with their transport to the PDO work site where we would all get onto the PDO 1 work barge to carry out all the maintenance on the SBMs. I was delighted, as I knew I would be working in Oman for at least a few months, which meant I could stay with Dee. I could see more of each other and spend some time together instead of travelling all over the Middle East and Asia, and seeing if we really could make a go of our relationship under one roof. We never paid for air tickets in this life of travelling around and expat parties all the time, living life and travelling on companies' air tickets. We were given air tickets as long as we had made a three-month trip, and the companies would provide us with the money to book our flights. If I had worked for six months, I could have received two payments for air tickets, which, at the time, covered my airfare and accommodation for my travels.

Chapter Twenty-one

Back in Oman for PDO, my last operation at ABK, onward to Salalah for one of the best diving operation adventures I've ever had.

I was delighted to return to Oman for the SBM operation. My diving supervisor was Simon Wiess, who was also living in Oman at the time. The operation involved replacing spreader bars, which were fitted across the SBM hoses to keep them separate, as well as inspection work on the SBM and all the SBM mooring chains from the SBM buoy down to the seabed, approximately 160 feet. We were only working during the day, and if we had any bad weather, we would get the day off, which was great as Dee and I would go off and explore more of Oman, which I found to be an incredible country to explore. I loved visiting Mutrah Souq, located just outside Muscat in Mina Qaboos Harbour. It was a fantastic place to explore for hours, as it had a labyrinth of alleyways containing various shops, and the scent of spices was everywhere. I thoroughly enjoyed the place, especially with all the friendly and helpful Omani people. I would go there when it was busy, as I loved the vibe and culture, and I would go there when it was quiet. Seeing all the shadows in the small alleyways when the sun shone down into the souq was fascinating. Mutrah Souq is one of the oldest markets in Oman, dating back several hundred years. It's just off the harbour, but you won't see it from the harbour. But if you keep looking, you will start seeing people going down alleyways, and if you follow them, you end up in a magical world of local Omani shops; it was wonderful to walk into that area. I always loved it when I went there.

I took some pictures inside the Mutrah Souq from midday until late afternoon when it was closed. I didn't take too many pictures when it was busy, as some locals didn't like their photos taken.

We had a great day just walking around the souq. I would walk around for hours, but I never found where all the alleyways went. They just seemed to go on forever and ever. I never got bored. I just loved exploring the market; then, I would go outside and wander around the harbour, looking at all the vessels in the harbour. However, one vessel always took my interest, and that was the Sultan Qaboos Dhow. It was a lovely vessel to look at. Naturally, you could not go near it, but I loved looking at it as I was still making my ships in a bottle, and I hoped one day I would get to make that dhow and put it in a bottle. Little did I know that I would get to board the Sultan's Dhow in Liverpool at the Tall Ships Race years later.

One of my jobs was to take underwater pictures of the SBM PLEM and its hoses; one of the marine life forms on the seabed was the seahorse. They always seemed to appear when I did not have an underwater camera, but on this dive, I got lucky. I was swimming down one of the SBM mooring chains, and when I got to the bottom, I had to take a picture of the chain connection link; just then, I saw a seahorse; at first, it was difficult to make out as it blended in with its surrounding, but as I waited for my eyes to adjust to the area, I just took some pictures, but was unsure if I had captured the seahorse. I would have to wait until I got the photos developed, which was a nervous few days until I got the pictures back from the local photo shop. I had got one photo showing the seahorse and a puffer fish. I was delighted and always smile when I come across that picture. As you can see, it is well camouflaged; I was also lucky the following day when I managed to get a picture of chicken fish as they swam across the SBM hose I was working on.

The Seahorse, the Puffer Fish, two Chicken Fish and a baby lobster.

Into the Blue and Beneath The Waves

The diving operation was going very well, and I had sorted out when the local taxis ran and how much extra I would give the driver if he did not get four locals to make up the numbers to travel to the white camp where the divers were staying. Replacing the spreader bars was going very well; however, we could no longer bring visitors onto the work barge, as security had tightened up, which was understandable. We were having a great time as we went ashore every day; additionally, after completing five dives, the client would not allow us to carry out any repetitive dives, as per the USN dive tables we were using.

Drawing of the SBM Hoses and where the spreader bar is fitted.

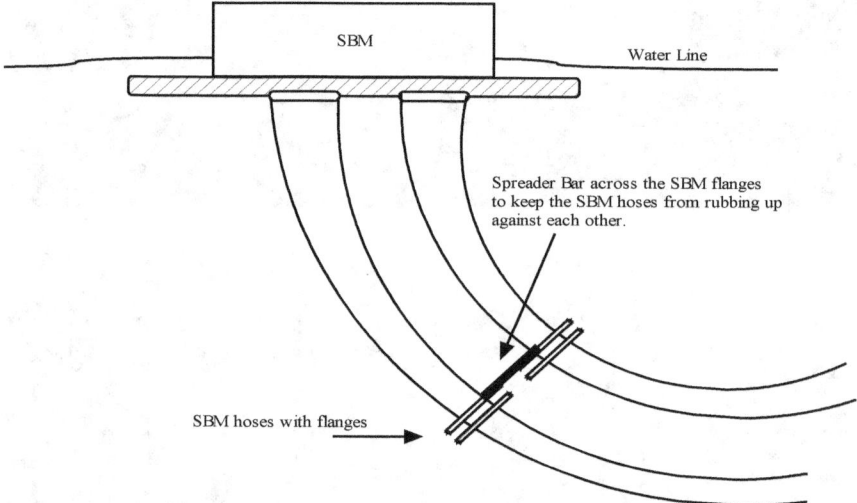

One of my jobs was to take pictures of the marine growth on the SBM buoy, as the sea water was very warm in the summer. The marine growth would cover the SBM in no time, but I didn't mind, as it would bring in loads of small, colourful fish; I loved taking pictures of them before we cleaned off all the marine growth, and the small fish swam away.

We had a couple of days of bad weather coming up, and Dee had a few days off at the same time, so we decided to go and watch the camel racing, which I had heard a lot about but had never been, so we got our cameras and lunch packed, and we set off. I was told that the camels are swift and do not stop for anything. At the end of each race, there are camel catchers, and as the camels pass the winning line, these individuals jump onto the camels' necks to slow them down and hopefully bring them to a stop. However, there were many times they would not stop, and they would continue running with a kid still sitting on them, tied on so they would not fall off. The camel race was exhilarating; all the local Omanis were thrilled, and the atmosphere was great. I was surprised by some of the sights; many of the camels were loaded into the back of pickups. The camels would then be lifted out of the pickups and prepared for racing. Dee and I would watch the start and then move down the race track to watch the camels go past us. It was a fantastic sight, but you would never get me riding a camel in a race. The pace was fast. I don't know how those kids stayed on, and how those guys jumping on at the end of the race to stop a camel running was some feat to watch.

We had a great day out, and a great time watching the camel racing and wondering how far those camels that did not get stopped carried on running. The truck on the right-hand side would drive alongside and follow any camels that never stopped, as they had to rescue the kids who were the jockeys. It was a fantastic experience, and not your typical day out. The SBM operation was coming to an end, and on June 8, 1988, I flew to Dubai and then on to Liverpool for the first time in 18 months. Dee was to follow and meet me in Liverpool after she had visited her parents in Cornwall.

I intended to see Rose, the kids, and my parents, as I had been away for a long time and did not know what to expect from anyone. I did not expect to be greeted well, which I understood, and I did not blame anyone. I wanted everyone to know that in early 1989, Dee and I would return to the UK to see if we could live in the 'real world' of dark and cold nights, rather than the warm, sunny days with everything paid for. I was unsure what work I would find as I had been away from the North Sea for nearly 10 years. The diving world had changed significantly with the introduction of various diving certificates, which I did not possess, and I had begun to notice this trend creeping into the Middle East diving work. It was becoming increasingly challenging to secure a spot in certain diving operations. The trip to the UK went as well as I had imagined, but I did not blame Rose. It was I who had left, leaving her with the two kids, whom I didn't get to see much. I don't blame anyone; I hoped to see them more once I returned to the UK, but I knew and understood it would be a slow process. Dee eventually met up with me in Liverpool and met my parents, who were glad to see that Dee and I were doing okay and would return to the UK in 1989. After a couple of days, Dee and I went to Inverness in Scotland to stay with one of Dee's friends for a few days before heading back to the Middle East until early 1989. On the 30th of July 1988, I landed in Sharjah to join a work barge called Conoco Four to work on a small operation around Das Island in the Arabian Gulf, and Dee returned to Oman for a few weeks before heading back to the UK to start looking for a home for us.

Life was simple and easy for us in the Middle East. You worked, had parties, and travelled worldwide, all at the expense of the companies you worked for. We both loved working and living in Oman. It was a beautiful country; we loved Oman, its history, and its people, but we had to head home to the UK to see if we could live in the real world. Dee was great with everything; she put down a hefty deposit on a house in Winsford, Cheshire, so we had a home to go to, and everything was set for us both to have Christmas in our new home and New Year away in York with most of our expat mates from the Middle East. However, before we met for the New Year, we still had a few months before Dee and I headed to the UK. I finished the minor operation on Das Island, which was a small construction job of laying screen frames down onto the seabed in 36 feet of water, which would then be filled with small stones to form a level base in which the concrete blocks would be laid onto the top and which would then be used to lay small pipes on which came from the island as out discharge pipes for excess water overflows. Once I had finished that operation, I returned to Oman for a few weeks. While there, I was asked if my ships in a bottle could go on display. At a marine exhibition, people saw my ships in bottles; a few even bought some from me. I was happy for my Ships in a Bottle to go on display, as it showed that the people in Oman liked my hobbies.

Some of my Ships in a Bottle. The Omani Dhow is one of my favourites.

 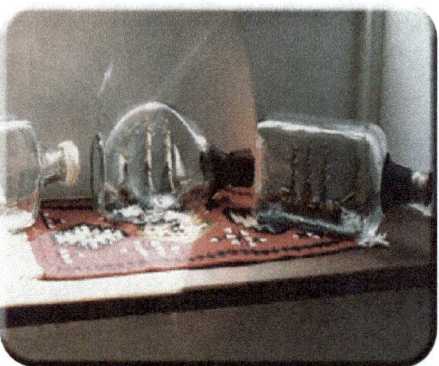

One Ship in a Bottle at the exhibition caught everyone's eyes, and that was the HMS Victory in a Dimple bottle, which was everyone's favourite bottle to have a ship in. It turned out it was a favourite of one particle person who stole it, much to the dismay of the people running the marine exhibition who did not discover it was missing until I went to collect my ships after the exhibition but after they had a look at the CCTV system they had they found out who had taken the bottle. He was stopped at the airport before taking it home.

My HMS Victory in a Bottle.

After a couple of weeks in Oman, I set off to Abu Dhabi to start my annual inspection operation at ABK, which began on September 14, 1988. All the regular divers I asked for were there waiting to board the Conoco 111, and it was great to see the guys again. We were also carrying out a new inspection operation, called Vibro Detection Scan, which was like a little robot we called K9 after Doctor Who's dog. The French engineers did not understand this, but they liked the name. It was a small unit with an umbilical to the surface engineers that we would fix to any members on the platforms; once it was attached firmly, we would press a button on the unit, which sent a signal to the topside engineers who then would operate the unit. To us, basically, it was a posh hammer as it would hammer the members which sent out a vibration along the platform support members which would register to the surface any anomalies the vibrations would find in the members and the welds. It worked well, as the engineers would then instruct us to inspect specific positions on the support members, which we would clean and inspect thoroughly. Each time, we would find anomalies, which saved us a significant amount of time by allowing us to examine the entire length of the support members. Once the Vibro detection unit had completed the inspection, a red light would come on, and we would remove the unit to its following location; what was funny was that one of the divers had attached a dog lead to it and started shouting, "Come on, boy, there's a good boy," which even the French engineers found funny.

The operation lasted a few months, and working with the Vibro engineers was fascinating. It surprised us what it could find and detect. It was also amusing as the hammering would disturb any marine life hiding on and around the support members. On this particular dive, I was working below one of the support members, getting hammered by the Vibro machine above me, when suddenly, two sea crawfish, also known as spiny lobsters, fell onto me. At first, I thought, what the hell is grasping my umbilical? When I looked, it was a crawfish, which surprised me at first. However, I was even more surprised when another one dropped onto the support member I was working on. I quickly grabbed it, put it in my other dive bag, and returned to the surface, as I was only 40 feet underwater.

I am with my two crawfish alongside Boyd Starzynski and Graham Watts.

It was a good way to finish off my last trip on the Conoco 111 at ABK as I realised my time in the Middle East was coming to an end. It was also for some of the guys in that operation they were planning on doing saturation course and inspection courses as diving operation certificates were coming in more and more in the Middle East and work was getting harder to get as priority was for the divers with all sorts of qualifications. We finished the inspection operation on the 26th of October,1988 and after a good run ashore with the guys, I set off to Oman on the 29th of October to start a diving oxy-arch operation, cutting up an old barge which could be seen when the tide was out. It was an ugly looking rusting cargo barge in an area called Salalah in South Oman as I had been cross hired by CCCUE for a diving company called Aqua Diving or as everyone in the Middle East called them, Aqua-Splash. The operation was not going to start for a week or so. However, it had to be completed before the Oman National Day as the Sultan of Oman would be visiting, and everything had to look good along the beach area, which was close to the harbour where the Sultan would be arriving. Additionally, it was interesting to note that we were to be flown to Salalah by a military plane, as commercial aircraft were not available to us. Obtaining a visa for Oman was not quick or easy, and Aqua-Dive could only provide a visa for one Filipino diver. My one-man dive team and I had to fly to Salalah to dismantle an old cargo barge that was over 250 feet long and 40 feet wide. All the diving equipment and oxy-arch equipment were already in Salalah, as dive teams had been there to cut up the barge. No one had managed to cut anything up, and now the local authorities were growing concerned, as they did not want the Sultan to see this old barge on the beach during his visit. On October 5th, my one-man dive team and I flew down to Salalah for what was to be one of the best diving experiences and adventures I had ever had.

When we landed, the Strong-Plant driver picked us up, the company that had been given the contract to remove the sunken barge. The driver took us to the only hotel in Salalah, an ancient building with lots of character. After checking in, I went to my room. I found it full of Heineken beer from floor to ceiling, so I thought, "Great, they've converted a store room to use as my bedroom." However, the room was fine apart from being full of beer. After unpacking, I went down for dinner and met with my other dive buddy, Romeo. I asked him how his room was, which was full of beer, and we both laughed about it. After dinner, we went for a walk around the town, which was fascinating as the locals were very traditional in their clothing, with their Khanjar (the local knives) tucked into their belts, and some of them carrying rifles. Most of the traffic consisted of old Bedford trucks held together with rope; some locals were travelling on horseback. It was terrific; I loved it. It was amazing to see that the living history of an old period in Oman was slowly changing, but Oman was not going to change its old ways. They wanted to blend in the old ways with the oncoming new world, modernising Oman. As I had learned in my time in Oman, Oman respected their old traditional ways dearly.

Some local shops sell a wide range of items.

The following morning, we were picked up by the plant operation manager, who asked us how the hotel was. I said it was fine; the food was good, and the room was pleasant and clean, but why were we put into a storage room? He looked at us, confused, and asked us what we meant. Well, I explained that both rooms were full of beer from floor to ceiling; he now looked confused and explained that he was told divers like a beer or two after work and as there was no bar, he filled up the rooms with enough beer to last us while we were in Salalah, which made us both laugh. He took us to the work site, which was the local beach. He explained to us that three diving companies had attempted to cut the barge in half, but without success. He was on a 'no success, no pay' operation, as the operation would fail, if it did not work again. It was unreal when we arrived at the beach area, with fishermen and their huts, camels, and old dhows all along the beach from which we would be working. We could see the old barge at low tide, and it was an eyesore that the local elders wanted to remove before the Sultan's visit on National Day; at high tide, the bollards on the barge would stick out of the water.

We could walk out to the old sunken barge at low tide.

One of our problems at low tide was that it was too shallow to carry out any oxy-arch cutting. Hence, we had to wait for high tide to start any underwater cutting, but it allowed us to have a snorkel dive around the barge to check for any problems we may encounter. The most significant issue I noticed was the bottom of the barge was under the seabed so all we could break down was the barge above the seabed.

A Plan View of the Barge

Not only did we have to oxy-arch along the length of the barge, but we also had to oxy-arch out the panel holding the chambers together. It was going to be a hectic time; a good job we had all those beers, as it would be long days with just the two of us doing all the diving and cutting.

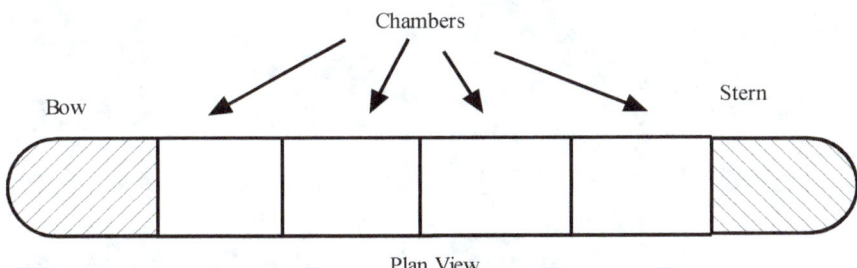

Plan View

Romeo and I are getting all our equipment ready before we start our two-man operation.

Side View of the Barge

The bottom of the barge is under the seabed plus the inside of the barge is filled with sand at the bottom of the barge.

As we were getting everything ready and tested, we noticed one of the camels had come over to check us out, which is not what you expect on a diving operation. It was very amusing, but what was even more entertaining after the camel left us was that he went over to where the local fishermen had their fish hanging out to dry in the sunshine and started eating them off the post where the local fishermen had left their fish.

The camel is coming to look at us before wandering off to find the fish on the hanging posts.

The camel was eating the fish from the handing frame, and the local fisherman was just wondering what we were doing.

At long last, on November 7, 1988, I started our first dive to test the oxy-arch cutting equipment and left Romeo to control the shoreside operation. I first started on the beach side, the port side of the barge. To begin with, the underwater cutting equipment worked very well; I would tell Romeo to make it hot, which meant switching the cutting equipment on, and then make it cold to switch it off. I was cutting along the seabed when, all of a sudden, a big wave hit the side of the barge. As I was only in 12 to 15 feet of water, I went with the oxy-arch cutting equipment going everywhere, and I shouted, 'Make it cold!' As I was in very shallow, I walked out of the water and up the beach to find out what was going on, only to find the area we were in, was where the local fishermen would bring their fishing boats and speedboats alongside. Hence, if we were to continue, we needed to communicate with the local fishermen to slow down when approaching the beach to drop off their freshly caught fish; they were great, as it was explained to them that we had to tidy up the beachfront for National Day. They stopped speeding around the barge, but they were interested in what we were doing, so they repaired their fishing nets next to us. I loved it; the whole experience was magical, and the local people were as friendly as the camels which roamed the beach.

The locals were great; they had never seen anything like this operation before, and they were as fascinated by us as we were by them; the whole operation was a one-off, just two divers, a sunken barge, camels and the local Omani people that were known as Dhofar Omanis that were once part of the Dhofar Rebellion and the forgotten war that British troops were involved in from 1963 to 1976.

The below information was referanced from Wikipedia.

The Dhofar War took place from 1963 to 1976 in the province of Dhofar against the Sultanate of Muscat and Oman. The war began with the formation of the Dhofar Liberation Front, a Marxist group that aimed to create an independent state in Dhofar, free from the rule of the Omani Sultan Said bin Taimur. Omani and British goals were to safeguard Oman from communism and halt the spread of communist ideology as part of the broader Cold War.

The war initially took the form of a low-level insurgency, with guerrilla warfare being used against Omani forces and the foreign presence in the country. Several factors, including the British withdrawal from Aden and support from the newly independent South Yemen, China, and the Soviet Union, contributed to the rebels' increased success, with the communists controlling the entirety of the Jebel region by the late 1960s. The 1970 Omani coup led to the overthrow of Sultan Said bin Taimur by his reformist son, Qaboos bin Said, who was backed by a British military intervention in the conflict. The British initiated a 'hearts and minds' campaign to counter the communist rebels and began the process of modernising the Sultan of Oman's Armed Forces while simultaneously deploying the Special Air Service to conduct anti-insurgency operations against the insurgents. This approach led to a string of victories against the rebels and was boosted by the Shah of Iran's intervention in the conflict to support the Sultanate of Oman in 1973. The war ended with the final defeat of the Dhofar rebels in 1976.

Mountains surrounded Salalah; it is where frankincense and myrrh come from. It's the sap from the local trees in the mountains. After our first day of setting up and having an idea of what we were doing, we got down to a few busy days of cutting along the side of the barge. Everything was going well; we had completed cutting down the outside of the barge on the seaside of the barge, but the internal pieces inside the barge were holding the sides up. I decided to carry out an oxy-arc cut down the middle of the internal plates. At low water, I would use a caterpillar machine with a bucket on it to see if it could rock the side of the barge plates that were cut back and forth. As they were so rusty, I hoped the plates would be too weak to hold on and would break.

The caterpillar headed out at low water to see if it could rock the cut sides back and forth.

The idea worked; the sides of the barge started to come away, the caterpillar driver was having a great time ripping the barge to bits, and the strong plant operations manager was made up as, at long last, he could see the barge being removed from the area. However, we still had a big problem removing the bow and stern sections, but we would come to that once we had cleared all the side sections of the barge.

Now that we knew we could remove the side sections, we continued our underwater-cutting operations. However, we knew we had to get the base of the barge out of the water, which was under the seabed, as well as the bow and stern sections. In the meantime, we carried on cutting up the sides and internal sections of the barge, plus I must admit we were making full use of the free beers back in our rooms.

We continued to cut both sides of the barge, working each dive between us as it was still only the two of us, but Romeo was a very competent, hardworking diver; the only time we couldn't dive was at low water, but then we would move the caterpillar into position to rip down the sides of the barge and by now we had an excellent routine going. Still, we were always concerned that the caterpillar would start skidding into the seabed, but it never did, and the driver was having a great time, even though, at times, we thought that was it. He was sinking; as you can see from the pictures below, the caterpillar had gone too deep into the water.

But no, he knew what he was doing, and when the water level got too high, he would dig his bucket into the seabed and drag his caterpillar to shallow water; the driver just loved mucking about in the water, and his boss wasn't bothered as he just wanted to get the sunken barge out of the sea before the Sultan arrived. We were now making good progress with removing the side of the barge as each piece came away at low water. We would attach wires to the loose pieces, and the caterpillar would drag them ashore, where another team of helpers would cut the metal into smaller pieces, which would then be loaded onto an HGV to be taken away. As each piece came away, the barge was getting smaller and smaller, but the significant issue was what we could do to remove the bow and the stern, and as yet, we had not come up with any ideas. In the distance, I noticed these bulldozers working away, but, as yet, had not thought anything about them. As you can see, the caterpillar was doing a fantastic job of pulling the cut pieces ashore, and so far, everyone was happy as everything was on target to remove the barge before National Day.

We had been so busy we forgot it was Friday on this particular morning, which was a day of rest for our caterpillar driver, so we went down to the beach as it was a busy day with many people buying fish and meeting up, plus our caterpillar driver helped pulled an old dhow ashore that needed some TLC for an exchange of fish which the Strong

Plant manager wanted to share out amongst his workers for them to enjoy on the Friday afternoon.

The Strong Plant manager buys fish from the local fisherman on a Friday afternoon.

That's me by the bow of the old Dhow that our caterpillar driver dragged ashore for some TLC.

Well, Friday was a lovely day off, but now it's down to the final big push to get the barge away this coming week. National Day was drawing closer, and the Strong Plant operations manager was getting a little nervous. We pushed on and completed all the underwater cutting, and all the side panels and internal panels were removed; all that was remaining was the oversized bow and stern sections, the base of the barge, which was still under the seabed, and the local elders wanted everything removed, nothing was to be left behind. Once more my eyes kept looking at the bulldozers in the distance knowing they had a pushing power of over 250 tonnes. I said to the Strong Plate operations manager, "It's a pity we cannot bring those bulldozers over and put one at the bow and one at the stern at low water and get them to push forward to each other, which would break the suction holding the barge to the seabed and hopefully start lifting the barge's ends off the seabed.

He looked at me as though I were crazy and asked me what I meant. I said the sides of the barge were gone; all that remained is the bow, the base of the barge and the stern; if we could build a path to the barge that the bulldozers could work on, we could use their pushing power of 250 tonnes at each end and it could lift the barge out of the seabed and then maybe we could drag the remains of the barge ashore. We would need to get those bulldozers. "Not a problem," he said, as they worked for him, and he was willing to try anything as time was running out. Soon after that conversion, the bulldozers arrived and built a road to the bow and the barge's stern.

Once the roads were completed and it was low tide, the bulldozers moved into position and started pushing at the bow and the stern, but nothing was happening; nothing was moving apart from the temporary road underneath the bulldozers, and the operations manager was starting to get concerned as he could not let these very expansive machines get stuck in the seabed. Then we heard a big crack and the bow began to lift. "Keep pushing," we were all shouting and then the stern started to lift. "Keep going, don't stop, keep pushing," everyone was screaming and then both ends of the barge just lifted and began to fall into each other like a big Swiss roll. All the locals on the beach were also getting excited. Everyone was now amazed as both ends of the barge just lifted up and then fell on top of each other. "Keep pushing," everyone was shouting and they did until each end of the barge was one big heap on top of the other. It was amazing to see that it all came together. Just me and one Filipino diver had managed to cut up an old barge that had been an eyesore for years, and now it was no longer an eyesore but just a big heap of rusty metal on the beach.

Two bulldozers are pushing the rusty heap into a single, massive heap of metal.

Everyone was pleased as more of the sunken barge was brought together, allowing some fabricators to cut it up on the beach. It was a great feeling to know we achieved what seemed impossible when we first arrived in Salalah, with just the two of us doing all the diving. I thought what a sight it was to see three bulldozers in the water, having a great time and a lot of fun.

Three bulldozers out at sea are not a sight that is seen very often.

As for me, I heard that Aqua-Dive and CCCUE were very happy with the news, as it was a no-fix, no-pay contract for them. So, everyone was pleased with me and Romeo, but I was not going to miss out on suggesting a bonus would be nice, as you should have had four divers, not two, which everyone agreed. I was to spend a few nights in a nice hotel in Oman with Dee, with everything paid for, including food and drinks.

I'm heading to the top of the rolled-up sunken barge.

Christopher de Beaufort

What a great way to finish a fantastic operation, climbing to the top of the Swiss roll of a sunken barge in southern Oman.

Top of the World on an old rusty barge in Salalah.

We started packing everything on November 11th. After a night of celebrating, Romeo and I flew back to Muscat for a few days' break before I resumed work on the PDO SBM maintenance operation. I couldn't believe the news coming from CCCUE, considering everything I had done in Salalah, that Pete would be the superintendent. He did not want me to be part of the operation. I could not believe it, nor could anyone else, as I still did not know what I had done, as I had never met him, and he did not want me on his operation. CCCUE asked me if I could at least stay on the operation until he arrived, as he was having problems getting a visa, and not to worry about anything, as CCCUE had another job lined up for me on the Conoco 111. "Okay, no problem," I said, as all the regular guys were on the operation and it was coming up to be my second-to-last diving operation before heading back to the UK with Dee. As the PDO operation was not starting for 10/11 days, Dee and I decided to go and explore more of Oman, as Dee had a week or so off, so all in all, we did not mind, as it allowed us to go and visit more of this fantastic country. Over the next few days, we visited the village of Nizwa, a great place to visit on a Friday, where we saw the goat market, the nearby freshwater stream, and the old town, which we both loved. It was a bustling place, as it was also market day, so all sorts of things were happening and a wide variety of items were being sold simultaneously. At one point, Dee could barely see me out in the crowd.

After visiting the market in the new town of Nizwa, we proceeded to explore the old town, which was equally fantastic, featuring a freshwater stream and numerous historic buildings. It was a ghost town, but fascinating at the same time; the locals still use the freshwater stream, as the water is clean and very cool. While we were there, a local appeared with his donkey to collect water and for his donkey to have a drink to cool him down.

We headed into the old town to have lunch. It was a great place to stop and try the fresh, cool water from the stream.

We visited another old village called Rustaq, where we saw locals dancing to their traditional music. Next to them was a camel just having something to eat. We had to stop and capture that moment, as it's not every day you get to see the traditional way of life in its proper form.

We enjoyed everything we encountered. Every time we moved on, we found something else of interest. As we approached Rustaq, we discovered more locals at a washing and watering area. Families were washing their clothes and watering their crops with water from the falaj systems, channels where water would run down and around the fields, their homes, and in the streets; the water flow could be diverted to any area. Water was flowing in from a large pipe, and it seemed to be flowing continuously in abundance.

I thought I would walk alongside the falaj, but flip-flops are tricky, so I gave up in case I fell onto the rocks below. Also, around the watering hole were a load of kids who were out for the day with their families and had delighted faces, which we had to take a picture of. I think they were laughing at me as I tried to walk along the falaj.

We continued towards Rustaq, and as we got closer, we could see a large old fort in the distance. It looked as though Beau Geste would come riding out on his horse in his French Foreign Legion uniform to greet us or shoot us.

Seeing this fort against the mountain backdrop was truly something special. What an adventure this was turning out to be. We were so glad we decided to venture out and explore more of northern Oman.

As we approached the old fort of Rustaq to get a closer look, a young boy came out to greet us, and luckily for us, we had learnt some Arabic to welcome him back. In Arabic, we asked him if we could take a picture of him. As he stood to attention with a big smile, we took a lovely picture of him standing outside his home. Although the fort was ancient, many local Omani families still preferred to live the old traditional way.

The Old Fort of Rustaq.

We continued, and as we got closer and closer, we could see Rustaq fort in the distance. It looked stunning, and we could not believe it was built in the 17th century. As we drew closer, we noticed a large number of locals walking with their cooking pots and clothes towards a tiled area filled with water. We decided to stop and observe where they were all heading, as it was close to the fort. We couldn't believe what we found – it was a hot water spring where you could wash your cooking pots. Everything that needed cleaning was crystal clear and was bubbling up from under the ground. It also had a falaj system going in different directions throughout the village homes and into the fort.

The hot water spring of Rustaq.

As we discovered, the old fort was terrific and is still in use. The fort was close by, so we walked over. The main door was open, so we walked in and followed the noise we could hear. When we realised the noise was the family living there, they were washing their cutlery in the hot water from the hot water spring that was running through the fort. We could not apologise enough, but the family was great and offered us tea and bread.

The walk to Rustaq Fort from the hot water spring.

Inside the grounds of Rustaq Fort.

We had a great few days exploring northern Oman. What a magical experience it was! I am sure all those areas would be slightly different today, not in the sense of being modernised, but for tourism and visitors, as they are fascinating places to visit. We are glad we saw it as it was then, but now it was time to head back to Muscat for a couple more days before I start one of my last diving jobs for CCCUE in Oman on the PDO SBM maintenance operation. For the next few days, we relaxed at Dee's beach club, which was a charming way of getting ready before starting work again, even if it was just until Pete arrived and I had to step down.

Chapter Twenty-two
My last operation for CCCUE in Oman was on the Conoco 111, and then I returned to the UK.

On November 24, 1988, I met all the guys at the CCCUE White camp to start work on the SBM for PDO. The guys couldn't stop laughing because I had to leave, but it became a joke about Pete and me, and we all laughed. I was told I would only be there for a few days until Pete arrived, but by now, I was no longer bothered, as I was packing up and heading back to the UK. There was supposed to be a lot of underwater photography to be carried out on the SBM hoses and under the SBM itself. I was asked to inspect the camera equipment over the next couple of days to ensure it was all functioning correctly, as none of the diving equipment had been inspected for over five months. That was not a problem, I told Simon Weiss, the supervisor at the time. I would review it all in a couple of days, once we had finished setting up all the diving equipment on the work barge. It took a couple of days to get everything up and running. On November 26th, I began my first dive, which involved conducting configuration checks on the SBM hoses to a depth of 110 feet and verifying that all floating beads were still attached to the SBM hoses. The weather improved after a few days, allowing us to dive. We had a couple of days off, and I invited all the guys for a meal and a few drinks as my goodbye, as I was told Pete was on his way. No problem, I knew it was coming, so I wasn't that bothered but that evening as we were having dinner and a few drinks Simon gets a phone call to say Pete is having problems getting approval for his visa and could I stay on a bit longer. Well we could not stop laughing and I was happy to continue. The following day, the weather improved, and we continued to dive on the SBM. At the same time, I asked Simon if he wanted me to check over the underwater camera equipment. "No, don't bother," he said. The PDO ops manager didn't need any photography this trip and had cancelled the underwater photography operation. OK, no problem with me, so the underwater camera was just left to one side. Eventually, Pete obtained his visa and arrived in Oman, and I had to leave the operation. However, I would be heading to Abu Dhabi for one more operation on the Conoco 111. Dee and I had a few days to go before I set off to Abu Dhabi, so we spent a couple of days relaxing back at Dee's beach club while we packed all our belongings and prepared them for shipment to the UK.

We had a great day just chilling out and headed back to our accommodation to continue our packing when there was a knock on the door, which surprised us as it was gone 21:00 hrs. I opened the door, it was Tommy Smith standing there laughing his head off, Tommy told me the operations manager had changed his mind and wanted the photos carried out the following day. They then discovered that the underwater camera, the Nikon Mark 5, was not working at all; everything was clogged up. They were unable to obtain another camera in time for the following day. They wondered if they could use Dee's underwater camera. I told Tommy to tell Pete that they could, as long as they bought it for 500 Oman Riyals, which was about 5,000 dirhams, or about £1,200; otherwise, forget it.

Pete was not very happy, but he had no choice; he had to pay Dee in person at their accommodation at the White camp while I stood there. Dee gave me the money, and I bought a drink for all the guys, other than Pete. I flew back to Abu Dhabi, and I was a very happy man. I landed in Abu Dhabi on November 29th and joined the Conoco 111 on the same day. That evening, we set sail for Mubarraz Island, where we carried out seabed surveys, riser surveys and thickness readings on a few platforms. It was a strange feeling knowing this would be my last trip on a vessel that meant so much to me, as I had supervised many diving operations over the years on the Conoco 111, as well as the missile attack and the rescue of all those rig workers from the ABK oil field. Still, it was only appropriate that my last operation for CCCUE was on a vessel that had given me many happy memories over the years. It was time to go back to the UK to see if Dee and I could live there, plus we had to find new jobs in the UK, as now we had given up our working life in the Middle East. Still, we were both looking forward to the challenge ahead of us in the UK and, hopefully, seeing more of Chris and Grace. However, we knew it would take time for them to get to know me, fingers crossed.

The Conoco 111 operation ended on December 3, 1988. I flew back to the UK on December 6, 1988, and headed to the house Dee had bought in Winsford, Cheshire, to spend our first Christmas there. We met up with most of our friends from the Middle East for a New Year's party in Marsh Chapel Lincoln at Tommy Smith's home. Our first Christmas in Cheshire was a quiet period for us as we had not been able to prepare much. The house needed decorating and furnishing, plus we were waiting for all our stuff to arrive from the Middle East, so we made the best of the Christmas time. We were looking forward to the New Year's party with our friends. We were to leave for Lincoln the day before New Year's Eve; we had put items in place around the house, and I accidentally put a nail through a water pipe in the kitchen. There was water everywhere, and trying to find the stopcock was great fun. Additionally, finding a plumber to fix the water pipe was a great challenge, as we didn't have anyone in the area. Eventually, we got everything sorted and set off for our New Year's party with our friends from the Middle East.

Simon Wiess Smithy RIP, and me in Tommy's man cave.

Dee's friend, Dee & I.

Over the many years I have been involved in diving, I have had some adventures working as a diver and supervisor; I met some great people who, like me, were looking for an adventure at work and travelling to different countries. It has been an education in life, and at times, a matter of survival. I had many great times and many low times, but all of them together allowed me to write my book, my story, my life, which, when I was growing up, if someone had said to me that one day I would write a book about my life I would have thought they were crazy. Dee had been telling me for years to write down my experiences, as there were many more than I realised. When a very good friend of mine asked me for some diving stories as he was putting together a book called 'A Dangerous Game' about the lives of divers offshore and inshore, I realised I had stories to tell that Dee kept reminding me about. What surprised me was that I still had all my diving logbooks and old passports, dating back years, and I found all my old diving photographs, which were tied in with my diving logbooks and old passports. It was my dyslexia that helped me remember everything. When I saw a dive or a picture, the stories flooded back. What I thought was stupidity, my dyslexia, gave me the ability to remember everything I had been through over the years. Once I knew what dyslexia was, it gave me a gift I never knew I had until Dee explained it all to me. I have to thank her for that help, I would also like to thank Geraint Williams for giving me the extra push I needed to sit down and write down the story of my diving career. I would also like to thank my cousin Tony Luxon whom I always described to everyone when talking about my diving career as the most intelligent guy I have ever known. Eventually, I could utilise his knowledge of the English language to serve as my proof-reader and advisor in helping me write down my stories in standard English, rather than my dyslexic English.

Most of all, I would like to thank Dee for continually encouraging me to write down my life story over many years. She always said I had many stories to tell Chris, Grace, and my grandkids. It has been some adventure. Tom Hooper, RIP, who made me realise there must be more to life. So, thank you, Tom. It has undoubtedly been some adventure. My diving career will continue, but I don't see myself repeating all those adventures as I move on to my new life back in the UK.

www.ingramcontent.com/pod-product-compliance
Lightning Source LLC
Chambersburg PA
CBHW052014070526
44584CB00016B/1753